The Second World War
Through Soldiers' Eyes

The Second World War Through Soldiers' Eyes

British Army Life 1939–1945

James Goulty

Pen & Sword
MILITARY

First published in Great Britain in 2016 by
Pen & Sword Military
an imprint of
Pen & Sword Books Ltd
47 Church Street
Barnsley
South Yorkshire
S70 2AS

ISBN 978 1 78159 298 4

Typeset in Ehrhardt by
Mac Style Ltd, Bridlington, East Yorkshire
Printed and bound in the UK by CPI Group (UK) Ltd,
Croydon, CR0 4YY

Pen & Sword Books Ltd incorporates the imprints of Pen & Sword
Archaeology, Atlas, Aviation, Battleground, Discovery, Family
History, History, Maritime, Military, Naval, Politics, Railways, Select,
Transport, True Crime, and Fiction, Frontline Books, Leo Cooper,
Praetorian Press, Seaforth Publishing and Wharncliffe.

For a complete list of Pen & Sword titles please contact
PEN & SWORD BOOKS LIMITED
47 Church Street, Barnsley, South Yorkshire, S70 2AS, England
E-mail: enquiries@pen-and-sword.co.uk
Website: www.pen-and-sword.co.uk

Contents

List of Plates

Acknowledgments

For agreeing to this project I thank Pen & Sword Books Ltd, and I am very grateful for the editorial support provided by Jen Newby, Eloise Hansen and my copy editor Stephen Chumbley. I also thank Lisa Hooson for her assistance with the illustrations. The staff at Tyne and Wear Archives, Durham County Record Office and Lincoln Central Library all offered welcome assistance and made research visits more pleasant. I thank the librarians at Newcastle City Library who were most helpful, particularly in digging out regimental histories from their store of reference works. Similarly, I thank Helena Bates and her staff at Wylam Library, Northumberland, who were kind and supportive, particularly when looking for books in their local history section.

Paul Ternent and the staff at Northumberland Record Office provided encouragement and assistance, especially when dealing with the oral history interviews. I am extremely grateful to Adrian Wilkinson and the staff at Lincolnshire Archives, not least for providing a draft catalogue of material relating to the Lincolnshire Regiment, and for being so efficient when ordering material on research visits.

It was a privilege to speak to the following wartime veterans during the course of my research: Bill Moylon; Bob 'Killer' Taylor; Bill Titchmarsh at Royal Hospital Chelsea; Bill Ness; and George Henderson from Newcastle upon Tyne. My thanks to David Bell (County Secretary Northumbria) and David Hayley (Chairman Newcastle Central Branch) of the Royal British Legion for putting me in touch with the latter two veterans.

Professor David French offered support, and I am especially grateful to him for alerting me to the availability of the Imperial War Museum's oral histories online. Likewise, I am indebted to former Royal Northumberland Fusiliers officer Sam Phillips, for drawing my attention to John McManners's excellent memoir *Fusilier Recollections and Reflections 1939–45* (Michael Russell Ltd, 2002).

Every effort has been made to use short quotes from printed sources in keeping with the guidelines on copyright. A full list of materials consulted during research can be found in the bibliography. The illustrations are sourced from the author's collection, and for their assistance in compiling this I thank: Clive Hardy; John Turner; Simon Murdoch (Tansy Murdoch Collection); and the staff at Fieldstaff Antiques, Rochester. For allowing me to photograph wartime military vehicles and equipment at their events and museums, I am indebted to the North East Military Vehicle Club, Muckleburgh Military Collection, Norfolk, and 2014 Victory Show, Leicestershire.

Last but not least I thank my family and Poppy the Boxer dog for their unstinting love and support during the research and writing phases of this book.

Introduction

The Second World War remains one of the most momentous events in human history. It claimed the lives of an estimated fifty million people, and inflicted physical or mental injury on countless more. Simultaneously, many areas of civilisation were ruined around the globe and the conflict led to the Cold War, the ramifications of which we are still facing today. This book focusses on the experiences of wartime British soldiers who fought in a variety of theatres, and women who served with the Auxiliary Territorial Service (ATS). They came from a generation that had grown up in the shadow of the First World War, and a Britain that had not yet relinquished her position as an imperial power. Many volunteered, but equally the army became increasingly reliant on conscripts as the war progressed, some of whom proved more willing warriors than others.

In September 1939 the British Army was unprepared for war, particularly one against a major European power such as Germany that involved modern weaponry and tactical innovations. Reflecting on the fall of France and the Low Countries in May/June 1940, Field Marshal Bernard Montgomery later commented, 'to our shame ... we sent our Army into that most modern war with weapons and equipment which were quite inadequate, and we only had ourselves to blame for the disasters which early overtook us in the field when fighting began'. Yet, by 1944 the army had evolved into an effective fighting force, that ultimately emerged victorious as part of the overall Allied war effort. This was despite lacking, what former American Army officer and historian Carlo D'Este described as, 'the soldierly instincts that characterized the German Army'.

Chapter 1 emphasises the role of training in the process of rejuvenating the wartime army, and considers what it was like for ordinary men and women when they volunteered for military service, or were conscripted. According to historian Hew Strachan, training was a multi-functional process that went beyond merely 'imparting the basic grammar of military service'. In the twentieth century it was widely used by armies to counter boredom within the ranks, and acted as a means to instil professional pride. Training also generated unit cohesion, when groups of soldiers trained together and went into battle together led by officers who had been responsible for that process.

Finally, as Hew Strachan highlighted, training could help soldiers assimilate changes in tactics and master new technologies. As Chapter 1 illustrates, battle drill was introduced by the British Army during 1941, and built upon previous teachings. It became an effective means of imparting an understanding of basic infantry tactics amongst wartime soldiers, and helped them cope psychologically with the pressures of combat.

As the war continued, the army had also to consider how it selected soldiers for training in particular trades, such as signallers and drivers needed to support the expanded wartime force. Likewise, the selection and training of sufficient officers to lead wartime units was a pressing concern. Chapter 1 considers these issues via the experiences of ordinary soldiers who undertook wartime selection processes or officer training.

The role of women is highlighted by two chapters. Chapter 1 covers the ATS, including the invaluable work that organisation conducted with Anti-Aircraft Command. By contrast, Chapter 5 on casualties and medical matters acknowledges the immense contribution of the Queen Alexandra's Imperial Military Nursing Service, particularly in caring for soldiers in hospitals overseas.

Understandably the Second World War is often portrayed as a war of movement. The German victories in Poland (September 1939), Norway and Denmark (April 1940), and France (June 1940) demonstrated the potency of Blitzkrieg tactics, at the heart of which was the effective synergy between airpower, armour, and mobile infantry and artillery units. The see-saw nature of the campaigns in the North African desert during June 1940–May 1943 were highly dependent on armoured forces, and further reinforce the view that combat during the war was often fluid and dynamic. However, as Chapter 2 on active service shows, many of the major campaigns involving British troops, particularly during 1943–45, involved prolonged periods of static warfare, notably in Normandy and Italy. Consequently, combat for ordinary soldiers during the Second World War often had more in common with the stalemate conditions that characterised the First World War on the Western Front than is popularly appreciated.

Battle was an extremely stressful and demanding experience. Chapter 3 considers how personnel were able to endure wartime active service, and highlights the danger posed by battle exhaustion, more popularly termed shell shock. For some soldiers, desertion or a self-inflicted wound offered an escape from military service, and these issues are discussed here as well.

Simultaneously, the chapter outlines factors that helped soldiers cope with life on active service, including access to food and alcohol, relationships and sex, plus the provision of welfare and entertainment. Attention is also drawn to the importance of discipline, and the role of the regimental system in fostering it. Special bonds of comradeship were experienced by many wartime soldiers, particularly those from combat units, and as the chapter emphasises this often helped personnel cope, and maintained the cohesion of small groups such as eight- to ten-man infantry sections.

Many thousands of British troops became POWs during 1939–45, and their plight is covered by Chapter 4. Discussion considers the bewildering conditions of being taken prisoner on the battlefield, the degradation often suffered while being transported to a POW camp, and conditions in the camps themselves. Experiences of soldiers held by the Germans and Italians are set out alongside those who endured captivity at the hands of the Japanese. Consideration is given to how prisoners coped, such as what they were able to eat, plus topics such as escape and evasion. Contrary, to the popular image, reinforced by the silver screen, there was nothing glamorous about becoming a POW during the Second World War. Typically, soldiers in all theatres who were captured, and especially those in the Far East, endured horrendous conditions, that many of us from younger generations that have grown up since 1945 might find difficult to imagine.

Finally, this book outlines the vital role played by the army's medical services during the war and Chapter 5 on casualties and medical matters draws upon the experiences of individual soldiers, army doctors and nurses. At the outbreak of war the army had one of the most advanced medical systems in the world, as exemplified by the introduction and development of an effective blood transfusion service, at a time when techniques for carrying out such procedures were still in their relative infancy. Advances were made in other areas too, including the treatment of broken bones and the introduction of penicillin for use by wounded or sick troops. The treatment of burns posed another significant challenge, particularly amongst tank crews, and soldiers burnt while cooking as they routinely relied on petrol-fuelled stoves.

Another element to the chapter underscores that significant casualties in all theatres resulted from accidents or disease, rather than enemy action. Ultimately soldiering, even when not in contact with the enemy, could be dirty, dangerous, and demanding. The importance of health and hygiene is therefore emphasised in Chapter 5, as the army went to some lengths to encourage troops to take precautions against diseases and insanitary conditions. This was particularly important when operating in awkward theatres such as North Africa and the Far East.

This book has relied on a variety of sources ranging from oral histories and memoirs, to War Office pamphlets/manuals, regimental histories and academic journals. A full list of the materials consulted can be found in the accompanying bibliography. Any reader wishing to delve further into the experiences of wartime British soldiers might like to employ this as an aid to his/her own research. It is now seventy years since the end of the war, and sadly the number of surviving veterans is diminishing rapidly. Consequently, it is more important than ever that we continue to respect their memory, and try to understand what that generation endured during the Second World War. I hope that this book has provided readers with a vivid impression of what it was like to be an ordinary British soldier, NCO or regimental officer serving with the wartime army.

James H. R. Goulty
April 2015

Chapter 1

Call-Up and Training

All units in wartime required effective training, which is the subject of this chapter. Initially this was difficult to accomplish, as the army was under-prepared for a major war, having spent the inter-war period policing the British Empire and conducting duties at home. John McManners, who enlisted in the Royal Northumberland Fusiliers (RNF) in 1939, stated that 'it wasn't the Army as it had been that we came into, but a former organic unity disrupted to function as a vast ramshackle training organisation'. After the evacuation from Dunkirk during the summer of 1940, it was fortunate that sufficient regular personnel remained to form a nucleus around which a mass conscript army could be forged from this 'ramshackle training organisation'.

Eventually the wartime army expanded to more than three million men and 300,000 women, around three-quarters of whom were conscripts. Forty-eight divisions were formed: thirty-five infantry, eleven armoured and two airborne. There were constant changes to the War Establishment (WE) of divisions, although they were considered the ideal-sized fighting formation because they comprised not only combat units, but all the necessary support personnel as well. At the start of the war the strength of an infantry division was 13,863 all ranks and this rose to 18,347 by the end of the war. The constituent parts of many divisions also altered during the war. For example, over a two–year period seventeen different armoured regiments and nine separate infantry battalions served with 7th Armoured Division, the famous 'Desert Rats'. Even so, individual soldiers tended to feel an affinity with the division to which they were attached and were proud to wear the relevant cloth insignia on their uniforms, such as the distinctive black cat emblem worn by members of 56th (London) Division, taken from the legend of Dick Whittington.

General Sir David Fraser, who was commissioned into the Grenadier Guards in 1941, observed that by 1945 the soldiers of the British Army had 'learned their trade and became entirely professional'. As will become apparent, recruits came from a variety of social, economic, educational and occupational backgrounds, and required training to mould them into effective soldiers. Almost all were subjected to the harshness of basic training, before commencing training in a particular trade, such as a signaller or infantryman. During the early 1940s the army also began employing scientific techniques in an effort to improve how it selected personnel for trades, and for training as officers.

Numerous soldiers did not actively seek promotion, preferring the relative anonymity and comradeship of the ranks. Leslie Blackie from Gateshead was posted to India in 1945 with 43rd Royal Tank Regiment (RTR). Writing home he explained that he was happy to remain a trooper (equivalent to a private) because he felt 'stripes make you disliked rather than liked'. However, as this chapter highlights, several wartime conscripts and volunteers became highly effective leaders at NCO or officer level alongside their Regular Army counterparts.

Many troops eventually served overseas, particularly after D-Day (6 June 1944) when the army became heavily involved in the Allied war effort. Yet, throughout the war large numbers of troops remained stationed in Britain. According to the military historian Jeremy Crang, more than 1.5 million troops, or over half the army, were based in Britain for much of the war, and even after D-Day approximately a million remained at home. These men were involved in home defence, and supporting those army units that were serving overseas. Military training was also one of their primary preoccupations, particularly leading up to the invasion of Normandy in June 1944.

A further part of this chapter outlines the importance of infantry training, with particular reference to the use of battle schools that came to prominence during 1941–44. With their emphasis on using live ammunition, coupled with physically demanding and realistic conditions, battle schools significantly helped transform men into fighting soldiers. Historian Timothy Harrison Place considers that 'they raised the British Army's game enormously'.

Recruits who volunteered for the army often proved eager warriors, whereas many conscripts simply longed to survive and pick up the threads of their civilian lives as soon as possible. Similarly, a divide existed between combat personnel and those whose job it was to provide logistical support working on the lines of communication rather than the front line. Historian John Ellis noted that for the latter the war typically comprised 'foreign travel tempered by excessive regimentation', whereas front-line troops often endured conditions as torrid as those encountered by their predecessors during the First World War. Often there was also a divide between regular soldiers who had served during the inter-war period, or even the First World War, and conscripts. Alan Wykes, who was called up into the Royal Hampshire Regiment, remembered that his Regimental Sergeant Major (RSM) would routinely berate his draft by stating: 'You are just a load of flaming amateurs' in his 'intimate voice (the one that merely traversed the parade ground at Brookwood, Surrey, as distinct from the one that that must have sounded to the slumbering souls in the nearby Necropolis like the Great Awakening)'.

Conscription for Men

Faced with the prospect of war during the late 1930s the British government began making preparations, including expanding the Territorial Army and re-introducing conscription. The Military Training Act, passed on 26 May 1939, compelled all males aged twenty and twenty-one to complete six months' service in the armed forces, followed by three and half months in the reserve. By the outbreak of war 35,000 of these conscripts (known as Militiamen) had been called-up into the army and completed their basic training.

Militiamen were notified by a letter from the Ministry of Labour in a buff-coloured envelope, similar to that received by John Elliot, who joined 4th Lincolnshire Regiment in late 1939.

Dear Sir,
In accordance with the Military Training Act, 1939 you will be required to present yourself for military training on Tuesday 17 October 1939 to 16 S/L Militia Depot Royal Artillery. A further confirmation will be sent to you later.

For most Militiamen basic training entailed square-bashing, rifle drill, physical training, and an introduction to infantry weapons, notably the Lee-Enfield rifle and Bren gun. Some men adjusted to this better than others. Ivan Daunt, who had worked on building sites, was conscripted into 4th Royal West Kent Regiment (RWK) in July 1939, and discovered he enjoyed army life, especially physical training. However, Leslie Crouch, who had worked as a carpenter and joined the same battalion, noted Militiamen tended to be more intelligent than the average regular soldier, and consequently proved less good at responding to military discipline. According to Leslie Crouch, you also always felt like 'a civilian in uniform' rather than a real soldier.

Another source of angst among Militiamen was that their pay was less than that of regular soldiers. Leslie Crouch recalled initially receiving 1 shilling and sixpence, although this was later increased to 2 shillings per day. However, soldiers of all types tended to be concerned about their pay throughout the war, particularly if they went overseas and had dependants at home. The conscript Leslie Blackie was delighted at having his pay as a trooper in the RTR increased in October 1944 from 3 shillings to 3 shillings and sixpence per day.

Once war was declared against Germany in September 1939, the Military Training Act was superseded by the National Service (Armed Forces) Act that made all males aged eighteen to forty-one liable for military service for the duration of the emergency. The upper age limit for compulsory military service was later raised to fifty-one years, and many older men were deployed on duties in Britain such as in anti-aircraft units.

Anyone liable for military service faced emotional and physical upheaval as they left their pre-war lives behind, and faced an uncertain future in the course of their duty. Citizens could only decline to serve if they were in holy orders, declared unfit under the Lunacy and Mental Treatment Acts, a registered blind person, or worked in a reserved occupation crucial to the war effort such as armaments manufacturing.

Conscientious Objectors had to put their case before a local tribunal, but could still be conscripted to fulfil non-combatant duties with the army, such as working as drivers, in stores, as medical orderlies, or even in bomb disposal. Alternatively they were employed as agricultural labourers, miners or served with the Fire Service or Friends Ambulance Unit run by the

Society of Friends (Quakers). Although there was still a great deal of social stigma attached to being a 'conchie', in contrast with the First World War men with long-term pacifist sympathies on ethical, religious and political grounds were usually respected and treated less harshly than during the earlier conflict.

Ken Adams was in his early twenties when he received his call-up papers and had been employed by the West Yorkshire Road Car Company. He attended a tribunal in Leeds during January 1940 and announced that, while he was prepared to join the Armed Forces, he 'wasn't prepared to kill a man in cold blood and wouldn't join the infantry'. Consequently, he was posted to the Royal Army Medical Corps (RAMC) and trained as a medical orderly. He still faced some disapproval as other soldiers perceived that he had wangled a comparatively comfortable position by registering as a 'conchie'. However, medical personnel who supported combat units frequently shared many of the discomforts that were a routine part of front-line life.

Even if the government considered it their patriotic duty to serve King and Country, other soldiers resented conscription, not least because it disrupted their civilian lives. In June 1939 Jack Brunton from Byker, Newcastle upon Tyne, was studying architecture at night school when he was called up. He had no aspirations for promotion and spent the next seven years as a gunner in the Royal Artillery (equivalent to a private in the infantry), bitterly resentful of the way in which the army had uprooted him and thwarted his efforts at obtaining an education. Before being commissioned into the Brigade of Guards, General Fraser served with 8th Royal Berkshire Regiment, and rapidly discovered that many of his fellow soldiers were criminals from Birmingham, who had been advised to join-up by magistrates and 'were totally uninterested in politics or the war'.

The actor Peter Ustinov became a reluctant infantryman in 1942, and confessed he was fearful of 'the brutalizing effects of military life', which he felt threatened to turn him into a 'robot'. On being called up into the Gordon Highlanders in 1939, Alistair Urquhart observed there was 'a lot of grumbling at lives turned upside down and becoming regimented, and no gung-ho euphoria'. Many were also wary, due to having grown up hearing unsettling stories from relatives about their experiences during the First World War, and were aware of the high casualty rate in the previous conflict.

As Reg Twigg, who enlisted in the Royal Leicestershire Regiment in June 1940, observed, 'a dark, collective memory sat in the corner of the pub like a ghost' as 'depressed eighteen to forty year olds' waited for the buff envelope.

By contrast, others were more understanding of the need for conscription, and even enthusiastic about what military service might entail. Bill Titchmarsh had served with the Home Guard and was working in an aircraft factory in Wiltshire when he received his call-up papers in December 1942. He could have claimed 'Reserved Occupation', but instead chose to join the army. As he recalled 'I sent them back and a fortnight later received an envelope with a ticket and One shilling postal order for lunch'. This was to cover the tortuous rail journey from his home in war-torn Southampton to Bodmin, where he was to undergo basic training under the aegis of the Duke of Cornwall's Light Infantry.

Eric de la Torre was called-up in October 1939 and selected for the Royal Army Service Corps (RASC), before later volunteering for the Commandos. He was excited about joining the army, having found his pre-war occupation as a desk-bound trainee accountant in London extremely dull. By comparison basic military training with its emphasis on discipline and drill seemed stimulating to him because it was so different from what he had experienced in civilian life.

Many young men were also swayed by the ideological nature of the war. When called-up in October 1939, Richard Phillips was already registered as a 'Militiaman', and eventually became the Intelligence Sergeant with 2nd South Wales Borderers seeing active service in Normandy and North-West Europe during 1944–45. As he put it 'someone had to stop Hitler's march across Europe' and as a soldier he was motivated by the need to win the war and defeat Fascism.

Regular Army Soldiers

Unlike conscripts, for regular soldiers the war provided the means, as Rifleman Victor Gregg commented, for them to 'earn their keep'. Some of these soldiers had seen service policing the British Empire during the inter-war years or even during the First World War, whereas as many others had only enlisted in the late 1930s and were still comparatively inexperienced.

As professional soldiers it was a chance for them to put their training and skills to the test on the battlefield. In 1939 Platoon Sergeant-Major Martin McLane, aged twenty-eight, was posted to France with the mortar platoon of 2nd Durham Light Infantry (DLI), part of the British Expeditionary Force (BEF). Although he missed his family, particularly his young daughter, he relished the challenge of being able to deploy his unit's mortars in an active role. The son of a shipyard worker from Tyneside, he was typical of the many young men who had enlisted during the 1930s rather than face unemployment, and who formed the bedrock of the wartime army.

Typically, men enlisted for seven years with the Colours, plus another five in the reserve, or 'seven and five' as it was known by regular soldiers. However, there was nothing to stop men signing on for longer terms of engagement if they desired, although as Victor Gregg cautioned men risked becoming institutionalised if they spent several years as a regular soldier, and could find civilian life awkward upon discharge from the army.

The outbreak of war witnessed a rapid readjustment within many regular units from a peace-time footing to mobilisation for active service. Cyril Feebery, who eventually rose to the rank of Regimental Sergeant-Major, enlisted in the Grenadier Guards in May 1937. When war was declared he noted, 'all the drill and boxing and spit and polish seemed pointless, part of another world'. Rapidly he and other guardsmen were ordered to hand in their highly-polished rifles and ceremonial kit, and re-equip themselves for war as part of 1st Guards Brigade, posted to the Franco-Belgian border.

Additionally, during 1940 'Young Soldier' volunteer battalions were raised and attached to each infantry regiment and given the prefix 70th. These tapped into patriotic enthusiasm and willingness to serve amongst those who were too young to be officially called up and young regular soldiers who had previously served with Home Defence Battalions. To be eligible boys had to be in top physical condition and ardent teenagers from a range of backgrounds flocked to these battalions, including troublemakers advised to join by their local police.

Often these youthful soldiers were highly motivated and several eventually became regular NCOs, were selected for officer training or volunteered for elite units. Eric Sykes from Huddersfield unsuccessfully attempted to join the army several times while under age, but in January 1943 was eventually accepted and posted to 70th DLI. The following September he volunteered for the Parachute Regiment, largely because he was fed up with the routine of guard duties and fatigues, and was eventually promoted sergeant.

As a sixteen-year-old in 1941, Stan Scott, who later joined Number 3 Commando, was posted to 'D' Company 70th Suffolk Regiment based in Ipswich. He recalled that they were issued First World War vintage weapons and equipment and conditions were fairly primitive. Their quartermaster provided them with 'three scratchy blankets, a big white bag and a little white bag. These had to be filled with straw for a palliasse and pillow.' No transport was available so they marched everywhere, including to a drill hall on the Portman Road near Ipswich Football Club's ground.

'Young Soldier' Battalions were frequently employed on guard duties and assisted in the construction of defence works at a time when the war was progressing badly for Britain. During 1943 they were disbanded, but as General Phillip J. Shears author of *The Story of the Border Regiment* (1948) opined, most troops from these units had proved keen to do their best and absorbed the spirit of the regiments to which they were posted.

However, not all soldiers serving within these battalions were willing volunteers. When Ernest Harvey was conscripted into the army in late 1942, he was posted to 70th DLI at Barnard Castle, County Durham. He found the 'NCOs charged you for almost anything' and was routinely punished by being confined to barracks, or given pack drill each evening after a days' work with the signal platoon. This entailed being made to run at the double along a river bank in full kit, complete with heavy pack, for lengthy periods.

Territorial Army Soldiers

During the late 1930s with war looming, numerous men aged between eighteen and thirty-eight volunteered for the Territorial Army (TA). Subsequently, many experienced active service during the war when the TA was embodied into the Regular Army under the control of the War Office. Most Territorial units had strong ties with particular geographical regions which boded well for their morale, even though these links were frequently diluted as the war progressed. On mobilisation in September 1939, 4th Royal

Norfolk Regiment for example, had its HQ at the Drill Hall in Norwich, and companies stationed at Yarmouth, Attleborough and Harleston.

Similarly, the Northumberland Hussars Yeomanry recruited predominantly from County Durham, Tyneside and Northumberland. Hugh Paterson, who volunteered for that unit in 1939, remembered, there were a wide range of accents on display from plummy public school to Standard English and broad Geordie dialect. Most officers came from the 'county or "coonty" set' and troopers were mainly 'townies'. By contrast, an officer from 6th Battalion DLI noted that in 1944 his platoon contained not only men from County Durham, but several from London, Liverpool, Wales and even Guernsey.

There were various reasons why men volunteered for the TA. Recruiting posters tended to appeal to men's sense of patriotism. One proclaimed 'Defend Britain and All That Britain Stands For. Join The Territorial Army'. Another from 1938 pictured a determined-looking rifleman with a fixed bayonet imposed upon a map of the British Isles, with the slogan 'Safeguard Your Liberties! Join The Territorial Army'. Yet another poster appealed to men to join the anti-aircraft units of the TA, which had a vital role to play in defending the country. It showed searchlights piercing the night sky and stated 'Make Britain a Stronghold of Freedom'.

As an eighteen-year-old miner's son working in a Chesterfield barber shop, William Sheppard was influenced by such posters, and inspired by sight of a group of soldiers in his home area, all appearing very smart in new uniforms, complete with puttees and spurs. During June 1939 this encouraged him to join 2nd/5th Sherwood Foresters, his local Territorial battalion.

However, although many Territorials were motivated to become 'amateur soldiers' out of a sense of patriotic duty, other factors also influenced men's desire to volunteer. James Donaldson, the son of a Scots electrical engineer, left school at fourteen and worked at sea and as a navvy before gaining employment at a quarry in Devon. He joined 4th Devonshire Regiment while underage, spurred on by a spirit for adventure because it represented 'something new'. By contrast, Derek Birch, who became a soldier with 6th Lincolnshire Regiment, recounted that he seemed 'not to have much say in the matter'. His boss at Catlin Bros. Ltd. Grocers and Tea Merchants, ensured that he joined his local TA battalion in April 1939, rather than wait to be conscripted, so that he could continue to work for the business.

Charles Andrews from Mortlake had various jobs after leaving school, including filling shelves at a shop in Hammersmith and working for a brewery. During the 1930s he volunteered for 6th East Surrey Regiment. Similarly, eighteen-year-old Donald Lashbrook, a keen footballer from Croydon, enlisted with 4th Queen's Royal Regiment shortly before the war, while working for his local Co-Operative Store. Both men were motivated by the financial incentives on offer. As *TA Poster Number 9* explained, a trained private soldier could earn a proficiency grant totalling up to £5 per year, a considerable sum in those days. Territorials could potentially receive other grants too, including up to 30 shillings per year for attending extra drill nights. The figure varied depending on how many extra drill nights they actually attended.

In the TA men learnt a variety of skills on regular drill nights, and at their annual summer camps which normally lasted between eight and fifteen days. This included instruction in foot and arms drill and physical training, plus how to handle various weapons. In some cases specialist training was provided in specific trades. Douglas Old served with the signals platoon attached to HQ Company of 4th Dorset Regiment. He recorded that in 1939 his signals training comprised the use of telephones, plus to a lesser extent signalling lamps and heliographs. However, as the war progressed various forms of wireless set were introduced, and he adapted to operate these, particularly on active service in Normandy and North-West Europe in 1944–45.

As Tom Barlow, who joined 2nd/4th South Lancashire Regiment during 1939, remembered there were distinct practical advantages to the TA part-time training regime. In his case it enabled him to continue his education via evening classes when not attending drill nights, a liberty he would not have had as a conscript. Jack Lock, who eventually became a sergeant with 4th RWK, explained the main reason he volunteered for the TA in 1938, was because he wanted to exercise control over his own destiny and have some choice as to where he served, rather than be conscripted and probably end up miles from home.

Another incentive for men to join the TA was that it provided sporting and social opportunities within an organised framework that they might not otherwise have enjoyed. One recruiting poster informed men that by becoming a Territorial soldier not only were they serving their country, but they were entering 'a fellowship of congenial companions'. Charles Andrews found that his annual camp with 6th East Surrey Regiment compensated for the lack of a summer holiday, something he couldn't afford in the 1930s.

In May 1939 Basil Levi volunteered for 4th Queen's Royal Regiment (TA) which later became 63rd Searchlight Regiment Royal Artillery and was involved in the defence of Britain before being posted to Norway in June 1945. As a keen footballer he was able to play for the army, and became involved in other sports, including organising table-tennis tournaments. Ray Ellis volunteered for the South Nottinghamshire Hussars and was tempted by the prospect of learning to ride and becoming a dashing cavalry trooper. Yet, as he soon discovered, his unit was destined to become part of the Royal Artillery, equipped with guns and vehicles rather than horses, although like most Yeomanry regiments it did retain much of its cavalry spirit.

The Auxiliary Territorial Service (ATS)

In September 1938, the Auxiliary Territorial Service (ATS), forerunner of the post-war Women's Royal Army Corps, was established by Royal Warrant. This offered the opportunity for young women to volunteer for training so they could be of use to their country in case of war. Many early ATS volunteers demonstrated Girl-Guide like enthusiasm for the challenges they faced on drill nights and at annual camps. After a strict upbringing, Carlotta Blanshard found service with 1st (Glasgow) ATS liberating, especially annual camp when she was away from home for the first time. Typically, drill nights and camps allowed women to learn and practice skills within a framework of military discipline, which boosted their morale. However, owing to their auxiliary status they did not learn to handle weapons like male soldiers.

By the outbreak of hostilities 17,000 women had voluntarily enrolled in the ATS, and as Eileen Bigland stressed in *Britain's Other Army* (1946), most did so with little idea of what their eventual pay would be, or the exact roles in which they would serve. All they could be certain of was that they had committed themselves for the duration of the war, however long that might be.

As the official booklet *National Service* (HMSO, 1939) explained, ATS personnel were to be employed in non-combat duties, primarily as drivers, in clerical jobs, or as cooks, store-women and orderlies. According to the historian Lucy Noakes all of these roles with the possible exception of drivers, 'fitted easily within the accepted definition of a female sphere of activity'.

Irene Salmon had joined the ATS before the war and on 3 September 1939 was required to report to the Drill Hall in North Shields near to where she lived. As an orderly one of her first jobs was to make sandwiches for anti-aircraft gun crews, but when an eagle-eyed officer spotted her neat handwriting on a laundry list, she was re-assigned to clerical duties. Staff Sergeant Jennie Warwick, who originally came from County Durham, was living in Brighton at the start of the war and spent much of her ATS service attached to the Royal Army Pay Corps in Radcliffe, Lancashire. Here, in an old mill which still stank of oily machinery, she helped run an office working out pay for the Royal Engineers.

Similarly, at Richmond Barracks, RHQ of the Green Howards, Number 40 Company (North Riding) ATS was ordered to take over clerical duties, and provide women to work in stores and as cooks and waitresses during 1939–40. While such roles may have appeared mundane, importantly by taking over from men the ATS were able to free up soldiers for postings elsewhere. However, as the war progressed a greater variety of jobs became available to the ATS. In late 1943 the ATS could boast 200,000 Auxiliaries and at least 6,000 officers, with approximately a third of these women having been trained in a trade. This enabled them to supplement soldier craftsman. Trades included draughtswomen, armourers, fitters, wireless operators and a wide variety of clerks and technical staff. In short, ATS women ultimately came to perform many of the functions that were necessary to effectively support a modern, mechanised army at war.

Notably ATS personnel were widely employed on communications duties, and by 1944 they had taken on the bulk of the work in signal and cypher offices, plus on switchboards. Throughout the war ATS women also served overseas, including North-West Europe, where by mid-1945 over

9,000 were deployed on various tasks including as drivers, signals staff and even supporting male gunners within mixed heavy anti-aircraft batteries.

During the winter of 1944–45 ATS Private A. S. Hall was employed working in shifts on a telephone exchange in Brussels, a vital part of the communications network supporting units of the British Liberation Army (BLA). Off duty her life was enlivened by walks in parks, visiting the Treveuren Forest and enjoying cafes. Similarly, in March 1945 Helen Hay was posted to Brussels to command 306 Switchboard Operating Platoon, Line of Communications Signals BLA, which as she recalled allowed her ATS women to replace male signallers in rear areas. As an officer she was billeted in a house with an army cook, and entitled to visit officers' clubs run by the British and Canadian Armies.

Often their work enabled ATS women to learn skills that they might not otherwise have been able to acquire. Training for those selected to operate searchlights with the all-female 93rd Searchlight Regiment Royal Artillery incorporated instruction on electricity, electronics, mechanics, map reading, Morse code and first aid, plus the general maintenance of searchlights. In 1940 former nursery nurse Joan Reeves who volunteered for the ATS, was posted to Wales and attached to a radar unit of the Royal Artillery. There as part of a team she learnt how to operate a GL receiver set, and was inducted into the field of radar location. Gwen Gillham, who served with the ATS during 1940–44, spent two years in the operations room at RAF Biggin Hill, where she helped co-ordinate anti-aircraft defences in South East England. This entailed relaying messages from the RAF to ATS personnel attached to anti-aircraft units who in turn communicated with the male gunners.

Wartime officer Elizabeth Stevens explained that women of the ATS were not integrated with other branches of the army, but rather loaned to them. Even so, many ATS women developed an affinity with the units to which they were attached, and appreciated being able to display the relevant insignia which was good for their morale. For example, from October 1942 ATS women attached to the Royal Electrical and Mechanical Engineers were granted permission to wear REME shoulder flashes on their uniforms, and trade badges such as the lightening zig-zag denoting an electrician. Similarly, as a qualified switchboard operator with Northern Command stationed at Catterick during 1940–41, Helen Hay was delighted to proudly wear the Royal Corps of Signals badge, nicknamed 'Jimmy', above her left breast pocket.

During the war women volunteered for the ATS for a variety of reasons. Ruth Aves (née Hawkins) was working in the aircraft manufacturing industry when she joined up as she longed for a more active part in the war. She was spurred on by having a relative in the army, and hearing the catastrophic news that Singapore had fallen in February 1942. Other women were motivated to join for patriotic reasons, or because they wanted revenge for a loved one killed during the war. Many women from less privileged backgrounds viewed the military as a means of escaping the drudgery of domestic service or factory work. The army appeared to offer a better future, especially if they were able to learn new skills and be trained in a trade.

Consequently, those with comfortable middle-class upbringings could find themselves rubbing shoulders with working-class girls, and all were subjected to army discipline. Pam Hoare, who volunteered as an eighteen-year-old before the war and was mobilised in 1939, remembered that in her unit were a variety of women, including shop girls, office workers, parlourmaids, a librarian and one or two older ones who appeared to be veterans of the First World War. With the passing of a second National Service Act in December 1941, that introduced conscription for unmarried women aged between twenty and thirty, the social diversity of the ATS was increased further, although many officers still tended to have middle- or upper-class backgrounds.

During late 1943, prior to commencing her officer cadet training, Helen Hay was ordered to assist in the training of ATS recruits, by which time female conscription had taken effect. Initially she had to deal with resentful women conscripted from the East End of London, many of whom needed a bath and lessons on personal hygiene on joining the ATS. Another draft she instructed comprised several French women who had volunteered and were extremely keen, but lacked adequate English, making communication a challenge so that she had to rely on her schoolgirl French.

To an extent military service offered all women, whatever their background, a chance to prove they could perform tasks as well as men. To do so, they often had to face the fact that in the 1940s women were largely regarded as second-class citizens. There was also a widespread perception that women in uniform were of loose morals. Historians Lucy Noakes and Virginia Nicholson highlighted that the ATS was invariably viewed badly, particularly when compared with the other women's services. Common slurs included that the other ranks were widely promiscuous, or 'officers' ground sheets'. Yet, as former army officer and historian Imogen Corrigan observed, 'far from being of low virtue', most ATS recruits 'were astonishingly naïve by today's standards'. Another deterrent against illicit sex was fear of pregnancy. Wartime ATS officer Elizabeth Stevens noted, falling pregnant resulted in an automatic discharge under paragraph 11 of King's Regulations.

Some soldiers initially found the presence of females nerve-wracking, or even disliked them. In 1939 Richmond Gorle, as regular officer in the Royal Artillery, was tasked with supervising the introduction of ATS personnel into his regiment. 'I was very ill at ease when I sat down to interview some forty or so young women … Dealing with women en masse was a new and uncertain experience for me.' Working on clerical duties in Dundee during 1941–42, Carlotta Blanshard, who had been promoted sergeant, recalled encountering married men who had been conscripted who were unhappy working with women who appeared to be stealing their jobs so they could be posted overseas. At RAF Biggin Hill Gwen Gillham discovered the men ATS women replaced were resentful, not least because most of them lived in nearby Bromley, and her first commanding officer was an elderly major who proved intolerant of females. As the war progressed men who were to work alongside women were often vetted so that SFM (Suitable For Mixed) or NFM (Not For Mixed) would appear on their documents, 'Mixed' meaning units comprised of male and female personnel, such as some of the batteries in Anti-Aircraft (AA) Command.

The only active operational area open to women was with AA Command that operated searchlights and a variety of anti-aircraft guns as part of the nation's air defences. At least 57,000 young ATS women served with AA Command, and performed every duty apart from actually firing the guns. The War Office, reflecting wider public opinion, deemed it unacceptable for women to be directly involved in killing. However, Brigadier Shelford Bidwell in *The Women's Royal Army Corps* (1977) suggested there were cases where women unofficially fired anti-aircraft guns. Likewise, defence writer

Georgina Natzio noted that ATS volunteers in mixed heavy anti-aircraft batteries posted to the Continent in 1944 carried small arms for personal protection, even though technically this was prohibited owing to their status as auxiliaries.

Recruits volunteering for AA Command had to be physical fit and highly-capable individuals. Gwen Gillham recounted that she was rejected from serving on a gun because of her small stature. However, Ruth Aves was selected for training on the box-like predictor, a primitive form of computer that required six operators. This used data on the height and previous flight path of a hostile aircraft to calculate its likely position when shells reached it. The information was passed onto the male gunners to enable them to set the correct fuse and elevation to engage the target. Other ATS women operated height- and rangefinding instruments, or early forms of radar used to provide warning of approaching aircraft, and worked in plotting stations that helped co-ordinate the anti-aircraft defences.

In gun positions ATS women faced harsh, potentially dangerous conditions alongside the male gunners they were assisting. Commenting on her service with 627th (Mixed) HAA Battery on Foulness Island, ATS Corporal Peggy Linington (née Hennessey) noted it was so cold there was sometimes a rum ration, they pitched their tents on boggy reclaimed land, and washing and sanitary arrangements were extremely primitive.

Ruth Aves, who became an NCO, remembered that once in her unit a round from a 3.7in anti-aircraft gun exploded prematurely, killing a young ATS woman working nearby. The first ATS casualty of the war was Private Nora Caveney, who was killed by a bomb splinter during an air raid on the South Coast, while working on a predictor attached to 148th Regiment Royal Artillery during May 1942.

Typically, women on gun batteries were required to demonstrate high levels of fortitude, efficiency and bravery. Former shop assistant Lance Corporal Golland of the ATS was awarded the British Empire Medal when in January 1944 she stayed at her post during a night raid on London and passed information to the gunners, despite her position receiving several near-misses from enemy bombs.

The operation of cumbersome searchlights for AA Command was another area that taxed women's abilities to cope both psychologically and physically, particularly when these were positioned in remote rural locations. Searchlights were used to illuminate enemy aircraft for anti-aircraft guns and night fighters, and acted as beacons to guide friendly aircraft back to their bases. It was strenuous work and potentially perilous, as the members of the all-female 93rd Searchlight Regiment Royal Artillery discovered. They had to regularly change the carbon sticks used by the searchlights, and risked being badly burned if these were not allowed to cool sufficiently. Another threat was that enemy aircraft sometimes tried to disable searchlights by firing down their beams, which could kill or maim their crews.

Despite all the challenges ATS women faced, particularly in AA Command, Monica Jackson, who became a signals officer, considered that 'generally morals and morale were pretty high'. She also remembered that there was a strong sense of comradeship, which increased later in the war when some of the dangers had declined which allowed personnel to feel more relaxed. According to Major George Whybro, who encountered several volunteer ATS personnel while serving with the Royal Artillery, they were hard-working and very efficient.

Medicals and Basic Training

All new male and female recruits were subjected to a medical prior to basic training. As Robert Fife, who was called up in 1939 and joined 49th (Northumberland Battalion) RTR, discovered, under the pressure of wartime conditions these were not necessarily scrupulously undertaken. His was at a local recruiting centre at a medical college in Newcastle upon Tyne, where men lined up, gave a small cough and were informed 'Right you're in'. Similar, scenes were repeated around the country. When Oliver Hardy volunteered for 6th Lincolnshire Regiment, he was sent to a local doctor's surgery where 'with sufficient clothing removed to allow a cursory examination, questions were asked and the answers noted, and in a very short time another batch of recruits was accepted for service'.

For young women the prospect of a medical examination was often more daunting because it was likely to be conducted by a male doctor. Pam Hoare came from a middle-class household and when she volunteered for the ATS, she felt that 'the worst thing was the medical. We had to strip to the waist in front of a young doctor with whom we'd danced and played tennis. Goodness knows what he was thinking. As embarrassed as we were, I expect.'

Soldiers also received a batch of inoculations, notably against Tetanus. On joining the DLI in 1942, Ernest Harvey discovered that 'TET TOX injections left an awful scar' and afterwards the Medical Officer advised recruits to scrub tables so as to keep their arms moving and prevent them stiffening up.

There followed a basic training programme which attempted to transform recruits from civilians into disciplined soldiers. For men foot and rifle drill were accompanied by PT, plus instruction in elementary tactics, map reading, fieldcraft and weapons training. This grounding in fundamental military skills and discipline paved the way for recruits to be further trained for specific roles such as infantrymen, tank crew or signallers once they had completed basic training.

At ATS barracks women were treated with equal harshness to men, often nursing swollen feet from hours of marching and drilling in heavy shoes. Besides foot drill and PT, instruction covered security procedures, how to cope with a gas attack, and social (a euphemism for sexual) hygiene. Many women had never been away from home before and had to contend with the misery of homesickness, compounded by strict rules forbidding them from displaying family photographs in their barracks. Although she never left her native north-east of England during her ATS service, Irene Salmon remembered suffering from homesickness and was once confined to barracks for running away.

Like their male counterparts, women were soon introduced to army discipline. On their first day at one ATS barracks recruits had to endure 'Latrine Parade'. Squads were marched to the latrines by an unsympathetic junior NCO and given precisely one minute each, before being issued with uniforms and personal kit. A skill many soon learnt was that of 'barracking' their beds by placing bedclothes in a symmetrical, perfect square at one end on top of three 'biscuits' or mattresses. The whole lot would then be inspected before they were allowed to make their beds.

For many male recruits their service began with an awkward rail journey under wartime conditions, before they were herded unceremoniously onto army trucks and transported to forbidding-looking infantry depots or other training establishments. An entrant to the Royal Corps of Signals noted, 'Catterick Camp was a bleak, lightless huddle of hut roofs, jagged against the night sky'.

Conditions at most barracks were tough. Stuart Hills was posted to 30th Primary Training Wing at Bovington Camp, Dorset. 'On arrival we had to fill our paillasses with spikey straw to sleep on'. Alternatively, recruits were issued with 'biscuits' and coarse army blankets with which to sleep on hard wooden beds. Colonel John Shipster joined the army as a private soldier at Willems Cavalry Barracks, Aldershot in 1940. 'The living conditions were appalling; there were twenty-four soldiers in one barrack room, heated by only one small coal fire in bitterly cold weather, with nowhere to sit and read or write.'

For men army life started with a severe haircut. Dirk Bogarde recalled at Catterick 'we queued in the drizzling mist to be shorn like sheep'. Likewise, Brian Harpur observed that within hours of joining the army we were shaved to 'within an inch of our scalps', the idea being that it reduced the individual to a 'cypher'. Similarly, ATS women were expected to have their hair clipped, or wear it neatly in a bun above the shoulder. Alternatively, as Jennie Warwick remembered, it proved popular to wear a hairnet at work so that you could wear it long for going to dances when off duty.

Recruits were rapidly assigned an army number which they kept for their entire service, even if they transferred to another unit. Lucky recruits were allotted a number that was straightforward to remember. Bill Titchmarsh was allocated 14396143, which he felt was easy to memorise as the first three and last three digits were the same. Under the terms of the Military Training Act, Fergus Anckorn was classed as a Militiaman, although owing to the outbreak of war he did not join the Royal Artillery as a recruit until October 1939. He recounted the process of receiving his army number with some poignancy:

We lined up to go to a table where there were two sergeant-majors with paper and pen and we were given our army number and told never to forget it. Mine was 947556. The man in front of me was of course, 947555. He is now a name on the war memorial in Westerham. If I'd been one ahead in the queue ... would that have been me on the memorial?

All recruits were issued a Soldier's Service and Pay Book or Army Book 64 (AB 64) as it was known. This was an essential document that had to be carried at all times. It contained a soldier's enlistment/attestation details, lists of training they had undertaken and kit issued, records of their employment both with the army and in civilian life, medical data, and importantly details on their next of kin, plus instructions on making a soldiers' will.

Often, those from sheltered or more comfortable backgrounds were for the first time living and working alongside less privileged individuals. On entering the depot of the Middlesex Regiment at Mill Hill in North London, Brian Harpur, son of a Protestant clergyman from Ireland, was confronted by 'prime examples of race, class, creed and villainy'. Yet, as Bill Bellamy who joined 58th Training Regiment at Bovington Camp in 1941 discovered, 'it was not always those with the purest of accents who proved most reliable'.

Within many intakes a diverse range of backgrounds were represented. Lieutenant Colonel Colin Mitchell joined the army as a private soldier in 1943, and noted that his fellow recruits at Maidstone Barracks included: an old navvy who kept his trousers up with an officer's Sam Browne belt, a pilot dismissed from the RAF for 'lack of moral fibre', a ballet dancer, several ex-policemen, a sprinkling of former convicts and even a veteran of the Spanish Civil War. Alistair Urquhart's intake to the Gordon Highlanders comprised farm-workers, servants, labourers, fishermen, apprentice engineers and plumbers, who all considered themselves expendable.

Rapidly all recruits, whatever their background or sex, would receive their uniforms and personal equipment. For male soldiers this typically included:

- a rifle and bayonet
- steel helmet
- knife, fork, spoon
- mess tin
- mug
- spare metal buttons
- a 'housewife' or needle and thread for repairing clothing
- washing/shaving kit
- three pairs of socks
- three khaki shirts

- vests,
- battledress blouse and trousers
- a duplicate set in denim for fatigues
- forage cap
- gaiters and boots
- belt and webbing equipment
- groundsheet.

One of the most important smaller items was a long string with a weight at one end and loop at the other, into which a flannel measuring 4in by 2in was inserted. This was known throughout the army as the '4 by 2'. Onto this flannel soldiers put a little oil and then repeatedly slid the weighted end down the barrel of their rifles until they were immaculately clean.

Battledress, described by military historian Sir Michael Howard as 'that most sensible of all uniforms', was introduced during the late 1930s. It was specifically designed as a military working outfit, although was smart enough to be worn for parades. As Captain Hugh Gunning of the King's Own Scottish Borderers (KOSB) explained, it had 'been scientifically designed with its pockets in all the right places in trousers and blouse'. Although battledress had no metal buttons requiring polishing, the associated gaiters and webbing equipment needed regular attention if they were to pass inspections.

However, ATS personnel were provided with clothing designed by army tailors that frequently proved uncomfortable, unfeminine and contrasted poorly with that issued to other women's services, notably the Women's Royal Naval Service with their stylish blue uniforms. The army issue underwear or 'khaki bloomers' were universally disliked together with cotton vests and bras which many women deemed extremely unflattering. As Joan Reeves remembered 'you had to wear stockings like bricks to put on' and these together with the underwear were often derisively termed 'passion killers'. It was quipped that if the entire ATS had paraded on the front line in their underwear, the war would have been over in a week because the enemy would all die laughing.

Initially many women were issued with ill-fitting garments, or lacked important items because the army was unprepared for a large influx of female volunteers. On joining the ATS in 1939 Irene Salmon had to wear a hat that was several sizes too big, a skirt too long for her, and Wellington boots because no shoes were available. ATS officer Elizabeth Stevens found nothing ever seemed to fit her, particularly trousers, because she was tall and slim. Despite this, like many ATS women she considered her uniform practical, even if it was not very flattering.

Some women opted to alter their shapeless ATS uniforms, especially the skirts, but this risked incurring the wrath of their officers who would hold a 'skirt parade' and insist that all garments were worn at the correct length specified by military regulations. Pam Hoare noted 'you really couldn't do a thing with those uniforms, not even the prettiest and slenderest of us'.

As the war progressed, the uniform situation improved for women and many were issued with ATS Service Dress, a form of utility uniform equivalent to male battledress. In 1943 an ATS handbag was introduced that enabled women to carry a modicum of personal items. At one billet in Newcastle upon Tyne, an issue of blue-and-white pyjamas even proved so popular amongst one ATS contingent that they danced a conga and would have continued into the street had an officer not curtailed the celebration.

Army boots issued to male recruits required special attention to achieve the obligatory sheen. There were three possible methods of achieving this: boots could be covered in a layer of methylated spirits and 'burned off' to give a superficial glossy skin. Alternatively, a coating of nail varnish could be applied, but if it cracked it could be disastrous. Although laborious, the safest approach entailed plenty of old-fashioned 'spit and polish', working polish into the leather inch by inch, then honing the surface for hours until it shone.

Kit inspections, where everything had to be laid out in the prescribed army manner could be a horrendous ordeal. Even the slightest deviation from the accepted layout resulted in soldiers being put on a charge or 'fizzer'. Punishment typically comprised being confined to barracks, or made to double around the parade square in full equipment, including a heavy pack. Peter Ustinov vividly recalled one inspection where his socks proved troublesome:

I did what I could to hammer them into the squareness demanded by military protocol, to no avail. The moment I left them alone, the wool expanded slowly into a voluptuous rotundity, and they lay there like buns on a breakfast tray. The sergeant-major entered my room in fairly jovial mood, but when his eyes fell on my socks, I fancied I saw smoke emerging from his flared nostrils.

Foot drill was another key component of basic training for recruits from both sexes. It was intended to instil discipline, a sense of pride and generally achieved this, although some found it easier than others to demonstrate the necessary precision. It included teaching recruits how to march and salute correctly. As John McManners recalled it was impressed upon recruits that the correct way to salute officers was 'longest way up, shortest way down'.

Mel Lowry, who eventually joined 12th Battalion RTR, recalled a hapless fellow recruit who had to be left in the barracks during their passing-out parade because he was so un-coordinated at drill. Similarly, even though he eventually became a sergeant with the Royal Corps of Signals, Reg Best admitted that he hated the discipline, drill, parades and fatigues that were an omnipresent part of army life. Whereas the film star Dirk Bogarde, another recruit with the Royal Corps of Signals, excelled at drill owing to his theatre training which had attuned him to taking stage directions or commands.

During drill soldiers and ATS women could expect to be treated with a mixture of sympathy and harshness by their instructors, and this was sometimes reflected in the language they employed. Ruth Aves found it difficult to believe some of the comments she heard during her ATS training. Squads were marched up and down and likened to apes or informed in no uncertain terms that they were a disgrace. When John McManners, underwent recruit training at Fenham Barracks, Newcastle upon Tyne, he encountered what he termed the 'sexual ambience of the barrack room', which stemmed from the routine employment of obscenities by NCO instructors.

Soon most recruits learnt that much truth applied to the old adage 'never volunteer for anything'. Army life resonated with ruses designed to secure the services of unwary soldiers for mundane chores. For example, if an NCO asked for musicians, then any recruit naïve enough to express an interest would probably be ordered to move the piano in the NAAFI rather than demonstrate their musical talents. Similarly, most recruits regularly had to endure irksome fatigues, such as peeling large piles of potatoes in freezing cold, greasy water, or mounting lengthy guard duties.

Yet during their square-bashing many drafts displayed levels of teamwork, corporate spirit and discipline that the army was keen to foster, and would prove beneficial on active service. As Ken Tout, who fought as a tank gunner with the Northamptonshire Yeomanry commented, 'discipline, learned through foot drill on parade or through endless shining of brasses and peeling of spuds does produce an instinctive reaction to commands in the heat of battle'.

Many men and women united against the tyranny of fatigues and developed ways of coping with basic training. Within some drafts a spirit of competition emerged, as individual recruits sought to outdo their comrades. Conversely, many recruits would help each other to prepare for kit inspections, or offer to clean their comrade's equipment in return for payment. Dirk Bogarde became an expert boot polisher and hired out his services for cigarettes. Jack Brunton brought a small electric iron into the army, which cost him 7/6d, and loaned it to other soldiers for 3d, rapidly recouping his investment.

Some recruits even enjoyed their experience. Former Defence Secretary Denis Healey served with the Royal Artillery, and noted basic training at Uniacke Barracks provided an

> escape from the demoralising consciousness of war and the constant peering into an obscure and dangerous future ... The war was rarely ever mentioned. I had no responsibilities to myself, and I positively welcomed the regimentation.

Recruits with previous military service in the Home Guard or Officer Training Corps (OTC) at school or university tended to cope better than those who lacked such experience. As a teenager from Tyneside, Bill Ness served in his local Home Guard unit which brought him into contact with several experienced older soldiers, including veterans of the First World War. Consequently, he learned much about army life that proved highly beneficial when he joined the Duke of Wellington's Regiment (DWR) in 1943, before later volunteering for the Parachute Regiment. In particular he explained these veterans taught him to respect authority and never question an order. 'Always do as you were told. If you couldn't, salute smartly, turnabout and disappear. Alternatively if you received an order that was stupid salute smartly and go away.'

Likewise, Sir Michael Howard discovered that OTC at Wellington School and Oxford University had familiarised him with important facets of the military, including drill and the handling and maintenance of small arms. Owing to his OTC background, Lieutenant Colonel Robin Painter similarly performed well during his basic training, and found that 'foot drill, rifle drill and weapon training presented no problems'.

Other Ranks Selection

Initially all conscripts and volunteers had to register with the Ministry of Labour and National Service before being sent to a local recruiting office for a medical and interview. If lucky they would be selected for training with the regiment or corps of their choice. The industrialised nature of modern warfare and the mechanisation of the British Army ensured that a wide range of trades were open to troops, ranging from a rifleman in the infantry to a skilled tradesman with the Royal Engineers.

Men with a mechanical bent or previous experience often opted for the Royal Armoured Corps (RAC), where they could eventually learn to operate armoured vehicles. Mel Lowry volunteered and was posted to 60th RAC Training Regiment at Tidworth, where he was determined to become a tank driver. At RAC Training Regiments personnel underwent a 24-week course intended to provide elementary military training and produce the necessary tradesmen for the Corps. These included gunners, wireless operators, driver/mechanics, fitters, electricians and administrative personnel. Driving and maintenance formed a vital component of training as any member of the RAC, whatever his trade, needed to be prepared to serve as tank crew.

Alternatively, the RASC proved popular amongst drivers and recruits who wanted to learn because they stood a chance of being trained to operate trucks and other military vehicles. On joining the TA Ray Close, who could already drive, was posted to 509th Company RASC, 44th (Home Counties)

Division, based in Croydon. He became a trooper driver and experienced active service in France during 1940. Similarly, John Blake was posted to North Africa in 1942 to drive a cumbersome 3-ton Chevrolet truck with 288th Company RASC, responsible for ferrying vital supplies from railheads to forward areas. Fergus Ankcorn had been used to driving his family's car before the war. When called up in 1939 he expressed an interest in becoming a driver with the RASC. Instead he was drafted into the Royal Artillery, but his experience was still useful when he was ordered to drive a variety of antiquated gun-towing vehicles.

Some units proved effective at harnessing conscripts' civilian skills. When 8th Battalion DLI mobilised for war it was able to employ several men who previously worked for County Durham haulage firms as drivers. Likewise, Alfred Sheppard, a stonemason, was conscripted in October 1939 and sought to join the Royal Engineers (RE). Owing to his background as a tradesman he was accepted and posted to Number 1 Training Battalion RE in Kent, where alongside basic military training he received instruction on bridging and demolition work.

By contrast, drafts posted to 12th RTR contained several men from the building trade whose skills were of debatable value for tank crew. As the war progressed it became increasingly apparent that existing selection methods were inadequate, given the rapid expansion of the wartime army. Men were required not only for combat roles, but also to perform numerous specialist functions, such as wireless operators and armourers, which had no civilian equivalent. Similarly, the various corps such as the RE and RASC offered a variety of jobs to recruits including storekeepers, clerks and drivers, as well as mechanically-skilled tradesmen.

As the historian Jeremy Crang has demonstrated, men often ended up being posted to units on the recommendation of the recruiting officer who interviewed them, rather than having their preferences, temperament and previous experience fully considered. This was because the recruiting officers were untrained in interview techniques, and to a large extent obliged to allocate personnel in accordance with the War Office's manpower requirements. Mel Lowry and Alfred Sheppard were fortunate in having their preferences met. Due to weaknesses in the selection process other soldiers proved military misfits. Given his self-confessed lack of technical prowess, Dirk Bogarde was surprised to be posted to the Royal Corps of Signals. He presumed the army noticed he had attended a technical school in Glasgow, even though he had been removed from lessons to pursue bookbinding, metalwork and pottery. As he admitted regarding his signal training: 'I was baffled, uncomprehending, lost … floundering in a mess of wires, bells, batteries and code'. Graphic designer Abram Games, who produced some of the most iconic wartime posters, discovered his skills were initially considered of limited value. As a lowly private soldier he was ordered to draw route maps for training schemes in the depths of Northumberland, and by his own admission lost more convoys than any other draughtsman.

Investigations within Northern Command and Scottish Command during 1940–41 revealed that personnel were often misemployed. Notably, infantry battalions and the RAC contained large numbers of personnel who proved unsuitable, either because they lacked the necessary aptitudes for these combatant branches of the army, or were capable of more skilled employment elsewhere. According to Jeremy Crang, army psychiatrists concluded that approximately 4 per cent of all intakes were unlikely to be efficient as combatants, and around another 5 per cent were only suited to less skilled combat requirements such as using a rifle in self-defence.

In 1942 the army sought to improve its selection process by introducing the General Service Corps (GSC). Under the GSC all recruits spent six weeks at a Primary Training Centre (PTC), before being posted to a specific regiment or corps. Here recruits endured the usual discipline and fatigues associated with basic training. As Lieutenant Colonel Colin Mitchell recalled, 'we were drilled, inoculated, indoctrinated with "British Way and Purpose" [official booklets on political issues], taught to fire weapons and generally converted from pyjama-wearing civilians into rough-shirted basic soldiers'.

However, while assigned to the GSC recruits also sat selection and intelligence tests designed to assess their suitability for training in a particular trade. These were presided over by Personnel Selection Officers (PSOs), frequently chosen from the teaching profession, and comprised questionnaires, plus oral and practical elements. Those with an aptitude for combat were selected for the infantry, RAC or artillery, while others with suitable technical abilities were chosen as army tradesmen in one of the corps.

Weaker recruits could be assessed by a psychiatrist to determine what function they might best fulfil. This included being allocated specific employment with a non-combatant unit such as the RAMC. Alternatively, those deemed to be suffering from a disability or psychiatric illnesses were often discharged by a medical board.

How well ordinary soldiers reacted to the employment of psychiatrists and scientific selection methods is open to question. Historians Edgar Jones and Stephen Ironside observed that there was a large degree of scepticism within the military, which is innately conservative, regarding the value of psychiatrists. In particular those employed direct from civilian practice were resented, as was evident by their popular army nicknames 'trick cyclists and pissy Christs'.

The experience of 2nd Fife and Forfar Yeomanry would seem to bear this out. That unit spent considerable time training in Britain before being posted to Normandy as an armoured regiment in June 1944. During 1942 many of its personnel, including tank driver Ron Forbes, were earmarked for psychiatric testing. He had previously worked in the art department of a printing firm and performed well in these tests, one of which asked soldiers to match up various shapes. However, most of his comrades were deemed unfit to serve as tank crew, and as he recalled the unit's overall reaction was to treat the tests scornfully.

Similar testing procedures were employed by the ATS. During her service as a switchboard operator at Catterick, twenty-year-old Helen Hay was surprised to be assessed by a psychiatrist who determined she had a top-grade IQ and would be better employed elsewhere. Initially she was promoted to lance-corporal in charge of three switchboard operators, as she was considered too immature for another posting, but she was eventually selected for officer training.

By summer 1945 over 700,000 male recruits had passed through the GSC: 6 per cent were identified as potential officers, 9 per cent as suitable for training as tradesmen, and 14 per cent referred to psychiatrists. As Jeremy Crang commented scientific methods 'revolutionised the utilisation of manpower in the army' and emphasised 'the recognition that recruits had different individual capabilities, temperaments and job needs'. Yet, on balance both the army as an institution and many individual soldiers remained wary of psychiatrists and psychologists becoming involved in military affairs.

Infantry Training

Having successfully passed their basic training, soldiers could expect to receive further training with the specific branch of the army they went on to join. Recruits selected as infantrymen during 1942–45, spent another ten weeks at an Infantry Training Centre (ITC) after completing their basic training. Here they were instructed in a diverse range of skills ranging from map reading to handling small arms.

Infantrymen required not only basic military knowledge, but also had to demonstrate initiative, physical fitness and discipline. Consequently, much training sought to foster these characteristics and particular efforts were made to expose men to realistic simulated battlefield conditions. This was intended to help them cope psychologically with the shock of combat.

In addition soldiers were imbued with the spirit and traditions of the particular unit to which they were posted, as each ITC was affiliated to one or more infantry regiments. For example, Number 6 ITC at Strensall, Yorkshire, trained drafts for the Lancashire Fusiliers, King's Own Yorkshire Light Infantry and West Yorkshire Regiment, whereas Number 4 ITC at Brancepeth Castle, County Durham, dealt exclusively with the DWR and DLI.

Bill Scully, a nineteen-year-old infantry recruit, recalled that 'we were well trained in the art of weapons'. The bolt-action Lee-Enfield rifle of .303in calibre was the principal weapon which soldiers learned to maintain and operate at section and platoon level. Much training centred on drills designed to perfect a soldier's ability to handle his rifle effectively in battle, both as a precision weapon at long range, and by firing or using the bayonet at close quarters. Sessions on the firing range with live ammunition were also important. John Hudson, who went on to serve in the Far East, noted soldiers were taught the following rifle drill 'legs spread-eagled–heels touching the ground–take aim–squeeze–rapid fire!' As he observed, rifle fire could be devastating, particularly against troops advancing in the open, when infantrymen used the above drill with 'their well-oiled bolts snicking rhythmically'.

Tests of Elementary Training (TOETs) were used to ensure personnel in all branches of the army reached a sufficient standard, and had particular resonance among infantrymen. Tests for the rifle included using rapid fire, where from cover and with bayonets fixed soldiers fired five aimed rounds at a target designated by their instructor. Four out of the five rounds had to be accurate for troops to pass.

Another significant weapon was the Bren light machine gun (LMG), introduced in the late 1930s which saw widespread use during the Second World War. Again this was of .303in calibre and as a magazine-fed weapon it was capable of rapid fire, although often troops were expected to fire in short bursts, or even single shots. It was heavy, at around 22lbs, but still light enough to be carried by one man. Consequently, with the rifle the Bren enabled British infantrymen to employ effective fire-and-movement tactics. As Richard Phillips remembered it was a fundamental principle of training that any movement would be protected by fire, so if a platoon was deployed in sections one would seek to advance, while the other two sections provided covering fire.

Some soldiers were issued with the Sten gun, a hastily-produced sub-machine gun that was potentially useful at close quarters, although it had a bad reputation owing to its unreliable magazine and safety catch. According to Herbert Harwood an NCO with 4th RWK, it always appeared to be 'slapped together', whereas the Bren had more sophisticated engineering. Tom Barlow witnessed a Sten discharge accidentally when a soldier jumped from a truck, and such incidents were common owing to the weaknesses in its design.

Various types of grenades were also employed, the most common being the high explosive Number 36 Mills bomb or fragmentation hand grenade, which could be thrown up to 35 yards depending on the skill and strength of the soldier concerned. These could prove awkward weapons for troops to master. Herbert Harwood recounted that during an assault course one recruit he was instructing threw a grenade at a pill box, only for it to hit an overhanging branch of a tree and land at their feet. They escaped injury but the butt of the recruit's rifle was blown away and there had to be an inquiry into the incident.

Initially infantry units were issued with the Boys anti-tank rifle, a cumbersome weapon over 5ft long that weighed 36lbs and when fired the recoil felt like a kick from a mule, which as Ivan Daunt discovered could easily hurt the firer's shoulder. Many soldiers felt it was of dubious value as it could only penetrate around 20mm of armour at 300 yards. It was later replaced by the Projector Infantry Anti-Tank (PIAT), which proved one of the most notoriously difficult infantry weapons to operate. It fired a 3lb hollow-charge grenade capable of penetrating a tank's armour at close range. To the uninitiated it resembled a piece of drain pipe and because it was spring-loaded it required two men to cock the weapon. Bill Titchmarsh was attached to 9th RWK in Blackburn, Lancashire for some of his training. He witnessed an instructor demonstrate 'how not to cock the PIAT' when 'unfortunately it went off and I heard he [the instructor] later died of internal injuries'.

Infantry units also relied on a variety of support weapons. The water-cooled, belt-fed .303in Vickers medium machine gun (MMG), had entered service prior to the First World War, and was still widely deployed during the 1940s, usually mounted on a tripod allowing it to provide sustained fire. John McManners noted that few topics appeared to be as well taught as the drill for operating the Vickers. Years after he left the army he still remembered the exact method for dealing with stoppages, along with the appropriate jargon: 'ease, pull, tap, new lock two' and 'never fail to realign sights before firing again'. Likewise, Brian Harpur observed, 'the machine gunner carried with him to eternity the three-word drill "ease–pull–tap" which was dinned into him incessantly from the very start of his apprenticeship'.

Further fire support came from mortars capable of firing smoke or high explosive bombs. The lightweight 2in mortar entered production shortly before the war and was intended to enhance an infantry platoon's organic firepower, as well as provide an illuminating round useful during night fighting. It had a range of 500 yards and could fire five rounds per minute, but as military historian David French states few wartime infantrymen 'had much to say in favour' of this little weapon.

The heavier 3in mortar was a more potent weapon, even though it lacked the range of its German equivalent. It could hurl a 10lb high explosive bomb up to 1,600 yards. As it was muzzle-loading with a high angle of fire it proved popular, particularly in awkward terrain, and it was light enough to be manhandled into action if necessary. As sergeant of the mortar platoon from 1st Battalion Hampshire Regiment, Jack Vardy fought in North Africa during 1942–43. He observed their mortars often provided fire support from behind advancing troops, sometimes even being grouped together and operating like an artillery battery. Another significant deployment of mortars was accompanying patrols, where their presence could 'keep the Germans' heads down', which helped save the lives of British troops desperate to get back to their lines.

Instructors imparted an appreciation of basic infantry tactics based around the above weapons using what was known as 'battle drill'. This had its antecedents in the First World War, and by the early 1940s had gained prominence within the Home Forces of the British Army, before being employed overseas. Essentially battle drill encouraged troops to react swiftly and appropriately under fire, using a series of standard moves. These were intended to be adapted in action, rather than be slavishly copied from infantry training manuals, and concerned both offensive and defensive operations.

As an experienced NCO, Martin McLane first encountered battle drill while training with 2nd DLI in India during 1942. He found it an eminently sensible method of controlling platoons or sections in action, not least because it encouraged fire and movement. Typically, in attack sections would be divided into a Bren group and a rifle group. The former manoeuvred so as to provide enfilading fire to pin down the enemy, which enabled the riflemen from the other group to advance and assault the enemy position, taking care that they re-grouped beyond the objective so as to avoid enemy artillery and mortars which might have it pre-registered as a target.

Captain Gunning commented battle drill 'began, like other drills, in formalised style on the barrack square'. Wartime infantry officer Major Frederick Myatt explained 'the instructor simply called out the situation, for example, "leading section under fire" upon which the soldiers under instruction carried out the appropriate movements'. In this case they would have been expected to shout out 'down–crawl–observe–aim–take-up fire position' as they envisioned conducting these moves against an enemy, before awaiting orders from their section commander. As General Sir Anthony

Farrar-Hockley, who joined the wartime army as a teenager, remembered these were concise such as 'Left flanking-Bren take up fire position there: riflemen give covering fire' followed by 'Bren group (once in position) give covering fire by observation. Remainder follow me'. During battle drill instructors would also indicate verbally to soldiers what type of terrain they were supposed to be facing.

Later, field training taught men to adapt battle drill to terrain and deploy it under a variety of different tactical situations, such as flank attacks or pincer movements by an entire platoon. Consequently, instruction in fieldcraft was vital alongside that dealing with infantry tactics. Soldiers were taught numerous methods of movement and camouflage, using both natural and artificial materials, designed to help them negotiate the battlefield and employ their weapons as effectively as possible. The War Office manual *Infantry Training Part VIII: Fieldcraft, Battle Drill, Section and Platoon Tactics* (1944) urged troops to appreciate that:

> Fieldcraft is offensive and does not mean using ground to cower in a hole out of the enemy's fire. Ground must be used as the hunter uses it – to get closer to the prey whom he is going to kill. You must use your knowledge and cunning to outwit the enemy.

Simultaneously, many exercises exposed troops to live fire intended to inoculate them against combat conditions. Such training, which normally occurred at specially-established battle schools in Britain or overseas, provided realistic training that was intentionally stressful and strenuous. As Major Denis Forman recounted:

> Everything was carried out at the double, live ammunition was used in exercises and fired very close to students to get them accustomed to its sound, there were lectures on the psychology of fear and on motivation, and there was a formidable assault course with casualties so high that an ambulance stood by.

Similarly, Captain Gunning provided a vivid account of battle school conditions experienced by soldiers from his regiment, the KOSB:

The man on the Bren gun, and his comrades laden with hand grenades and full quota of rifle ammunition, accompanied by a sweating team carrying the mortar and 'smoke' bombs, had to move quickly and often under 'hostile' machine-guns on fixed lines which spat out their bullets a few feet away from the safe lane of approach towards the objective. And all the time there was the fiendish instructor urging his men to get a move on or reminding them of the infantryman's classic duty to [care for] his rifle.

Initially means were devised to inculcate troops with a sense of loathing for the enemy via what was termed 'hate training'. Battle school trainees were taken on visits to slaughterhouses and sometimes animal blood was liberally splashed around during exercises. The idea was that this would help to condition men to the horrors of battle. Such training was of questionable value, especially when dealing with troops who had volunteered for war service and were well motivated. During his infantry training John McManners considered efforts to 'instil gratuitous hatred' were laughable. Moreover, as wartime army psychiatrist R. H. Ahrenfeldt noted, exposing men to 'the more sadistic aspects of war' frequently proved counter-productive. Many troops found that rather than toughening them for the rigors of the battlefield, the use of blood was extremely upsetting, and consequently 'hate training' of this type was discontinued.

However, battle school instruction remained important in preparing troops for action. As most were entirely inexperienced it provided a practical means of training them under fire. Brian Stewart served as a junior officer with the Black Watch and acted as an instructor at 49th Division Battle School. Prior to seeing action in Normandy he recalled:

Students were stretched physically: crawling under barbed wire as Bren guns fired live rounds over their heads on fixed lines; clambering over ten-foot walls, crossing rivers on ropes, clambering up and down cliffs. We fired lots of blank cartridges and threw thunder flashes; the air was filled with smoke and noise. We practised night fighting ... the human bridge method of crossing barbed wire [leading man throws himself over the obstacle allowing the others to cross]. The Battle School risks were justified and we were preparing to take on the battle hardened soldiers of the German Army.

Officer Selection and Training

Another pressing challenge facing the army was sourcing enough officers to lead its wartime units. During the inter-war period the officer corps was largely comprised from a narrow segment of society from the middle and upper classes, who had attended public schools. Purely owing to their schooling and OTC training they were deemed to have the requisite leadership potential. Historian Jeremy Crang observed that in 1939 85 per cent of entrants to the Royal Military College, Sandhurst and 91 per cent of entrants to the Royal Military Academy, Woolwich were drawn from public schools.

Sir Michael Howard who was granted a wartime commission into the Coldstream Guards remarked, most of his fellow officers 'had been to Eton, and many were interrelated over many generations. This had some advantages. As he recalled, they believed that 'cowardice or misbehaviour – "putting up a black" – would thus taint them for life, so it simply did not happen'.

Yet, as had been the case during the First World War, by the early 1940s the army was forced to cast its net wider in an effort to find sufficient personnel to be trained as officers. Captain 'Toby' Taylor of the East Surrey Regiment noted that after Dunkirk new men with new skills came into the army such as bank managers, solicitors and schoolmasters. Usually in their late twenties and university-educated, these men often made excellent leaders, and were in Taylor's opinion less hidebound than many regular officers who had known no life outside the army.

Potential officers were at first recommended by their commanding officer and interviewed by a small Command Interview Board comprised of senior officers. The board assessed each candidate on their merits and successful candidates were selected for officer training. It was an unscientific system and continued to favour soldiers with a public-school background.

At these boards, the intelligence, personality of soldiers and their powers of leadership were placed under scrutiny. Those with an appropriate background, not only in terms of their schooling, but also any experience with the TA or OTC had an immediate advantage. As Lord Whitelaw recalled 'I ... did an attachment [via his University OTC] that summer [1939] with a Scots Guards battalion at Windsor before war broke out ... I was granted a commission in the Scots Guards soon after war started in September, without having to undergo further officer training like many of my friends'.

According to psychiatrist R. H. Ahrenfeldt 'complaints which had most frequently been made about ... Selection Boards [Command Interview Boards] had been allegations that candidates were asked at interview about their school, their father's occupation and income and so on'. Despite the obvious snobbishness of such questioning it had some reasoning behind it. Even in wartime there were various costs entailed with becoming an officer, particularly for those who aspired to join prestigious regiments.

As Major General Dare Wilson, who was commissioned into the RNF on the eve of war, commented, 'it was necessary to know the level of private means which many regiments recommended junior officers should have before seeking acceptance. Sometimes mess bills alone would exceed a young officer's pay.' The unfortunate Christopher Bulteel, who desired to follow in his father's footsteps and become an officer with the Coldstream Guards, discovered that 'the cost of buying the uniform had made me more miserable than ever. The official grant was £30, but I had spent over £200, cash which I did not possess. I had no private means ... Guards officers in peace-time were expected to pay to look beautiful; and the practice still stuck.'

However, as the war progressed it became clear that a more scientific approach was required when seeking potential officers. During 1942 War Office Selection Boards (WOSB) were established, including one for the ATS, which employed psychiatrists and psychologists on their staff. Candidates posted to a WOSB were assessed over a few days, which proved a more thorough means of gauging leadership qualities, rather than solely relying on an interview. Within months of instituting the WOSB system, it was reported that there had been a rise in the number of soldiers seeking commissions.

Typically, attending a WOSB was a demanding experience as personnel sat a series of tests, interviews and physical challenges intended to assess their suitability for training as officers. As Private Bill Titchmarsh who attended a WOSB at Catterick recalled, 'We had night exercises and came back about 3.30 am. We were then up at 7 am, breakfast at 7.30 am and then straight into lectures at 8 am. You were so shattered you found it difficult to remain alert and concentrate.'

Successful candidates were posted to an Officer Cadet Training Unit (OCTU), where they underwent further general military training and received specialised instruction. Typically, conditions were extremely arduous for all officer cadets, both male and female. Helen Hay was posted to an OCTU in Edinburgh where hours were spent polishing shoes and preparing for kit inspections, when not attending lectures or being drilled. Lieutenant Colonel William Weightman, who served with 2nd DLI in Burma, attended an OCTU in Bangalore, India. Here the cadet's day started at 5 am with 45 minutes physical training, then instruction in foot and arms drill, all before breakfast. Instruction followed in a variety of topics including military law, man management, Urdu lessons, infantry tactics, weapons training and fieldcraft. At all OCTUs cadets lived with the constant fear of being returned to unit (RTU'd) if they failed to perform adequately. As Eric Lomax who was granted a wartime commission into the Royal Corps of Signals stated, 'being RTU'd, was the worst humiliation'.

Despite the wartime innovations in selection and training, the officer corps continued to favour those with a public-school background, who were often perceived to possess the most desirable leadership qualities. In 1944 the Commandant of Number 164 OCTU, Barmouth, Wales, commented:

The public school boys took to the training like ducks to water. They were used to being away from home and a system in which they were trained both to give and to accept orders. The grammar school boys, to begin with, were less independent, able to give orders but less at home taking orders from their equals ... The promoted sergeants were sound material. The winner of the Sword of Honour [awarded to the best cadet on passing out] at the end of the course was seldom a sergeant but a sergeant very seldom failed the course.

Typically, officer cadets drilled relentlessly under fearsome NCOs, such as the burly RSM Copp of the Coldstream Guards, who had a booming voice and became a well-known figure at Number 164 OCTU. Distinct practical reasoning lay behind the emphasis on drill. As Denis Healey, who became an artillery officer, discovered, 'drill which seemed so senseless at the time, enabled me to carry out standard movements without thinking, thus freeing my mind for more important tasks in a crisis'.

Trainees moved rapidly from parades to lectures or other instructional activities, and any transgression, however minor, was punishable by some form of extra drill. The tempo of training was intentionally very high as ultimately officer cadets were being trained to become leaders on the battlefield. As General Fraser, who was posted to Number 161 OCTU at the Royal Military Academy Sandhurst, noted, there were 'ferocious warrant officers and unceasing drill, physical training, weapon-training, inspections ... lectures, tactical training of an elementary kind, and instruction in the rudiments of military administration'. Similarly, at Number 164 OCTU Brian Stewart recalled 'nightly sessions, polishing and cleaning' personal kit, which 'ensured attention to detail, and capacity to work on a minimum of sleep', a valuable skill once on active service.

Many soldiers were struck by the physically demanding nature of their officer training, particularly when on exercise. The future broadcaster Alan Whicker attended a course at Number 164 OCTU, before leading an army film unit covering the invasion of Sicily. He recalled 'the natural splendour of Merioneth never got through to me; a mountain merely meant something to run up with a full pack. A river was to wade through, a sun–dappled rocky chasm a place to cross while balancing on a rope, white with fear.'

Eventually all officer cadets hoped to pass their course, which was a proud moment. The hapless Dirk Bogarde had been transferred from the Royal Corps of Signals to the Royal Artillery, before being posted to an infantry regiment. After being selected by a WOSB he attended a course at RMA Sandhurst and recorded in his memoirs the moment he passed out:

I finally achieved greatness and marched solemnly off the parade ground at Sandhurst a fully commissioned second lieutenant. In my splendid uniform, fitted for weeks by a gentleman from Hawes and Curtis in a wooden shed near the barracks, wearing my father's Sam Browne, with the badges and buttons of the Queen's Royal Regiment, flashing like the Koh-i-noor, my head held high, and before my somewhat astonished but proud none the less, parents ...

Having passed out from an OCTU and become a junior officer, or completed some form of trade training within the ranks, soldiers faced an uncertain future. Many spent lengthy periods in Britain and continued to train with their new units prior to seeing action once the Second Front opened. Others were rushed overseas shortly after completing their training to serve as replacements in combat zones.

Infantrymen who passed out of an ITC, for example, were usually held in reserve for five weeks' continuation training, during which time they honed their skills, before being posted to a battalion overseas or in Britain. Either way personnel, especially in combat units, would sooner or later experience active service in some form. Their training was often all they had to fall back on, as they faced the battle-hardened soldiers of the Axis powers for the first time.

Chapter 2

Life on Active Service

Combat during the Second World War was not necessarily as rapid or decisive as is commonly supposed. In fact much of the fighting involving British troops had more in common with the stalemate conditions of the First World War than is widely acknowledged. As military historian Paddy Griffith astutely noted, many wartime battles were 'protracted, gruelling, nerve-wracking and costly', especially when conditions were static for long periods as in Normandy and Italy. Advances in weaponry and communications ensured that the battlefield had become an increasingly dangerous place for ordinary soldiers when compared with earlier conflicts. For untested troops, combat was a grim ordeal, overshadowed by confusion and anxiety. Private Bill Titchmarsh fought with 2/6th Queen's Royal Regiment in Italy, including at Anzio, which he later described as 'a slaughterhouse'. In addition to the bloodshed of battle, troops typically experienced close comradeship and an emotional cocktail of fear, humour, uncertainty, boredom, frustration and excitement tinged with sorrow at the loss of friends.

Unlike the First World War, during 1939–45 the army was not continuously involved in one major operational theatre, but rather fought in a series of campaigns around the globe in countries as diverse as Norway, Egypt, Holland and Burma. Consequently, fighting occurred in varied conditions, from the hot and fly-ridden North African Desert to the freezing, wintery terrain of North-West Europe, and the jungles of Burma. Learning to cope with such contrasting conditions frequently proved as important as dealing with the enemy. Individual soldiers could potentially experience a wide diversity of operational theatres, particularly if they fought with a prestigious formation, such as 51st Highland Division or 7th Armoured Division, as these were deployed in more than one combat zone during the war. Consequently, if he had avoided being captured, seriously injured or killed, a soldier from the legendary 51st Highland Division could conceivably have served in France during 1940, North Africa from 1942–43 and France and Belgium in 1944, before ending his war in Germany in May 1945.

Troopship Life

The provision of transport links between Britain and the various operational theatres was vital and, given that mass air transportation was impractical during the 1940s, most soldiers travelled by sea. By 1941 convoys leaving major British ports such as Liverpool for far-flung destinations became an accepted part of wartime life. Until the Mediterranean was free from the threat of Axis submarines, convoys had to sail via the Cape, ensuring that passages to the Middle and Far East in particular were lengthy affairs. Troops usually had little idea of where they were headed owing to security concerns, although the issue of items like tropical kit might yield clues as to their eventual destination. India was especially unpopular, as ultimately a posting there was liable to lead to deployment in the Burma campaign and the prospect of fighting the Japanese, who were widely feared as a tenacious foe, well versed in jungle warfare.

During the 1940s many volunteers and conscripts had never previously left the UK, and voyages were as anxiety-ridden as they were exciting, the tension heightened by uncertainty over whether they would survive active service. As England and Preston North End football legend Tom Finney, who served as a tank driver in Italy, recalled 'When you were sent abroad, you knew you were likely to be going into action and your thoughts were on whether you'd ever come back – you know, would you get killed.'

On longer voyages shore leave was often granted at Freetown in Sierra Leone, which troops usually found unpleasantly hot, and as there was little there to occupy them it proved unpopular. In contrast, Durban and Cape Town had more to offer as soldiers usually had the opportunity of being entertained by local white South African families during what were termed 'Convoy Weeks'. Typically, South African families would line the quayside while bands played and eagerly offer troops lifts back to their houses for a few pleasant days away from military discipline. Private Stan Scott (2/7th Queen's Royal Regiment) remembered being driven to 'a house with a front garden the size of Hyde Park', in Cape Town. His hosts made him feel welcome as he sat with other soldiers 'in the garden drinking iced lemonade'. During his stay he also enjoyed a trip to Elizabeth Bay and ascended 'Table Mountain for a night-time picnic'.

Similarly, as a young officer cadet en route to India, Lieutenant Colonel Robin Painter enjoyed stopping at Durban where he visited a snake farm which was considered 'one of the sights of the town'. However, in South Africa troops faced two potential hazards. Firstly, there was the racial segregation or 'colour bar' that pervaded South African society and all soldiers were instructed not to discuss the issue of race while ashore. Neither were they permitted to mix with black South Africans, especially females. Secondly, troops were advised to avoid sampling the local Cape brandy, an extremely potent beverage. Of course this does not mean that all soldiers complied. As Lieutenant Colonel Painter commented 'warnings tended to stimulate many private soldiers to do exactly what they had been told not to do as soon as they set foot on shore'.

Even under wartime conditions military convoys presented a grand spectacle. Personnel from 128th (Highland) Field Regiment Royal Artillery aboard the *Duchess of Richmond* in June 1942 observed an impressive array of liners covering the surrounding ocean, including the *Stratheden*, *Empress of Australia*, *Empress of Asia*, *Orion* and *Durban Castle*, plus an escorting battleship. Shipping companies converted their liners and mail ships to military purposes, especially as transports. HMT *Stirling Castle* (25,000 tons) of the Union-Castle Line had been designed to carry 780 passengers but, after a refit, became capable of transporting 5,000 soldiers, albeit packed in like sardines. Certain vessels gained a reputation amongst troops such as the *Duchess of Bedford*, nicknamed the 'Drunken Duchess' on account of her tendency to roll, while liners like the *Queen Mary* tended to be viewed as majestic despite being largely shorn of their luxurious fittings.

Although living conditions aboard such vessels varied according to soldiers' rank, certain general factors of life at sea remained constant, including boredom and seasickness. As an artillery officer bound for Algiers in April 1943, Denis Healey recalled racing through 'novels by Evelyn Waugh, Graham Greene and C. S. Forrester' plus any autobiographies and poetry he could obtain, as there was nothing to do 'except read and sleep'.

Writing letters home and card schools proved popular leisure activities and took men's minds off their predicament.

Yet on most troopships, especially during longer voyages, there was scope for training and drill parades, even though deck space was limited and it was necessary to contend with seasickness and the roll of the ship. During the day physical training sessions and sporting contests, such as boxing competitions, helped occupy men as well as proving beneficial to their morale and fitness. Often while at sea it was also possible for personnel to hone specific military skills, such as wireless procedure or map reading. When 2nd Field Regiment Royal Artillery sailed to North Africa in February 1943 for example, a new system of calling down the concentrated fire of all twenty-four guns in the regiment known as a 'Mike Target' had to be learnt. Consequently, as one officer recalled, many hours were spent in the saloon echoing to the sounds of the new drill: 'Hello Roger 12, message for Roger, Dog and Sugar, Mike Target, Mike Target, Mike Target, over.'

While at sea British officers destined for service with an Indian Army regiment normally received some form of instruction in elementary Urdu to help them communicate effectively with the men they were to command. Another corollary of troopship life was that when different units sailed together and undertook shared activities, mutual understanding and friendship was acquired, which boded well for their cohesion and co-operation under fire. Even just the act of officers from different units messing together could prove advantageous. While at sea close ties were forged between 128th (Highland) Field Regiment Royal Artillery and battalions from 152nd Infantry Brigade all from 51st Highland Division, who would eventually endure harsh conditions together in North Africa.

Most convoys faced the threat of attacks by aircraft and U-boats, something that the soldiers were powerless to prevent. However, at least one enterprising commander arranged for loudspeakers on ships in his convoy to inform the men what was happening in case they came under attack. As Colonel H. C. B. Rogers explained, this was done much in the manner of 'a BBC football type commentary', which might have calmed men's nerves as they followed the 'action'! Unsurprisingly, given such threats lifeboat drills were an integral feature of troopship routine. Even so, the chances of surviving a sinking ship were negligible owing to the size of most vessels and their overcrowded conditions. Wartime Signaller Brian Aldiss sailed to India aboard the *Otranto*, where he was accommodated on H Deck. Christened 'Doolally Deck', it was 5ft below the water line, the lowest level on the overcrowded ship. He later acknowledged 'had a torpedo struck us, no one of H Deck would have stood a hope in hell of survival. We knew it.'

To take soldiers' minds off the dangers they faced, quiz games were frequently played as they assembled on the troop decks between alarms. In keeping with maritime tradition when reaching Equatorial waters, humorous 'crossing the line ceremonies' were presided over by sailors dressed as 'King Neptune and Queen Amphitritie' – another distraction. The presence of nurses, or other female service personnel destined for an overseas station, was equally valued. As Major General Dare Wilson recalled while a young, single officer in the Royal Northumberland Fusiliers he encountered several Wrens aboard his troopship who were 'intelligent, full of life and quite delightful'. For 'practical and common sense reasons they were treated as first class passengers' and thereby able to socialise with army officers. It would be naïve to think that more amorous relationships did not sometimes ensue from such contact, especially under wartime conditions. Richmond Gorle an artillery officer shared his voyage to North Africa with a Field Ambulance Unit that included eight nursing sisters, whose 'scarcity' as the only women aboard gave them 'greatly inflated value, of which some of them made full use'.

Rations formed another distinctive aspect of troopship life. Although Jake Wardrop, an NCO from 5th RTR, recalled that aboard his troopship 'we ate like lords: there was beer, whisky and gin on board', such an experience was not universal. Typically, troopship routines, especially relating to food, tended to accentuate the social divide between the officer class and other ranks. Sir Michael Howard, who served as a junior officer with the Coldstream Guards, remembered being 'absurdly comfortable' aboard a Dutch cruise-liner complete with 'Javanese stewards, elegant dining saloons' and lounges in which to play cards after dinner and berths to sleep in. Officers tended to be treated to lavish dining, unlike anything they had recently experienced under rationing in war-ravaged Britain. Aboard HMT *Banfora* in March 1943, officers from 48th RTR were served breakfasts of porridge or cereal, followed by haddock, bacon and egg, and white bread with plenty of butter and marmalade. Lunches consisted of: soup; macaroni cheese; steak and chips or Melton Mowbray pork pie; Sago pudding; plus cheese and biscuits. Additionally, good quality pre-war cigarettes could be purchased at 4d for a pack of ten, a distinct luxury in wartime. However, any pleasure derived from smoking on the deck of any ship was strictly forbidden for all ranks at night, because the glow of a cigarette could be discerned by an observant U-Boat for several miles.

In contrast, other ranks tended to endure crowded, unpleasant conditions and had to queue up for unappetising army rations, eaten in relays at crude wooden benches and tables. Private Steve Lonsdale (British Army Dental Corps) recounted particularly horrific conditions aboard the *Orbita*, which was used to transport troops from Durban to the Middle East. The men were 'herded like cattle' to eat on crowded mess tables and the food was 'crawling with maggots'. The whole ship was filthy, made more unpleasant by the heat, and even before leaving port the troops being ordered to sail in her were in a mutinous mood owing to the dire conditions.

Unlike officers, other ranks were frequently required to sleep in hammocks in order to save space and they existed amidst an overpowering atmosphere of stale sweat, bad air and vomit. To improve their conditions some soldiers managed to sleep on the decks of their ships, but as Leslie Crouch, who served with 4th Royal West Kent Regiment (RWK), recalled, they then risked being hosed down in the early morning by seamen cleaning the decks. Washing and toilet facilities were primitive, with most vessels providing some form of salt water shower and makeshift lavatories to supplement those already on board. Aboard one ship conditions were so bad that an enterprising officer had army tradesmen build extra lavatory seats with ropes attached, so that his soldiers could steady themselves in rough seas.

Despite unequal living conditions, it should not be thought that officers willingly wallowed in luxury while their men suffered. As wartime artillery officer Sir Robin Dunn admitted, many of his contemporaries were extremely embarrassed by the prevailing situation and admired their soldiers for their fortitude.

The Prospect of Action

Assuming a troopship was not torpedoed or sunk by aircraft, what could soldiers expect after surviving their passage overseas? Reinforcements were often placed in reserve at a holding unit, where typically they swapped the foetid conditions of troopships for an equally primitive atmosphere of military discipline, albeit in a theatre of war. John McManners, an officer from the RNF was briefly posted to the Infantry Base Depot in Egypt, which he later described as 'an institution of mindless discipline and highly organised boredom'.

Similarly, at 1st (Guards) Infantry Reinforcement Training Depot (IRTD) in Philippeville, North Africa, levels of what soldiers termed 'bull' (short for bullshit) were much in evidence. Normally associated with peacetime postings, 'bull' applied to anything that was excessively regimented, and not necessarily considered by ordinary soldiers to be of direct military value. At 1st (Guards) IRTD tents were perfectly aligned with one another, uniforms starched and pressed, webbing scrubbed white and brass fittings highly polished. Guardsmen could expect to be drilled as if on the parade square at home. Additionally, PT sessions, route marches and military exercises were employed, which would have been more useful in acclimatising personnel to combat conditions.

Alternatively, if posted to the front line rather than languishing in reserve, soldiers were often apprehensive at the prospect of experiencing their 'baptism of fire'. Private Ernie Leggett fought with the Royal Norfolk Regiment in France 1940, and as an infantryman he could not bear the prospect of close combat. The thought of being wounded by a bayonet or having to stab an enemy soldier with one made him 'feel cold inside'. For other raw troops the prospect of joining a combat unit full of experienced soldiers was almost as frightening as having to face the enemy. In early 1944 Private Peter Cuerdon admitted he was 'terrified – absolutely petrified', when posted from a holding unit to 1st Hampshire Regiment. This battalion had been earmarked as one of the assault units for D-Day, and comprised many seasoned veterans of the campaigns in North Africa and Sicily.

Along with fear, men often felt an element of excitement and pride, particularly young officers newly appointed to lead an infantry platoon or tank troop. Having joined the Regular Army in the late 1930s, Peter Vaux served with the BEF in France during 1940 and prior to action confessed to a feeling 'of anticipation and excitement and a sense of going into the unknown'. Four years later prior to D-Day, Bill Bellamy, a twenty-year-old recently commissioned officer with 7th Armoured Division, felt enthusiastic at the prospect of embarking on 'a crusade' and the 'sense of heroism at being part of it'.

Even so, young, inexperienced soldiers tended to feel differently about the war than combat veterans and older soldiers. When he enlisted aged eighteen in 6th Green Howards in 1939, Private Bill Cheall quickly discovered that reservists, usually older men in their thirties with families, 'crawled their way into jobs where they felt sure they would not take part in any battles'. Men who had seen action often tended to become reflective and quiet, distinct from the confident young recruits fresh from a depot. Many were fatalistic or even distanced themselves from fellow soldiers. Rifleman Victor Gregg, a regular soldier in his early twenties, vividly remembered a period of service in North Africa during late 1941, when in his unit 'older hands tended to keep aloof from the new lads fresh out from Blighty'. Equally, many old soldiers developed a kindly, paternalistic attitude towards inexperienced comrades, especially reinforcements, many of whom by 1944 were drafted into infantry units from elsewhere, as the army had become short of manpower. In all theatres officers, soldiers, and their units often had to contend with such differences in outlook between personnel.

When commencing action soldiers were typically gripped by what Battery Sergeant Major Ernest Powdrill of the Royal Horse Artillery (RHA) termed 'a surge of adrenaline as the panorama of battle surrounded us'. Such feelings could be extremely invigorating, especially for youthful troops, replacing any fatigue or tension they may previously have felt, but this rapidly subsided when they were faced with the realities of warfare. As a platoon commander in Italy during 1945, Lieutenant Colonel Colin Mitchell described how: 'exhilaration was soon tempered by the first signs of war'. Similarly, John Elliot who first experienced action in Tunisia with 2nd Coldstream Guards noted, 'the whine of the shell and the hissing of a bullet quickly dispels' any 'youthful eagerness'. Lord Whitelaw, who fought in France and Germany in 1944–45 with the Guards Armoured Division, confessed that 'away from the action one longs for battle, and as soon as the horrors of the battle are experienced one secretly craves to leave the action again as soon as possible'.

Initial shocking sights included encountering wounded or dead soldiers (both friendly and enemy), and even the destruction of civilian property and livestock, all of which could prove distressing to the uninitiated. Private Stanley Whitehouse of the Oxfordshire and Buckinghamshire Light Infantry vividly recalled the sight of dead cattle, which were a distinctive feature during the battle for Normandy. The air was frequently thick with 'the sickly-sweet smell' of their corpses 'bloated ... and festooned with fat maggots, and the fetid odour of soured milk from their ruptured udders'.

Life on the Battlefield

As indicated above, many soldiers suffered from what military historian Richard Holmes termed 'pre-contact apprehension'. Stuart Hills, an officer with the Nottinghamshire Sherwood Rangers Yeomanry (NSRY), remarked 'Survival was the hope and prayer of all, but duty and the task drew us on'. While the risk of being killed, wounded or captured were prominent concerns, in the minds of many troops, the fear of demonstrating cowardice or 'letting the side down' was an even greater worry. Watching Sword Beach grow closer from his landing craft on D-Day, Private Stanley Whitehouse observed that faced 'with its general tumult and violence, I began to have doubts about my confidence and eagerness'.

For some, the pressures they endured during combat were too much to bear. Captain Lewis Keeble of 1/4th King's Own Yorkshire Light Infantry recalled an attack in Normandy where one of his 'platoons ran away and were brought back at pistol point'. Even more serious was the disintegration of the entire 6th Duke of Wellington's Regiment (DWR) during that same campaign after a period of heavy shelling. Stuart Hills witnessed them 'burst from the wood in front of us [NSRY tanks], every man Jack of them running for his life'. As military historian David French explained, 6th DWR's behaviour was largely due to the fact that it had suffered heavy casualties, including among senior officers, over a much shorter period than other battalions deployed in Normandy. Consequently, its morale was in a particularly brittle state. It is testimony to the resoluteness of British troops, especially the infantry, that incidents like this were not recorded more frequently during the war.

Even so, all soldiers were liable to experience levels of fear and anxiety owing to the stressful nature of combat. Stanley Ferguson fought as NCO with the Carrier Platoon from 9th DLI in the Middle East, North Africa, Italy and North-West Europe. He recounted how the pressure began to fray soldier's nerves, and he was particularly disturbed in Normandy by hearing a badly-wounded young soldier calling for his mother. Military historian John Ellis highlighted many of the main symptoms resulting from fear including: an intense pounding of the heart; shaking or trembling; feeling faint; vomiting; breaking out in a cold sweat; and losing control of the bladder and bowels. Troops returning from prolonged periods of combat could sometimes be identified by their clenched jaws which sagged when open giving them an idiotic appearance. Mental tunnel-vision, or the concentration on one issue at the exclusion of all others, was a further symptom of stress during battle. In the worst cases men suffered a complete mental breakdown requiring evacuation from the front line. These men were frequently considered to be suffering from 'battle exhaustion', a catch-all phrase for psychiatric conditions which would previously have been classed as shell shock, and will be explored further in a subsequent chapter.

Waiting at the start-line for any assault was particularly fraught with tension, even for experienced troops. Peter White, a platoon and company commander with 4th KOSB in North-West Europe recalled, that he experienced 'an empty feeling at the pit of one's stomach'. This tended to subside once in action, when the order 'advance' had been given and the agonising wait was over. Likewise, a private from 7th Green Howards in Normandy, where casualties amongst infantry were heavy, commented that when ordered to prepare for attacks, 'the stomach sinks and a leaden feeling spreads throughout the body'.

Given the dangers they faced in battle there was a natural tendency amongst soldiers to seek refuge from enemy fire when possible. Rifleman Reginald Crimp, a veteran of the desert war, wrote in his diary 'Of course I always take all the cover that's going, and keep my swede down as long as possible.' While Private Bill Titchmarsh recounted that when under a German artillery bombardment during assaults in Italy, he would always 'get down more or less in the "guttering" and I always took my pack off and put it over my head when we got down like that and kept an eye on the man in front so that I was ready to advance'.

These were practical, understandable actions for soldiers to take when under fire, but sometimes risked slowing down any advance and incurring unnecessary casualties. As the commanding officer of 9th DLI in Sicily during 1943 observed, under heavy fire men were prone to bunch together and shelter behind the stone walls that were a particular feature of the Sicilian landscape. This could cause more casualties than the situation warranted. Consequently, as he stressed, officers and NCOs had to 'maintain the interests of their men in the enemy throughout battle. If curiosity and observation are lost morale will suffer and the general picture gone.' Even so, military historian Stephen Bungay considered that throughout the war one of the main challenges facing officers was getting 'men to close with the enemy'.

In order to achieve this, tactics had to be adapted to suit particular terrain, and take advantage of the available firepower. Fire and movement, as highlighted in the previous chapter, was important, especially at platoon/section level. Equally, the ability to move effectively over differing forms of terrain even when not in direct contact with the enemy was vital. Herbert Harwood, an NCO with 4th RWK who fought in the Arakan during 1943–44, remarked that one of the most difficult things was learning to deploy flanking movements against Japanese positions. His unit felt compelled to check most hills to determine whether they were occupied by enemy rearguards that might hold up their advance, and even if little opposition was encountered, they often suffered casualties because these hills were usually registered by Japanese mortars.

During the Normandy campaign of 1944 the terrain was again a major issue. The thick hedges of the 'Bocage' imposed a natural barrier on movement and were incorporated into German defensive lines. The narrow lanes and patchwork of fields were ideally suited to ambushes, infiltration and the use of mines and booby traps. James Bellows, who served with 1st Hampshire Regiment in Normandy, remembered German troops often hid in holes in the ground before firing on British soldiers' rear as they passed by, and deployed determined snipers who tied themselves to trees. Consequently,

James Bellows and his comrades tended to fire on any ground deemed to be suspect. To counter threats in Normandy still further, British units evolved methods of deploying tanks in close co-operation with infantry, backed when possible by artillery and aerial firepower. Even so, progress was often painful, not least because the attackers' fields of fire and observation were severely hampered by the labyrinthine nature of the Norman countryside.

In contrast, in North Africa during 1942–43 British tank units and the infantry they were supporting tended to enjoy greater freedom to manoeuvre. A significant lesson from that theatre was that it proved possible to employ tanks from hull-down firing positions, so as to limit their exposure to enemy anti-tank guns, and by moving from one such position to another they were able to support the infantry. Stuart Hills noted how desert veterans in the NSRY tended to yearn for the 'open spaces' of North Africa when faced with such awkward conditions in Normandy.

Similarly, many soldiers found that methods of fighting in the close country encountered in parts of Italy during 1943–45, differed from those they had previously experienced in North Africa. In his diary desert veteran Sergeant Jake Wardrop (5th RTR), alluded to the need for greater co-operation between infantry and armour: 'A troop of three [tanks] operated with a platoon or company of infantry. We had never tried this before, but it was the way we carried on all the time … , except for the times when we took the lead and scorched along the roads.'

As Chapter 1 demonstrated, by late 1941 conscription was having significant impact on the army, so that the majority of personnel were not professional soldiers. In 1944 film star David Niven served with the GHQ Liaison Regiment (Phantom) whose primary task was to conduct long-range reconnaissance patrols and ensure information was swiftly sent to Army HQ by wireless. He recalled that his squadron was composed of former 'bank clerks, burglars, shop assistants, milkmen, garage mechanics, schoolmasters, painters, bookmakers, stockbrokers and labourers'. Such individuals did not necessarily have any patience for what Sergeant Charles Murrell of the Welsh Guards described as 'the bull and baloney, the spit and polish, the drill and display, the *esprit de corps* and all the rest of it'.

Yet many conscripts proved effective in combat, while graduates and those with professional backgrounds who became officers often made good leaders and tended to be less hidebound by tradition than older regular officers. Some even rapidly attained high rank, including Paul Bryan, who enlisted as a private in 6th RWK during 1940 and went on to become an NCO, then ultimately lieutenant colonel, commanding the battalion in Tunisia and Italy during 1943–44.

Under Field Marshal Montgomery in particular, the British Army developed a methodical approach towards battle, reliant on set-piece attacks based upon elaborate logistical, intelligence and deception plans. As Second World War veteran General Sir David Fraser admitted, this approach sometimes lacked dynamism. However, these operational and tactical methods attempted to harness the full weight of Allied resources and firepower in an effort to reduce the likelihood of heavy casualties. Central to Montgomery's approach was the development of a doctrine based on harnessing the benefit of the massive levels of artillery support that became increasingly available during the war. The idea, especially in Normandy, was to seek out and neutralise the enemy with overwhelming firepower to enable infantry to assault and occupy vital ground, without incurring heavy casualties, which subsequently would be held against inevitable counter-attacks. The Germans were noted for their ability to launch rapid counter-attacks and, if troops were successful in taking a position, it was likely to already have been registered by enemy artillery. Consequently, it was vital for infantry to 'dig in' and co-ordinate their actions with the available fire support provided by other arms.

Improvements in communications during the war ensured that gunners could deliver rounds with increased precision, accuracy, and flexibility, which also supported the British approach. The Standard Regimental Concentration or 'stonk' comprised a 525-yard block of fire set to a predetermined template and was deployed to support assaults or break up enemy attacks. The term became a byword amongst infantry for any form of sudden bombardment whether launched by friendly or hostile forces. By 1945 'pepper pot' tactics had developed whereby divisional commanders employed every available weapon, including machine guns and anti-aircraft guns alongside conventional artillery pieces, to harass and demoralise defenders.

Even in difficult terrain artillery and armoured firepower was frequently employed, and during the Burma campaign proved very useful in helping to neutralise Japanese bunkers. Military historian Tim Moreman notes that, by 1944, the British approach to warfare in the Far East had become 'increasingly wedded in to artillery as gunners displayed greater skill in bringing forward a greater number of guns firing a larger weight of shell and adapted established techniques to the jungle'.

The 'firepower approach' was intended to minimise casualties, but the humble infantryman still bore the brunt of the bloodshed. In Normandy during June–August 1944 'footsloggers' accounted for 14 per cent of the total British force deployed, but received 70 per cent of the overall casualties. In all theatres it was ultimately the infantryman who had to 'close with the enemy'. While armoured and artillery personnel drove into battle, infantry often marched, as their predecessors had done in earlier conflicts. At the Battle of El Alamein in October 1942 Captain A. Grant Murray witnessed an infantry battalion commence its advance: 'Line upon line of steel helmeted figures with rifles at the high port, bayonets catching in the moonlight, and all over the wail of the pipes … As they passed us they gave us the thumbs-up sign, and we watched them plod towards the enemy lines.'

Alternatively, depending on the tactical circumstances, infantry could be transported by 'Troop Carrying Vehicle' (TCV), usually a truck, or even on the back of a tank. During the later phases of the war, especially in North-West Europe and Italy, infantry sometimes deployed specialist vehicles, including Kangaroos. These were improvised armoured personnel carriers based on turretless Canadian Ram tanks. Typically they were uncomfortable, with soldiers having to sit on cramped bench seats and anyone who needed the lavatory prior to action had to relieve himself in his empty mess tin. Yet they provided a considerable degree of protection from shell- and small-arms fire. During January 1945, while serving as an NCO with 4th Wiltshire Regiment, Eric Wheeler witnessed a Kangaroo receive a hit from a German anti-tank gun that knocked out two of its bogies, but the crew and soldiers inside were unharmed.

Major amphibious assaults, such as those in the Mediterranean and Normandy during 1943 and 1944, were even more daunting, not least because many soldiers endured a stomach-churning journey aboard various types of landing craft even before reaching a beachhead and engaging the enemy. On D-Day, Donald Rose from 'A' Company 5th King's Regiment sailed across the Channel aboard a landing craft infantry (LCI), that was transporting around 200 soldiers. He reckoned 50 per cent became violently seasick during the voyage. While during the crossing to Sicily in July 1943, Stanley Ferguson (9th DLI) recorded that conditions aboard his vessel were so bad 'even the sailors were sick'.

Typically, armoured and artillery personnel would travel aboard specialised landing craft capable of transporting their vehicles. One of the major types of vessel deployed was the Landing Ship Tank (LST), often dubbed 'large slow target' by servicemen owing to its size, over 300ft in length and maximum speed of around 12 knots. These were powered by diesel engines, had a shallow draft to enable them to approach gently sloping beaches, but which simultaneously made them roll, especially in bad weather. George Henderson, served as a crewman aboard LST-8 during amphibious landings in the Mediterranean and Normandy in 1943–44, and recalled 'in the bows was a large door and a hinged ramp, and we would run directly onto beaches to off load men and vehicles, and even evacuate wounded'. Alternatively, as at Anzio, in Italy, LSTs could make use of harbour facilities to offload their cargo. Usually lighter vehicles such as jeeps and trucks were transported on the upper deck via a hydraulic ramp, while tanks occupied the lower deck. According to George Henderson the relationship between the sailors crewing LST-8 and soldiers was normally very good, and 'we liked to look after them', which included sharing navy rations that were normally much better than those issued to the army.

In contrast, during amphibious operations many infantrymen sailed in ships to approximately 5–10 miles off shore, then climbed down scramble nets into a smaller landing craft, such as the Landing Craft Assault (LCA), that would ferry them to the beach–a potentially hazardous operation. Private Bill Cheall served with the Green Howards on D-Day and described getting down into his landing craft as 'hair-raising'. Once aboard, many troops immediately had to reach for their sick bags as the little craft was buffeted about in the swell. Subsequently, troops had to endure the run in to the beach often under enemy fire, and if their landing craft ran into difficulties en route or let its ramp down too early there was a chance that men might drown, sinking under the weight of their equipment.

Whether during an amphibious assault or other operations, troops tended to quickly become aware of the sounds of battle. This included the noise made by friendly artillery shells flying overhead and exploding on enemy positions. Rapidly other sounds would emerge, notably the rattle of small-arms fire, and with experience troops learnt to differentiate between friendly and enemy weapons. The German 7.92mm Maschinengewehr 42 or Spandau, had a high rate of fire and tended to sound like 'calico being ripped' whereas the British Bren gun had a more measured tone that some soldiers found 'comforting'. In the Far East the Japanese employed the 7.7mm Heavy Machine Gun Type 92, nick-named 'Woodpecker' by British and Commonwealth troops, after the highly distinctive sound it made on firing.

Bullets might whizz past overhead, which some veterans likened to the sound of the 'chatter of birds', or 'angry hornets'. Under fire from machine guns or other small arms, many soldiers experienced a sensation of 'time slowing down'. Instincts honed by training were supposed to come to the fore, so that they were able to take cover and, if possible return fire using suitable battle drills. The War Office manual, *Infantry Training Part VIII: Fieldcraft, Battle Drill, Section and Platoon Tactics* (1944) stressed that when soldiers came under effective fire they were (unless ordered otherwise) to drop flat and crawl forward or sideways into a firing position, observe and return fire. The mantra, encouraged during training was 'Down–Crawl–Observe–Sights–Fire'. With experience, soldiers were able to distinguish between the 'crack' of passing bullets as they broke the sound barrier, and the 'boom' or 'thump' of the explosion as they left the gun. Christopher Bulteel, an officer with 3rd Coldstream Guards explained, 'This always matters, when one is under fire … the "crack" is far more insistent, far more terrifying; but it does not reflect the path of the bullet, or where the fire comes from.'

Ultimately, infantry might be have to undertake close combat using grenades, small arms, knives, bayonets and possibly even their bare hands. Lieutenant Colonel Robin Painter experienced hand-to-hand fighting in the Far East:

Everything happened so quickly that there was little immediate fear; more a determination to survive by killing the enemy and afterwards a feeling of enormous relief and very little thought for the human you had killed. Fear came in retrospect ... During the actual encounter, things were done by instinct in response to the very thorough training we had all been given in hand-to-hand fighting and an enormous amount of luck was also involved. We helped one another by instinct and the so-called 'bravery' for which medals are given did not really come into it at all. It was just a matter of survival and killing by instinct and training- and frankly little to be proud of but a lot to be thankful for afterwards. The relief we felt after close combat was the selfish thankfulness to have come through unscathed and this was tempered by retrospective fear and horror.

A thirst for revenge motivated some soldiers to kill under such circumstances. Rifleman Victor Gregg, whose unit was predominantly comprised of Londoners, noted that in the Western Desert during 1940–41: 'We were beginning to read about the plight of our families and the terrible bombing they were enduring. Many a poor, hapless Eyetie felt the agony of a bayonet going in, wielded by a Rifleman who had just got a letter from home bearing bad news.'

A related form of killing soldiers sometimes witnessed was when men became driven by 'blood lust', even to the extent of ignoring pleas from their officers to take prisoners. This could occur at moments of extreme tension, such as when troops felt they were walking into a trap, or if they were fired on by an enemy who moments before had appeared to be surrendering. Private Bill Cheall recalled how, after witnessing a machine gun shoot a popular NCO in Tunisia, his section immediately stormed the enemy post and slaughtered all the Italians they found cowering in the bottom of their trench: 'We were consumed with rage and had to kill them to pay for our fallen pal.' During the North African Campaign of 1940–43 it also became common for tank crews to be considered 'fair game' by both sides, so that men seen escaping from stricken vehicles were shot rather than captured. In Normandy the fighting was frequently so savage that the Guards Armoured Division discovered that German prisoners from 9th SS Panzer Division referred to them as 'Churchill's Butchers'.

Rifleman Victor Gregg witnessed instances of comrades 'going berserk' and killing prisoners and no doubt this may at times have occurred in other units. Usually German and Italian POWs were rounded up and treated comparatively humanely, aside from some 'manhandling' as they were despatched rearwards. Near the River Senio, in Italy during late 1944 Private Bill Titchmarsh was tasked with escorting a captured German colonel through British lines. He 'prodded' the colonel along at bayonet point in the pouring rain. 'I only had tin hat [helmet] on and KD [khaki-drill] denims, summer stuff and I was soaking wet through.' Suddenly a senior British officer saw them and grabbed the gas cape the German was wearing and 'threw it to me before getting hold of this German and kicking him. He did not like Germans!'

Sergeant Jake Wardrop recorded that when his tank crew encountered columns of POWs in the Western Desert, 'we nipped out, pinched their watches, binoculars or anything they had and carried on'. In contrast, until late in the war the Japanese rarely surrendered, but their decaying corpses could often be seen by soldiers. Whilst serving with the Royal Corps of Signals, Brian Aldiss witnessed a pile of dead Japanese (or possibly Koreans conscripted into the Japanese Army), whose corpses 'had turned black and purple in the heat. Some seemed to have burst ... awaiting the bulldozers which would plough them into the ground, far from their native land.'

With any enemy, especially the Japanese who were noted for their fanaticism, there was always a danger that soldiers would pretend to surrender, before reaching for a hand-grenade or opening fire as British troops approached. It would be naïve to think that British soldiers did not take matters into their own hands under such circumstances and seek immediate retribution. For example, personnel from 4th RWK, who served in India and Burma during 1943–45, soon discovered that when fighting the Japanese it was safer to avoid taking prisoners rather than risk losing men to a desperate final act by an enemy soldier.

Similarly, in the heat of battle it was all too easy for soldiers to respond instinctively and kill anyone in an enemy uniform, even if their hands were raised in surrender. With regard to the harsh realities of combat it is worth considering wartime SAS officer John Tonkin's comment: 'I have always felt that the Geneva Convention is a dangerous piece of stupidity, because it leads people to believe that war can be civilised. It can't.'

For most soldiers one of the most terrifying parts of combat was being subjected to bombardment by artillery or mortars. Shells, particularly those of larger calibres, could kill or maim by their blast alone, and if a man received a direct hit then little trace of him would remain. Owing to their accuracy and versatility, mortars, with their high trajectory fire were considered even worse. Mortar bombs had greater fragmentation effect than artillery shells, and were frequently difficult to detect in advance. Approximately half of all British casualties suffered in the North-West Europe campaign of 1944–45 were thought to result from mortar fire alone. Poet Vernon Scannell, who served in the Middle East and Normandy with the Gordon Highlanders, provided a vivid account of how it felt to be under bombardment:

The full fury of artillery is a cold, mechanical fury but its intent is personal. When you are under fire you are the sole target. All of that shrieking, whining venom is directed at you and no one else. You hunch in your hole in the ground, reduce yourself into as small a thing as you can become, and you harden your muscles into a pitiful attempt at defying the jagged, burning teeth of the shrapnel. Involuntarily you curl up into the foetal position except that your hands go down to protect your genitalia.

Developments in weapons technology rapidly produced other horrors, notably the German Nebelwerfer, christened 'Moaning Minnies' or 'Screaming Sisters' by the British. These were multi-barrelled rocket-firing field artillery, introduced in 1942 and encountered in most theatres thereafter. Private Stanley Whitehouse recalled being 'unable to master' his fear of them. 'I could face ordinary shelling quite well but these devils had me quivering from head to toe.' It was not just the explosive impact of their rockets that was threatening, but also the weapon's fearsome 'whoo-whoo-whoo' noise on firing, which some soldiers likened to a 'cow with whooping-cough' magnified many times over. However, as 9th DLI and other units discovered, it was possible to counter this weapon because its distinctive noise provided advanced warning, giving troops time to seek cover, and enabled sound bearings to be taken so as to pinpoint Nebelwerfers for retaliation by British artillery.

Yet another threat came from ground-attack aircraft, particularly during the earlier campaigns of the war when the Axis powers had aerial supremacy. Being dive-bombed by the infamous German Junkers Ju 87 (Stuka) was a harrowing ordeal, not least because of their howling engines, supplemented by sirens as they dived. Troops with the BEF in France and in North Africa were sometimes plagued by swarms of 100 or more dive-bombers. Military historian Stephen Bungay noted 'the shout of "Stuka!" could reduce a group of soldiers to paralysis'. As with artillery, there was a point at which any bombardment could feel personal, as though an individual Luftwaffe pilot was specifically targeting your trench. In fact bombs normally had to land within 100 yards to cause serious damage, but their psychological impact was significant and demoralising, particularly when soldiers witnessed refugees caught in the carnage, as frequently occurred during the French campaign in 1940.

It was routinely said amongst experienced soldiers that you had to 'dig in or die', particularly when establishing a position, as for infantry in particular this was the only means of obtaining adequate protection from artillery and aerial bombardment. Consequently, depending on the terrain, soldiers might have encountered what Major Denis Forman (6th RWK) termed the 'woodpecker principle', whereby 'as each bout of shelling began every man would start digging frantically with entrenching tool [an essential piece of kit], and all around and far into the distance one would hear a cacophony of striking and hacking. As the shelling ended, the noises diminished in volume until one heard only one or two determined soloists still at work.'

Defensive positions consisted of hastily constructed slits trenches or more elaborate arrangements depending on the tactical conditions. The standard weapon pit, as laid down in the manual *Infantry Training Part VIII: Fieldcraft, Battle Drill, Section and Platoon Tactics* (1944) was to be capable of holding two or three men, two feet wide at the bottom, with sides as straight as possible. It also needed to be well concealed, with a good field of fire. However, in practice soldiers found that a degree of latitude was necessary as they adapted to local terrain and soil conditions. During the winter of 1944–45 infantry in Holland endured waterlogged conditions, which as

Captain Peter White (4th KOSB) noted 'meant excavating a mud parapet round the hole with grass-sodden sides as camouflage'. In parts of North Africa, the Mediterranean and anywhere where the ground was difficult to excavate adequately, troops constructed sangars, stone 'walls', around their positions which offered a degree of protection.

How long infantry had to hold a position depended on the tactical circumstances they faced. However, they might have had to sleep, albeit probably not comfortably, in their trenches as well as live and fight. In this case periods of 'Stand to' when everyone was on the alert and 'Stand down' when men had time to 'relax' would be instigated. If not actually fighting or grabbing some sleep, then sentry duty, cooking and washing were important activities. Soldiers also added improvements to a position, taking measures to make slit trenches more rain-proof, such as digging drainage ditches around their tops and sump holes in their bottoms to keep them bailed out.

Some soldiers gained pleasure in reading enemy propaganda material while in their trenches. In Normandy one German leaflet maintained that the British were like 'foxes caught in a trap'. Another proclaimed 'Life is short, but death is quicker' alongside a pretty girl on the telephone, unfortunately captioned 'You'll never hear her sweat [sic] voice again'. Yet another issued in Italy depicted an attractive blonde being kissed by a man with the caption 'Gentlemen prefer blondes', but on the reverse was a wounded soldier on crutches entitled 'but blondes don't like cripples'. Often these were put to practical use as additional lavatory paper or kept as souvenirs and pin-ups.

In action many soldiers also encountered a phenomenon termed the 'empty battlefield'. The prevalence of indirect fire weapons, such as mortars, during the Second World War ensured that the battlefield became an ever more dangerous place. Accordingly, soldiers went to great lengths to remain concealed and it was sometimes possible to seldom see the enemy. Indeed, for some troops, their immediate environment may have appeared 'empty', even in the front line. Normandy veteran Richard Phillips noted that in that theatre it was quite possible think that you were in a calm area devoid of enemy activity, only minutes later for 'all hell to break loose'.

According to military historian Paddy Griffith the 'emptiness of the Second World War battlefield was possibly a more significant change from First World War conditions than any development in armour'. In the eyes of soldiers, the landscape, except for urban areas, could also appear comparatively untouched by war because artillery had become increasingly accurate to enable gunners to hit specific targets with high volumes of fire, rather than laying waste to an entire area.

Mines of all types added to battlefield casualties caused by shelling, mortaring, and small arms fire. For anyone on foot, the prospect of encountering the dreaded German 'Schrapnell-Mine' or S-Mine was terrifying. These mines could maim and kill, often with little warning when an unwary soldier stepped on one. Only the prongs of the igniter were visible at ground level and, once triggered, a shrapnel canister was fired approximately four feet into the air before exploding, sending steel balls in all directions. Private Stanley Whitehouse witnessed a sergeant receiving the full blast from one of these: 'His face was destroyed and his throat torn apart by the ball-bearings. Mercifully it was too dark to see the full scale of the horror as we dragged him back.'

Typically, British troops never ceased to be impressed by the skill with which Axis soldiers employed mines, particularly in North Africa and Europe. Even anti-tank mines proved deadly to infantry, as although they might only blow tracks or wheels off vehicles, soldiers nearby were liable to be killed by the blast. During the Tunisian campaign a 'mine museum' was established by Royal Engineers attached to 46th Division HQ, intended to teach soldiers about the threat these weapons posed. There were various German and Italian mines on display, including 'ones to disintegrate a tank, and mines just big enough to drive a bullet through a man's foot; Teller mines; Schu mines; bar mines; box mines' and even 'rifle grenades that could be left in the grass' for a careless soldier to kick.

Booby traps were another threat, as Axis forces, often being on the defensive, planted devices on corpses, or left them behind in positions they were vacating. These tended to be cunningly sited and demonstrated greater skill than British attempts to adopt similar practices. As an infantryman Donald Rose witnessed mines in Normandy that were operated by a ratchet, so that it took a certain amount of pressure before they went off. He found these particularly disturbing as several vehicles and men might unknowingly pass over one before it suddenly exploded. Similarly, at Catania, Sicily, Major Roy Griffiths (9th DLI) encountered a roadblock that was 'very professionally built, consisting of Teller mines, stick grenades and other booby traps, which spread across the road and into the verges and ditches, which were laid with entangled very fine wire'.

In the Far East the Japanese didn't employ mines to the same extent as the other Axis armies. However, they were skilled at using primitive but nonetheless potentially lethal booby traps such as the *punji*. These were sharpened wooden stakes smeared with excrement or other filth, designed to inflict injury and induce blood poisoning. As an infantryman with the Border Regiment in Burma, George Macdonald Fraser encountered one while examining an abandoned Japanese bunker: 'Just inside the doorway where an unwary foot would tread on it, was a *punji*, ... set in the ground point upwards, that point usually being smeared with something nice and rotten.'

Patrolling

When you think of combat during the Second World War, naturally famous battles such as El Alamein, Kohima or Anzio come to mind. While these were major events, not least for the troops involved, much front-line soldiering usually involved more limited contact with the enemy. Patrolling was the essence of campaigning in all theatres, especially for infantrymen, and served a variety of functions. During defensive warfare, or in particular in quieter periods when there were no major operations, it enabled battalions to keep abreast of enemy movements, and conduct small-scale actions. As Rifleman Henry Taylor recalled, this also acted as a means by which it was possible to maintain 'the fighting spirit of platoons' and keep up morale.

Consequently, patrols tended to be organised with specific objectives in mind. Reconnaissance patrols sent out to observe and gather information on the enemy usually required relatively few men as they were not intended to establish contact. In contrast fighting patrols mounted ambushes or raids against the enemy and could be up to platoon size (thirty men). Whatever type of patrol troops undertook, it taxed soldiers' appreciation of fundamental infantry skills, including minor tactics, fieldcraft and weapon handling. These were liable to be tense affairs, especially if conducted by night, and if something unexpected occurred such as being ambushed.

During the Italian campaign Rifleman Henry Taylor was once forced to carry a wounded soldier back to British lines, after his patrol had run into the Germans and they were the only survivors.

Patrols were physically gruelling as well. In Burma Lieutenant Colonel Michael Lowry gained considerable experience as a company commander with 1st Queen's Royal Regiment during 1943–45. He recounted that at times 50 per cent of his unit were ready for action at night when they were surrounded by the Japanese, which 'combined with a considerable patrolling programme, meant sleep was in short supply'.

Likewise, enemy tactics had a heavy influence on patrolling activity. In Italy where the front line was often based around a series of strongpoints rather than continuous defences, the Germans were adept at employing infiltration tactics. These disrupted forward units and caused confusion and casualties in rear areas. As a result it became important for British units to attempt to dominate 'no man's land' via aggressive patrolling and so deny the Germans freedom of movement.

Alternatively, depending on conditions, patrols might prove more benign events, especially if little or no contact with the enemy was made. During 1943, 12th Royal Lancers (Prince of Wales's) were deployed to the Sangro Valley in Italy. In contrast to patrol operations elsewhere in the Italian theatre, one of their officers considered patrols here 'had all the qualities of a poaching expedition – just enough danger to add spice and purpose, and the exhilaration of walking through the lovely country in spring'.

Troops on patrol sometimes experienced 'live-and-let-live', a phenomenon well documented during modern warfare, notably by Tony Ashworth in *Trench Warfare 1914–1918*. This could make life more bearable for ordinary combatants because it lessened the chance of violence occurring by enabling limited fraternisation with the enemy. As Rifleman Victor Gregg, who was aware of it in North Africa, observed patrolling was exactly the kind of low-level tactical activity that provided an opportunity for informal agreements with the enemy to flourish. The reader can picture the scene: a small patrol of six to eight men, about the size of an infantry section, are tasked with conducting a reconnaissance mission. Most of the soldiers would be in their late teens or twenties while the junior NCO in charge might be a little older. They hear movement ahead of them and stop, only to find it comes from a similar German patrol. Instead of firing on one another the two patrols converse and barter rations for cigarettes, before heading back to their own lines.

Doubtless other soldiers experienced it, even if they did not always report it for fear of being castigated by their officers. Rifleman Henry Taylor experienced a sort of 'live-and-let-live' situation while enduring a patrol in Italy during late 1944 where they 'took shelter in a sty to avoid the foul weather'. Later that night a small unit of German mountain troops occupied the same sty. Neither side noticed the other until in the morning the Germans waved and attempted to steal one of the pigs. The British troops prevented this as they wanted the pig, and Henry Taylor remarked, 'I don't think for one minute either side even thought about firing'.

Fighting with Tanks

Compared with the infantry, tank crews might seem to have had a less strenuous war. After all they did not have to travel on foot, and fought enclosed behind a protective layer of armoured plate. However, frequently they endured torrid conditions, and at times experienced high casualties. Arguably one of the worst fates to befall a soldier in wartime was to be wounded and trapped inside a burning tank full of fuel and ammunition. Under such circumstances crewmen were roasted alive and their body fat might be heard to sizzle or even seen dripping from a tank. As military historian Stephen Bungay remarked 'if they were lucky, the ammunition would explode, caking their remains to the inside of the tank in a black, sticky paste' and so saving them from a prolonged, agonising death.

As an officer with 4th KOSB, Peter White found the cries of stricken tank crews were 'infinitely terrible', made worse because infantry could seldom help because they were pinned down. The American-manufactured Sherman tanks, which saw widespread service in the British Army during 1942–45, demonstrated an unfortunate tendency to easily catch fire or 'brew up' when hit, leading the Germans, with dark humour, to christen them 'Tommy Cookers'. Subsequently, army chaplains and the Pioneer Corps tended to face the grisly task of extricating the charred remains of tank crews for identification and burial. Major Stuart Hamilton (8th RTR) had been burnt in a pre-war training accident, and, on seeing action in North Africa, confessed: 'I was always terrified of being wounded and trapped inside a burning tank and swore that I would shoot myself if that happened.'

The British Army entered the war with a doctrine that specified there needed to be different types of tank for different functions. Light tanks were thinly armoured, comparatively fast and only armed with machine guns. They were intended primarily for reconnaissance, but by the 1940s armoured cars proved just as effective in this role. Even so, light tanks comprised a significant portion of the army's tank strength during the early phases of the war.

Infantry tanks, such as the Matilda and Churchill, were slow, heavily-armoured and intended to provide close support to infantry units. In contrast, cruiser tanks, such as the Crusader, were fast and designed for mobile operations where they performed tasks traditionally associated with the cavalry. Correspondingly infantry tank units fielded the former type, while armoured regiments were equipped with cruisers. However, wartime experience demonstrated that producing two types of tanks to perform these functions was flawed. Rather what was required was a single tank that could both support infantry and fight like a cruiser, or what Field Marshal Montgomery termed a 'capital tank'. Reflecting on the experience of the North-West Europe campaign in October 1945, he commented the 'ubiquitous use of armour is a great battle-winning factor'.

The various makes of tank employed by the British throughout the war also tended to exhibit their own foibles, and it is worth considering a few contrasting types here. Andrew Dewar and Harold Brown served with 2nd Fife and Forfar Yeomanry (F&FY), a proud Scottish Territorial unit. Initially this was equipped with Vickers Mk VIB light tanks intended for the reconnaissance role which had been designed and manufactured during the 1930s. Both men observed that these were notoriously difficult to steer, especially when going down-hill, because the Vickers was a rather top-heavy design, and their road speed exceeded their engine speed, compelling drivers to rapidly shift between gears in order to maintain control.

Many soldiers experienced the Covenanter, a comparatively modern-looking tank of the cruiser type. It was never deployed in action, but widely used as a training vehicle in Britain where it proved awkward for trainee tank crew to master. Not only was it mechanically unreliable, but it had air brakes, which as Captain Ian Hammerton, who served as an instructor with 61st Training Regiment (RAC), recalled caused numerous accidents when they ran out of air while driving downhill. Several unwary crewmen also caught their fingers in the Covenanter's hatches, or injured themselves by slipping while working on the tanks in wet weather.

Despite its faults, the Sherman proved popular with many crews owing to its ruggedness and mechanical reliability. During the breakout from Normandy in July 1944, tank troop commander Stuart Hills reckoned 'the Sherman's greater speed and endurance came into its own'. Although it fell short of being a 'capital tank' as envisioned by Montgomery, standard models of Sherman mounted a dual-purpose gun, capable of firing high explosive and armour-piercing ammunition. Consequently, they were able to support infantry and fight other tanks, albeit hampered by their comparatively thin armour and flammability.

Although designs varied, conditions inside most tanks and armoured vehicles were uncomfortable, smelly and claustrophobic, particularly when the hatches were battened down under fire, with crews relying on periscopes for observation. Ken Tout, a Sherman tank gunner with the Northamptonshire Yeomanry, was wedged in the turret when in action, much in the manner of 'a Victorian boy sweep jammed inside a dark, tight flue'. Trooper Dennis Bunn drove a Humber armoured car with 15th Scottish Division and recounted that inside the vehicle he experienced 'intense heat and darkness', while he gripped the steering wheel and 'peered through a small aperture at the ground in front'. Fighting in North African, an NCO from 3rd RTR described conditions inside his tank as, 'stinking and thick with cordite fumes from the two guns going hammer and tongs and our eyes were red rimmed and streamlining. You could taste the explosive.'

In contrast to their rest of their crew, many tank commanders liked to fight with their heads out of their turrets if possible. Despite the obvious hazards this improved their observation. As Lieutenant Colonel John Gilmour (2nd F&FY) put it this 'gave them a much better idea of what was going on'. Veteran tank officer Major Bill Close (3rd RTR) even liked to wear his headphones for the intercom around his neck, as he felt this way he 'could better judge the direction from which shells are coming'. As Robert

Boscawen, an officer with the 1st (Armoured) Battalion Coldstream Guards discovered it also proved wise for tank crews to learn each other's roles so that in an emergency they could readily change places.

Crewmen had to share their tanks with bulky radio equipment and large quantities of ammunition for the various guns. Major Stuart Hamilton described his Valentine tank as being akin to 'a travelling ammunition dump', after he and his crew had filled it with over 100 rounds for its 2-pounder gun. Soldiers often crammed in items to make life more bearable, including rations. War poet Keith Douglas commanded a Crusader tank in North Africa and he went into action with 'Penguin books, chocolate or boiled sweets if we could get them, a tin of processed cheese, a knife and some biscuits'. A first aid box was another necessity, as burns and injuries to feet and fingers when the gun recoiled or as the turret turned were as much a hazard as enemy fire. It was wise to hang onto a few spent shell cases for the crew to urinate into during combat. However, as Stuart Hills recalled after prolonged periods of action, when it was impossible to leave their tanks, crews tended to develop severe constipation.

Just as infantry might be required to 'dig in', tank crews had to live alongside their vehicles. This might have entailed excavating 'living quarters' and using a tank as a 'roof'. Sergeant Trevor Greenwood (9th RTR) recorded that, in France, his crew dug a long hole 2ft deep, 5ft wide and 12ft long, to sleep in beneath the safety of their Churchill tank. However, there were cases in soft ground where tanks used like this sunk, killing the men sheltering underneath. Consequently, another method of sleeping favoured by tank crews, especially in North Africa, was to employ a 'tank bivouac', which, as Sergeant Jake Wardrop (5th RTR) explained, comprised:

A crew bed of all the blankets laid on top of one another and the whole thing was covered with a tarpaulin. The drill for retiring was that we all removed our boots, counted from the top, one, two, three, four, five and in. In the morning we rolled it all up and tied it the back.

On the back of tanks, rations and other stores would also be kept, along with tools and spare wheels to help maintain it in action, plus any useful scavenged items. In Italy, Major Stuart Hamilton even 'liberated' a toilet seat, which he carried on his tank and had made into a special portable commode. As wartime photographs demonstrate, tank crews, particularly on the Sherman, often carried several lengths of spare track as additional armoured protection against anti-tank weapons, as well as replacements for their own tracks.

Despite advances made in armoured fighting vehicles by the 1940s, the tank was not master of the battlefield. Anti-tank guns, notably the dreaded German 88mm which could easily punch through the armour on Allied tanks, proved a perennial threat. As Stuart Hills wryly commented, tanks 'were big and made natural targets for enemy artillery'. Similarly, anti-tank mines were a significant threat, especially in the Western Desert where both sides laid huge minefields. As the war progressed, hand-held anti-tank weaponry improved too, so for example a single German soldier with a Panzerfaust firing a hollow-charge projectile could knock out a tank at close range, particularly in terrain favourable to the defender. At the other extreme, tank crews in the Far East sometimes encountered fanatical Japanese soldiers prepared to blow themselves up underneath their tanks. Awkward terrain, such as mountainous areas of Italy further reduced the potency of armour as a mobile strike force in its own right. Even in the Western Desert, often misleadingly perceived as a tank paradise, the going proved inconsistent, as rocks and varying types of sand hampered mobility, not least by damaging tank tracks.

These factors combined to ensure that tanks of all types were often required to co-operate with infantry if they were to be effective in battle, especially in awkward terrain. This was as much to protect them from anti-tank weapons as to provide fire support to infantry and could prove difficult to accomplish in practice. A War Office pamphlet, *Notes from Theatres of War Number 16 – North Africa* (November 1942–May 1943) admitted that co-operation between tanks and infantry in that theatre was not always 'sufficiently close'. Part of the problem as Patrick Delaforce, a veteran from 11th Armoured Division who fought in North-West Europe, identified, was that: 'most infantrymen disliked the sight of their large "friends". They were noisy, smelly, tin-can monsters which nearly always attracted incoming fire, not only on themselves but also on the nearby infantry'.

However, co-operation often improved when tank units were able to consistently work with specific infantry units on more than one operation so that they built-up mutual trust. In North-West Europe during 1944–45, 11th and 7th Armoured Divisions together with Guards Armoured Division had their own armoured and infantry brigades which fostered close relationships under fire. In contrast, as Patrick Delaforce highlighted, few British infantry divisions had permanent armoured support attached, and individual battalions were sometimes deployed with little training or experience in tank infantry co-operation.

Another challenge facing tank crews was dealing with Axis armour, and tactics varied depending on the terrain. A major lesson for wartime tank crews to appreciate, particularly based on experience in North Africa, was the value of adopting hull-down positions, where tanks exposed just enough of their turrets to fire the main gun. At Beda Fomm in North Africa during February 1941, such positions enabled 7th Armoured Division to destroy several waves of Italian tanks.

Alternatively if a hull-down position was impractical, tanks were expected to engage while on the move. Major Bill Close remembered that 3rd RTR evolved a method known as 'sprint–stop–shoot tactics' in North Africa. A tank was to be driven flat out towards an enemy tank, with the gunner doing his best to stay on the target while moving. When the driver was ordered to halt, the gunner would fire as soon as he was on target without waiting for another command. The sound of that shot was the signal for the driver to speed forwards and repeat the process. With practice tanks were only stationary for a short period. While the tactic could prove effective against enemy armour, it seldom could do much to allay the threat posed by anti-tank guns that the Germans tended to skilfully deploy in harness with their tanks.

Likewise, in the close, awkward terrain such as in Normandy, head on cavalry style or charging tactics such as these were rarely effective, particularly against thickly-armoured, well-armed German Panther and Tiger tanks. Owing to their thick frontal armour and powerful guns these were formidable opponents, especially under defensive conditions. A skilful or lucky tank gunner might, as Robert Boscawen noted, be able to deflect a round off a Panther's gun barrel downwards so that it penetrated the weaker armour of the driver's hatch. Generally, it proved more practical for British units equipped with less powerful tanks, like the Sherman, to manoeuvre around Panthers and Tigers if possible, and hit them in the flank or rear where their armour was weaker.

The Gunners' War

Serving with artillery units seemingly removed men from many of the dangers faced by infantry and tank crews, yet conditions could still be extremely tough on active service, requiring much physical, often dangerous work. As an NCO with 112th Field Regiment Royal Artillery, Ronald Clack served throughout the North-West Europe campaign, and experienced the harsh winter of 1944–45 in the Ardennes, with its 'slush, mud and snow' that proved 'very uncomfortable' to soldiers living and fighting in the open.

Another serious threat to gunners was posed by enemy artillery seeking to locate and neutralise them, using what was termed counterbattery (CB) fire. Comedian and musician Spike Milligan served with 56th Heavy Regiment Royal Artillery, deploying 7.2in howitzers in North Africa and Italy. During the latter campaign in January 1944, he witnessed a direct hit on a gun position. 'It was a terrible night, four gunners died and six were wounded. All suffered burns in varying degrees … It was terrible to see the burnt corpses.'

Like other branches of the army, casualties to artillery personnel also resulted from accidents and disease. As a junior officer with the Essex Yeomanry, Noel Hair caught his hand in the breech of a 25-pounder field gun, which required hospitalisation. Many soldiers posted to the Far East, including, Albert Brooke, an NCO with the Royal Artillery, succumbed to bouts of dysentery that temporarily put them out of action. By the climax of the North African Campaign in 1943, 2nd Field Regiment Royal Artillery had suffered a steady stream of casualties: three officers and twenty-seven other ranks, equating to roughly 5 per cent of its total strength.

Much of the gunners' workload was of a greater technical nature than that experienced by other soldiers. Consequently, they required a high standard of training and the Royal Artillery could justifiably claim to have been one of most professional branches of the wartime British Army. In Normandy during 1944 German prisoners were reputed to have been so effected by British bombardments that they asked if they could view the 'magazine-fed 25-pounder field guns', yet these weapons were manually operated by well-drilled crews. A further idea of the technical sophistication of the Royal Artillery can be gleaned from the experience of Ronald Case who served with 2nd Survey Regiment in Burma during 1943–45. Unlike a field regiment and other artillery units, his survey regiment did not possess any guns. Rather it existed to help establish positions for the guns of other regiments and so comprised a survey battery tasked with establishing gun sites, plus flash-spotting and sound-ranging batteries. These last two batteries sought to locate enemy artillery by taking bearings on the flash and sound that they made on firing, so that this information could be used to provide CB fire.

Along with gun positions, provision had to be made for accommodating personnel and establishing command posts (CPs) and observation posts (OPs). This was often done in trying conditions, such as the Tunisian mud, cold of an Italian winter, or jungle terrain of Burma that frequently hindered mobility and the concentration of firepower. Moreover, many guns used during the war were towed, so required man-handing to ready them for action, and regular checking to ensure they remained on target.

As the war progressed conditions were partially eased for units that converted from towed artillery to self-propelled guns (SPGs), artillery pieces mounted on a tank chassis. These were highly mobile and obviated the need to construct gun pits or man-handle guns into positions. Even so, this often required a period of retraining, as Sir Robin Dunn who commanded 16th Battery 7th Field Regiment Royal Artillery, found ahead of D-Day when his unit was issued the M7 Priest that mounted a 105mm gun on an American tank chassis. These had different sights to the 25-pounders they had previously used, and because they were armoured vehicles men needed instruction on driving and maintenance as well as ordinary gunner tasks.

Another characteristic of SPGs was that they only provided limited protection for their crews. Battery Sergeant Major Ernest Powdrill experienced action with the Royal Horse Artillery in Normandy and North-West Europe, using the Sexton, a vehicle similar to the Priest but mounting a British 25-pounder field gun. 'The armoured sides of our guns were only waist high so one had to crouch down on one's knees to escape lethal splinters coming parallel to the ground, but we could not escape shrapnel from above, so we were covered in muck and dust and enveloped in acrid smoke.'

Establishing adequate communications was another vital task, as artillery units needed to be in contact with those they were to support. This was not necessarily as straightforward as it sounds. Friendly tanks might tear up telephone lines as they manoeuvred past gun positions or mountainous terrain interfere with wireless signals. Spike Milligan recalled at one position having to haul a 'twenty-foot-long pole [radio aerial] through a complex of branches and boughs … like trying to thread a giant darning needle and I wasn't trained for that'.

Working as part of a gun crew was strenuous, particularly when significant ammunition expenditure was required. At Monte Camino, Italy, 346 guns fired 22,000 rounds in a single hour, and at Anzio a British 4.2in mortar platoon fired 2,600 rounds in two hours. Fergus Anckorn fought with 118th Field Regiment Royal Artillery in Singapore, before being captured by the Japanese. As he remembered apart from actually firing the guns there was also much else to learn, and typically in training men practiced all the roles of a gun crew. On the 25-pounder, the standard field gun in the army, there was a Number 1 who was in charge; Number 2 operated the breech; Number 3 was the gun layer who controlled the sights, and responded to instructions from officers; Number 4 was the loader; and Number 5 provided the ammunition. Generally field guns fired high explosive shells, and soldiers would adjust the fuses and charge being used depending on the range of the target.

Soldiers not serving the guns had also to perform other duties, such as manning OPs or working as signallers. Both of which, although not necessarily as physically demanding as manning the guns, frequently entailed equally lengthy shifts. Similarly, Forward Observation Officers (FOO) and their assistants had to accompany infantry or armoured units so as to co-ordinate their fire support. These soldiers were frequently exposed to the same dangers as other front-line personnel. While acting as FOO accompanying 1st Royal Norfolk Regiment in Normandy during 1944, Sir Robin Dunn received a serious head wound that eventually saw him evacuated to Britain.

As indicated above a direct hit on a gun position or SPG could be devastating. Matters were made even worse if gunners had become lax in their discipline. Negligence in the construction of positions, when faced with the likelihood of enemy shelling, was a cardinal sin. This included failure to provide sufficient overhead cover, or correctly store combustible items like charge boxes. A 'premature', where a round exploded in the breech of a gun or near to another friendly position, was especially dreaded. These could result in serious injury or the death of gun crews. Spike Milligan recounted an agonising incident within his unit in Tunisia where:

> ... the entire crew of A sub section lay dead, dying and wounded around their gun. At first we all thought it was a direct hit by Jerry, but it was an even bitterer pill to swallow. B Sub Gun section in the lea of A Sub had fired and their shell had prematurely exploded as it was level with A Sub Gun causing havoc.

Ultimately, combat during the Second World War was stressful, uncomfortable, dirty, physically demanding and often costly. During the Tunisian campaign, for example, over 35,000 British soldiers perished. While in Normandy, according to military historian Gary Sheffield, 'Overall, the casualty rate for the Allied armies was higher than for the British Army (including Royal Flying Corps) at Passchendaele in 1917' and served as 'a brutal reminder of how bloody modern industrialised warfare could be'.

Even before they even set foot on the battlefield most soldiers had to endure a torrid voyage by troopship or some form of landing craft, or aboard a TCV, clouded by uncertainty over their future. Once in action, they faced an assault on all their senses when they came under fire. Whether from sophisticated modern weaponry such as Nebelwerfers, or from comparatively primitive booby traps like *punji*, the prospect of death or mutilation constantly overshadowed troops' lives. Contrary to the popular conception that the Second World War was a conflict of bold, rapid movements, most soldiers in Europe and elsewhere, endured lengthy periods where conditions had much in common with the deadlock of the First World War. Even the advent of modern battlefield equipment, such as Sherman tanks and SPGs, did not necessarily alter this from the perspective of front-line soldiers as they sheltered in their muddy slit trenches, manned gun positions, or drove armoured vehicles under heavy fire.

For many soldiers comradeship forged under fire helped to keep them going, along with the *esprit de corps* fostered by the regimental system. Bill Cheall was particularly proud to serve in his local regiment, the Green Howards, and claimed 'we were like brothers and would go through hell for each other'. Likewise, many servicemen and women were inspired by the need to defeat Fascism and thwart Hitler, and as Helen Hay discovered while serving with the ATS, there was still considerable animosity towards the Germans that stemmed from the experience of the First World War.

However, although these factors were important, British soldiers were influenced by several other factors that enabled them to endure active service. This included discipline and morale, access to alcohol and sex, the quality of rations, medical care, welfare and entertainment, and rest arrangements. These and other issues form the subject of the next chapter.

Chapter 3

Enduring Active Service

Combat was a demanding and stressful experience, tinged for some soldiers with moments of excitement and exhilaration. As this chapter demonstrates, personnel risked psychological as well as physical injury on the battlefield. Equally, for soldiers from non–combatant units, not directly involved in the fighting, active service typically entailed a lack of comfort and sometimes they too came under fire. Consequently, anything that helped troops cope with the conditions they faced was welcomed, not least because this also helped boost their morale.

Lieutenant Colonel John H. A. Sparrow served as Assistant Adjutant-General at the War Office, and was responsible for compiling numerous wartime morale reports. He defined morale as those factors which made 'the soldier more, or less, keen to carry out his job of soldiering, and readier, or less ready, to endure the hardships, discomforts, and dangers that it entails'. These included the supply of food, contact with home, welfare provision, entertainments, relationships, and access to alcohol and sex, all of which will be explored here.

In addition, this chapter highlights the role the regimental system performed in instilling discipline and morale, amongst an army that was largely reliant on conscripts. By 1944 the British Army was suffering from a serious shortage of manpower, and this had particular impact on infantry units. In order to maintain sufficient fighting strength some units were disbanded, and it became necessary to find personnel from elsewhere in the army, notably from the Royal Artillery, who could be re-badged as infantry. As Geoffrey Picot discovered ahead of D-Day, 'all anti-aircraft officers under a certain age and below a particular rank' were hurriedly sent on infantry training courses and on completion posted to infantry battalions. These conversion courses were tough, and as wartime artillery officer Major George Whybro, who attended one on the Isle of Man, discovered only around one in three men were graded fit enough for service as infantrymen. In some cases Royal Navy and RAF personnel were even re-mustered as soldiers in an effort to ease the manpower problem.

Potentially such upheavals could have had a deleterious effect on army morale, and no doubt some units faired-better than others. However, despite being heavily eroded during the war, the regimental system proved it still had a part to play in maintaining *esprit de corps*. As the historian David French emphasised, during the World Wars when localised recruiting collapsed, unit commanders had to foster 'a sense of community' even where 'none had previously existed'. In late July 1944 to provide reinforcements for other units, 1st Buckinghamshire Battalion (Oxford and Buckinghamshire Light Infantry) was broken up. Many men opted to be posted to 1st Black Watch, and as Private Stanley Whitehouse remembered his old platoon was wisely allowed to remain intact 'which was a tremendous fillip' to their morale.

Battle Exhaustion, Desertion and Self-Inflicted Wounds

With prolonged experience of combat conditions, soldiers risked suffering from battle exhaustion or fatigue, which during the First World War had been termed shell shock. Although stress-related symptoms could vary from one soldier to another, many became familiar with what they dubbed 'bomb happiness', when a comrade exhibited little concern for his personal welfare, and seemed to have lost interest in life. Combat veterans were often more at risk than inexperienced troops, because they already knew how awful war could be, and had to continually ready themselves for action, knowing their luck might finally run out. After months of combat in North-West Europe, Private Stanley Whitehouse confessed, 'I was having to dig deeper and deeper into those innermost resources of resolution, endurance and zeal to combat the gnawing, nagging fearfulness that filled my waking, and often sleeping, hours'.

Stuart Hills, a tank troop commander in Normandy during the summer of 1944, provided a vivid description of coming under artillery bombardment while inside a Sherman tank.

We cowered in our compartments under the intensity of these bombardments, knowing full well that there were was no safer area to which we could try to move. Claustrophobia and the inability to escape from it were an added strain on our nerves – one literally felt hemmed in by the prospect of death or serious wounding and quite unable to end the onslaught.

Exposure to conditions such as these could contribute toward soldiers suffering from battle exhaustion, the worst cases requiring medical evacuation, and assessment by psychiatrists. To give further indication of the level of stress soldiers were under in combat units, historian John Ellis highlighted that during the North-West Europe campaign in 1944–45, officers from 1st Royal Norfolk Regiment had a 72 per cent chance of being wounded and a 17 per cent chance of being killed, while for other ranks the comparable statistics were 65 per cent and 17 per cent respectively.

Major Bill Close witnessed an incident while serving in the Western Desert, where a tank driver refused to obey orders and climb into his tank. The soldier had a good disciplinary record, but had previously survived bailing out of numerous tanks hit during combat. Eventually, he was court-martialled, but as Close put it his 'bank of courage' had simply run out. Geoffrey Picot, who served as junior infantry officer in Normandy observed, 'most men have a finite amount of this commodity [courage] and it can it can get used up. Very few have an inexhaustible supply.'

Likewise, in Italy during 1943–45, the Germans mounted a skilful strategic withdrawal making full use of the awkward terrain, and conditions were frequently highly stressful for the combatants. Although the Allies had vast amounts of artillery, tank and aerial firepower at their disposal, it ultimately fell upon the humble infantryman to assault enemy positions and throw him off the high ground. Private Bill Titchmarsh remembered at the River Senio his battalion had to rescue a soldier, who on returning from a patrol, refused to cross back into the safety of British lines, because 'his nerves had gone'. On another occasion he encountered a corporal wandering in a dazed state towards the German positions. 'I said "Where are you going? You're going the wrong bloody way" … he wandered on and I tried to bring him back, he had gone bomb happy.'

Another veteran of the Italian campaign, Spike Milligan, who served with the Royal Artillery, recorded how it felt when he was returned to his battery, having been evacuated and diagnosed with battle fatigue. 'As soon as our guns start to fire, I start to jump. I try to control it. I run to my dug-out and stay there. I suddenly realise that I am stammering. What a bloody mess!' Later he was on duty in the Command Post where his stammering became so bad he was no use at 'passing wireless messages or Fire Orders'. Instead he just copied down Sit-reps (situation reports) before being put on the telephone exchange.

Jack Vardy, an NCO with 1st Hampshire Regiment, received a minor head wound at Salerno, Italy during September 1943, leaving him feeling dazed and shaky. He was later diagnosed with battle fatigue, hospitalised and given the 'twilight treatment'. This entailed patients being sedated for twenty-four hours under artificial blue lighting, and they were only woken to administer further medication and visit the lavatory. The process was repeated for as long as was deemed medically necessary.

Other soldiers chose desertion as a last resort. Historian Richard Holmes in *Firing Line* (1985) maintained that this 'remained within manageable proportions', the British Army suffering over 100,000 cases during the Second World War. The motives and fears which compelled soldiers to desert may have differed, although all had in common a desperate need to escape the army.

Worries about their families may have influenced some soldiers, especially for those serving overseas while Britain was being subjected to heavy aerial attacks by the Luftwaffe. While serving in North Africa during 1940–41, Rifleman Victor Gregg observed how several of his comrades, the bulk of whom came from the London area, were disturbed by letters from home which indicated the suffering civilians were routinely enduring. Equally, soldiers might have attempted to desert because they were suffering from battle fatigue, fear, or simply because they could no longer endure the privations of the front line. Company Sergeant Major Herbert Harwood (CSM) ('C' Company, 4th Royal West Kent Regiment) encountered a soldier in Burma who had left his post, potentially a serious offence. As there were too few soldiers available to keep him under close arrest, CSM Harwood opted to take a practical approach. He kept the man with his ration party and returned him to his unit the following day, advising him that he should claim to have become lost in the jungle and so avoid having to face a charge for desertion.

Poor living conditions, lack of recreational facilities and the unappetising food that most soldiers had to endure in Britain during 1939–42 might have induced some to desert. These might appear relatively trivial reasons, but they were regularly highlighted as matters of concern by contemporary morale reports based on the questioning of units stationed at home. During the early years of the war troops had also to contend with the frustration of being stuck in Britain, while the rest of the army suffered numerous defeats overseas, and morale suffered as a consequence.

As historian David French highlighted, an official study conducted by psychiatrists on behalf of the War Office revealed, that of 200 deserters from 21st Army Group in North-West Europe during 1944–45, only 43 per cent had what could be termed 'normal or stable personalities'. Over 20 per cent were classed as immature, and among the group surveyed were also numerous 'dullards', psychopaths who displayed anti-social tendencies and men with inadequate personalities. In other words, these were all men who had problems prior to enlisting in the army, and this probably made them more likely to desert.

Private Stanley Whitehouse recorded an unfortunate but popular individual in his battalion, who was always petrified when he heard gun- or shellfire, even if it was very distant. It came as no surprise before one action, when 'word went round he had gone on the trot'. By contrast, Vernon Scannell served with the Gordon Highlanders and deserted during the North African campaign. The final straw for him had been the sight of the bodies of freshly-killed British and German soldiers being ransacked for valuables by men from his battalion.

Yet soldiers who chose to desert faced numerous challenges, not least of which was coming to terms with any guilt they felt for leaving their comrades to face the dangers of the front line. Private Bill Titchmarsh explained, before going into action the officers usually read out the 'Battle Orders and once they were read out, if you went missing [for whatever reason] you were automatically branded AWOL, or a deserter in the face of the enemy'.

Another problem, as historian John Ellis noted, was that there were relatively few safe places to hide, and even in Europe many towns and villages were ravaged by war making it comparatively difficult to scavenge off the local population. Moreover, the scale and complexity of modern warfare ensured that any deserter would have to travel for miles through rear areas, before he was free from the clutches of the army he was trying to avoid, and this entailed constantly dodging military police patrols.

If caught and convicted of desertion, a soldier could potentially face a lengthy prison sentence, although in some cases sentences were suspended to allow individuals to return to their units in time for the Second Front. *Divisional Routine Orders Number 35* issued by the commander of 50th (Northumbrian) Division on 13 August 1944, highlighted sentences passed by Field General Court Martials in the Normandy campaign. This included soldiers being sentenced to three years penal servitude for 'cowardice in the face of the enemy', 'desertion' and 'disobeying a lawful command to go to a forward area'. Typically, punishment would be conducted in military as opposed to civil prisons, with all that this implied.

Having been found guilty of desertion in North Africa, Vernon Scannell was sent to Number 55 Military Prison and Detention Barracks in Egypt. Here soldiers under sentence (SUS) faced an extremely harsh regime, with an array of degrading and vicious punishments, including the deployment of body belts and strait-jackets as a means of restraint. Further unpleasant features of prison life included:

Punishment Diet Number One: eight ounces of dry bread at 07.30 hours and a further eight ounces at 16.00 hours. A bucket of drinking water will be placed in the cell. The SUS on PD One will undergo solitary confinement. Punishment Diet Number Two is the same as Number One except that a pint of gruel is given with the first eight ounces of bread.

For other soldiers the pressure of combat was such that they resorted to giving themselves a self-inflicted wound in an attempt to be evacuated. However, this could still result in a court martial. *Divisional Routine Orders Number 35* issued by the commander of 50th (Northumbrian) Division in

Normandy emphasised that the standard punishment for soldiers convicted of wounding themselves deliberately was two years imprisonment with hard labour.

The most common method was for a soldier to shoot himself in the hand or foot. As the British Sten sub-machine gun and German Luger pistol, large numbers of which were captured, had notoriously unreliable safety catches, it could prove difficult to differentiate between a genuine accident and a deliberate wound.

Sir Charles Evans served as an army doctor in the Far East and encountered the phenomenon:

I had seen too many self-inflicted wounds [SIW], usually in the foot. What could you do about them? I dressed them; they might have been accidents … the position of the wounds in the hand or foot and the man's attitude to it [sometimes] made me suspicious. I wrote them down as accidents, not SIW, and took care not to publicise them. The man's companions always knew what had happened … and were slightly contemptuous but not censorious. I never noticed that a SIW had a bad effect on others; they were only sorry that a man had been brought to do this to himself. My attitude was that the sooner these men were out of the battalion the better.

Some soldiers resorted to more inventive means of obtaining a self-inflicted wound. This included waving their arms in the air while sheltering from artillery fire in a slit trench in the hope that a shell splinter might hit them. They hoped this would give them 'a Blighty one', a wound serious enough to be evacuated homewards, but not so serious as to be life-threatening. Alternatively, an NCO from an armoured regiment deliberately inhaled the fumes from a petrol-powered battery charger, so that he had to be evacuated unconscious from the front line.

Given the nature of their task and the pressures they faced, infantry soldiers tended to be the most likely to desert or resort to self-inflicted wounds. During their service infantrymen on active service routinely experienced constant exposure to danger, lived in muddy slit trenches while enduring the elements, lacked sufficient food except when pulled out of the line, suffered from fatigue, and witnessed the death or mutilation of comrades at close hand. This could take a severe toll on soldiers and act as a mental catalyst, forcing them to take desperate measures. Although he relented from giving himself a self-inflicted wound, the combat-weary Private Stanley Whitehouse candidly described the moment when he contemplated it:

> I tested the mechanism of the Sten ... My cover story was that I had been hanging the Sten up by its sling when it slipped and as I went to grab it the butt hit the floor and it went off. I decided to aim for my hand and wrapped a field dressing around it to hide any powder burns.

However, the vast majority of soldiers, no matter how bad the conditions, chose to continue, helped in large part by the loyalty of their comrades. Another former infantryman and Burma veteran George MacDonald Fraser remarked that on active service the regimental system with its sense of family was most strongly evident at section level. 'Those seven or eight other men were his constant companions, waking, sleeping, standing guard, eating, digging, patrolling, marching and fighting, and he got to know them better, perhaps, than anyone in his whole life except his wife, parents, and children.'

Units tended to have their collective spirits further fortified by any soldiers within their ranks who were particularly popular or notable personalities. According to Robert Woollcombe, a platoon commander with KOSB, they had a cheerful, pipe-smoking company runner, who was older than most of his comrades and had previously worked on a Dumfriesshire farm. He proved a 'perennial source of comic relief' who 'slept in his tam o' shanter; a worn floppy object pulled at a special angle and endowed with almost supernatural qualities' throughout the North-West Europe campaign.

In addition many combatant units adopted a scheme termed 'Left out of Battle' (LOB) that to a limited extent helped them deal with the strain of operations. Its purpose was two-fold. Firstly, as Peter White, an officer with 4th KOSB, explained, 'a few officers and NCOs, plus a handful of men would take a turn out of battle from each company', providing a nucleus around which a unit could be rebuilt with reinforcements if it suffered heavy casualties. Secondly, LOB offered a means by which small numbers of soldiers, identified as being battle-weary by their commanders, could be posted for a brief spell of recuperation behind the front line. Lieutenant Robert Boscawen commanded a tank troop with 1st (Armoured) Battalion Coldstream Guards, part of Guards Armoured Division. On 5th September 1944 he recorded in his diary, 'I was sent for by Colonel Dickie who told me I must be LOB, and go back to the Echelons [rear areas] for a rest for two or three weeks.'

Discipline in the Field

Discipline was instilled during basic training and subsequently reinforced by the military hierarchy throughout service. In addition, every soldier, no matter what their background, subscribed to a code of conduct enshrined in the King's Regulations, appreciated in particular detail by the hard core of senior NCOs vital to the management of every unit. These covered a multitude of issues including forbidding all serving soldiers from partaking in any form of political activity.

Ray Meads was called-up into the Royal Army Medical Corps (RAMC) in 1939 and served in Britain, Italy and the Middle East. He maintained that any soldier could be hauled before a senior NCO or officer, and found guilty of an offence on his 'Army Charge Sheet No. 252 ... without ever having seen a copy of King's Regulations, let alone having read them'. Consequently, the 'tyranny of the 252' ensured soldiers could be placed on charges for offences which sometimes seemed comparatively trivial, given that there was a war on.

Ray Meads faced a charge for 'possessing and defacing Government property' in relation to an old army belt he used as a back support that he had obtained second-hand, and from which he had removed the original buckles. The charge was later dismissed. According to Bill Ness, who eventually became a sergeant in the Parachute Regiment, there was something pantomime-like about the whole process, whereby a young soldier would be marched in front of an officer by an officious NCO and have charges read out. As a refugee from Nazi-occupied Europe who had joined the Territorial Army shortly before the war, Bob Taylor was surprised to be castigated by his commanding officer for 'urinating in an improper manner', after he had answered the call of nature outside.

However, discipline was a serious issue, particularly in assisting personnel to cope with the rigors of active service. Rather than be placed on a charge, a soldier who required disciplining on active service could potentially face some form of field punishment. This might entailed being made to run in circles, wearing full equipment, under the watchful gaze of the Provost staff. In one case in Normandy a soldier who pilfered a tin of cigarettes was charged with stealing rations and given ninety days' field punishment.

Frequently discipline on active service lost much of the formality associated with service in Britain or peacetime deployments, and instead was replaced by comradeship forged by soldiers of all ranks sharing common hardships. John Crawford described what it was like serving as a driver with the RASC in the Western Desert:

> Officers no longer issued orders in the old manner. They were more friendly and more with the men. They realised this was a team. We, for our part, never took advantage of this new association. While orders were given, except in an emergency, more in the nature of requests, they were obeyed even more punctiliously than under peacetime conditions. It was a case of every man pulling together, willingly ... The new officer who tried to be high handed or a know-all quickly found himself in trouble, and sooner or later had to come down to earth and fit into the general scheme.

Similarly, Major General Dare Wilson served as a young platoon commander with 8th Battalion Royal Northumberland Fusiliers during the fall of France in 1940, and discovered a certain type of discipline was needed in combat units. During those trying times he 'learned the true importance and value of discipline, which is so often misunderstood outside the army, and how it can be both effective and humane ... in the last resort it is discipline, the maintenance of high standards under all conditions, which lies between success [or] survival on the one hand and failure on the other'.

Military historian and wartime Guards officer Sir Michael Howard recalled an incident at Salerno where standards of discipline became extremely strained. His unit relieved another that 'had obviously had a very bad time'. They were 'nervous and insubordinate and the young platoon

The British Army fought the Second World War as a highly-mechanised force that included thousands of motorcycles. Orders were tendered by the War Office to numerous British manufacturers, and motorcycles were widely deployed by despatch riders and for reconnaissance purposes. (*Author's collection*)

The Bedford MW 4x2-wheel drive truck entered service in the late 1930s, and was the most numerous of the British built 15 cwt models to see service during the war. This restored example is a Bedford MWD variant with the standard General Service (GS) body. (*Author's collection*)

Three soldiers enjoying a smoke: the habit was popular in the 1940s and people were less aware of the health dangers than today. Many soldiers discovered that smoking offered some respite from the stress of active service and the drudgery of military routine. All three wear Battledress and Field Service or side caps. The man on the right has a medal ribbon, difficult to tell in black and white but probably that of the Africa Star awarded for ninety days' or more service in that theatre between 10 June 1940 and 12 May 1943 (*Author's collection*).

Soldiers from the Royal Artillery in Norway during 1945, demonstrating that Battledress was very much a working uniform as well as one suitable for parades. (*Author's collection*)

A portrait of an ATS private serving with AA Command. Just visible are the flaming grenade badge of the Royal Artillery on the left breast of her tunic, and the shoulder flash of AA Command, an archer firing towards the sky. (*Author's collection*)

Soldiers pose for the camera while off duty in Jerusalem during 1943. Men from combat units captured in North Africa and the Middle East tended to be at an immediate disadvantage as all they wore were uniforms like these that rapidly wore out. Notice the man on the far right making a Winston Churchill-style 'V' for victory sign. (*Author's collection*)

An ATS platoon proudly passing out at Number 7 Training Centre, April 1945. By then women were being issued better uniforms than earlier in the war, but they still received only two-thirds of male pay rates even when directly replacing men in various trades. (*The Tansy Murdoch Collection*)

A crowded troopship scene: The soldiers aboard such vessels often had little idea of their final destination or whether they might ever see home again. (*Author's collection*)

A well-constructed machine-gun pit employed during the North African campaign – the ability to dig in was essential, particularly for infantry, and formed a common strand of experience amongst soldiers in all theatres. (*Author's collection*)

Another view of the machine-gun pit in North Africa. The weapon is a Vickers K machine gun, originally designed for use on RAF aircraft, but many were used by the army, especially in the anti-aircraft role as seen here. The soldier in the foreground is armed with a Thompson submachine gun, an American weapon, large numbers of which were supplied to Allied forces, including the British Army. (*Author's collection*)

A relaxed, cheerful-looking group of British soldiers enjoying a moment off duty in a rear area, probably somewhere in the Mediterranean. The vehicle they are riding in is an American-built half-track, several of which served with the British Army. In the background is a jeep, another American vehicle large numbers of which were purchased by the British under the Lend-Lease scheme. (*Author's collection*)

Hygiene was vital in all theatres, and the army went to some lengths to promote it, including expecting soldiers to keep clean and wash regularly when on active service. Here two soldiers in Egypt go about their ablutions. (*Author's collection*)

Even in the desert where water was scarce, soldiers were expected to wash and shave regularly. Officially a gallon per man per day was the ration, but in practice soldiers seldom ever received that much. Typically, vehicles' radiators were topped up first, and the rest was used for drinking, cooking, washing soldier's bodies and clothes, in that order. (*Author's collection*)

Light utility vehicles were manufactured in Britain using civilian pre-war chassis that were less rugged than Jeeps. Known as a 'Tilly' they were intended for light general transport duties. This is a restored example of an Austin 'Tilly' in desert camouflage. (*Author's collection*)

A restored example of the 'Tilly' produced by Standard, displaying what was known as Mickey Mouse Ear patterned camouflage, where dark, roughly circular blobs were applied over the base colour. (*Author's collection*)

Much of military life, including when on active service, centred on set routines. Here a soldier in North Africa readies himself for guard duty, equipped with his rifle, 'tin hat' or helmet and gas mask/ respirator stowed on his chest. (*Author's collection*)

A smiling soldier equipped for life in the North African desert. The antiquated-looking sun hat or topee formed part of the tropical kit issued to troops in North Africa and the Middle East, but was not universally popular as it could be heavy and uncomfortable to wear. (*Author's collection*)

The American 'Jeep' was one of the iconic vehicles of the Second World War. Around 640,000 were produced by Willys-Overland and Ford, and many served with the British Army under Lend-Lease and were deployed in a wide variety of roles. (*Author's collection*)

During the war several British bicycle manufactures produced military models, including folding ones like this intended for airborne forces. On D-Day many British units, including the Durham Light Infantry, were also issued with bicycles to improve their mobility. Most veterans remember that these were deeply unpopular, being uncomfortable to ride, and were often rapidly discarded. (*Author's collection*)

Soldiers enjoying a drink in North Africa. When available, alcohol provided many with relief from the privations and stresses of active service. (*Author's collection*)

Reading material of all types was valued by troops in all theatres. Here a soldier enjoys reading a newspaper while off duty in Egypt during 1941. (*Author's collection*)

Daimler Scout Cars, or 'Dingos' as they were known, were capable of 55mph, and had a range of 200 miles. They had a two-man crew and were widely deployed for reconnaissance and liaison purposes, with over 6,000 eventually produced for the British Army. (*Author's collection*)

The Universal or Bren Gun Carrier was a light full-tracked reconnaissance and combat vehicle powered by a Ford V8 engine. Developed in the 1930s it was widely deployed by British and Commonwealth armies in a variety of roles, including reconnaissance, troop transport and as a mortar carrier. (*Author's collection*)

The American-manufactured Sherman tank served with the British Army during 1942–45. It was rugged and reliable, but had an unfortunate tendency to 'brew up' when hit, leading the Germans to dub them 'Tommy Cookers.' This surviving example resides in the Muckleburgh Military Collection, Norfolk. (*Author's collection*)

The Sexton was developed during late 1942 to meet British demands for a self-propelled gun. It mounted a 25-pounder field gun on a Canadian Ram tank chassis, but had an open-topped fighting compartment so the crew only had limited protection. (*Author's collection*)

The dreaded '88' was the scourge of British tank troops. This 88mm dual-purpose anti-aircraft and anti-tank gun was employed in France during 1940, but came to the fore during the Libyan campaign of 1941–42, and widely feared thereafter. (*Author's collection*)

The Pak 40 was another formidable German anti-tank gun encountered by the British. It was of 75mm calibre and could fire an armour-piercing shell to an effective range of 1,968 yards. (*Author's collection*)

Bombardier Basil Levi, described as a 'hard working, trustworthy and very capable NCO', pictured in Norway during June–December 1945. (*Author's collection*)

The Austin K2 was the standard heavy ambulance in British service. Affectionately known as the 'Katy', it could carry four stretcher cases, eight sitting cases or a combination of both. (*Author's collection*)

commander only maintained control with difficulty. "If you don't do what you are told I'll shoot you!" he hissed in exasperation – and sounded as if he meant it.'

Equally, discipline applied to mundane but nonetheless important tasks, such as the maintenance of equipment which assisted soldiers in coping with front-line conditions. A corollary of maintenance sessions was that, not only was it vital for equipment to be in good working condition, but they helped maintain morale and occupied soldier's minds when not actually fighting. Ken Tout, a Sherman tank gunner in Normandy and North-West Europe, explained that like all armoured vehicles his tank needed regular maintenance checks. The 75mm gun for which he was responsible relied on 'endless cleaning, servicing, checking, pampering' and it was a two-man job to scour the inside of the barrel with a long brush like a chimney sweep might employ. Simultaneously, other crew members had to check the state of the engine and the wheels or tracks, which could pick up unwanted debris.

Discipline was also required in the construction of defensive positions to ensure they provided both adequate protection from enemy fire and the elements. As one battalion commander in Tunisia observed, 'it was generally only the careless or lazy who got wet'. Wartime artillery officer Major Peter Pettit, saw extensive combat service, including in Normandy, where 'a slit trench is the first thing we do on arriving anywhere – it's like taking your hat off entering a house'.

Habituation to army regulations was equally important in other theatres. Brian Harpur, a junior infantry officer in Italy remarked 'if one was up front the first thing one did, and I mean the first thing, taking precedence even over the urgency to go to the lavatory, was to dig in'. As an inexperienced Guards officer during the Tunisian campaign, Christopher Bulteel rapidly discovered that, depending on battlefield circumstances, it was common to either dig a shallow slit-trench, known as a shell scrape, or one deep enough to stand up in. These both proved 'safe against anything but a direct hit', but this was an unusual occurrence, so most soldiers felt relatively comfortable holding such positions.

Even so, the commanding officer of 1st Lincolnshire Regiment in the Far East admitted that many of his troops proved 'poor diggers'. It was fortunate during the fighting in the Arakan in 1944–45, that his unit were able to employ tactical positions from previous actions and so 'find our defence more or less ready for us'.

A related issue while living in the field was hygiene, which again required a disciplined approach to be effective. Typically, communal latrine facilities would be constructed downwind from slit trenches for platoons or companies to use. Some units achieved quite sophisticated arrangements, with soldiers even making use of toilet seats from ruined civilian dwellings. In Normandy Ken Tout found the Northamptonshire Yeomanry enforced 'rigid sanitary regulations'. These necessitated 'those responding to the baser call of nature dig, and fill in, a hole at least 25 yards from the nearest tank'. This worked well provided conditions were peaceful. Another Normandy veteran, tank commander Sergeant Trevor Greenwood from 9th RTR recorded, that he crawled to the rear 'with a spade and dug a hole … just as I was hitching up my pants, there came the ominous "whining" [of German mortars], followed by crashes dangerously near. I simply dived head first further beneath the tank and stayed there, literally with my pants down!'

Similarly, soldiers were expected to keep themselves as clean as possible, regularly washing and shaving, even in close proximity to the enemy. Rubbish and any waste that would attract flies was normally burnt or buried. Even so, as Brian Harpur commented 'there were few soldiers who by the end of the war had not suffered dysentery or some other fly-borne disease at one time or another'. Major Stuart Hamilton described climbing down from his tank in Italy, when he landed amid the rotting carcass of a cow: 'There was the most appalling, disgusting smell that I have ever smelt in my life and I was immediately covered with hordes of the foulest and most filthy flies.'

In all theatres flies were especially hated by soldiers, and it was impossible to eradicate them despite taking precautions against them. According to Troop Driver Crawford of the RASC who served with the Eighth Army in the desert, 'flies produced more casualties than the Germans' and it was 'impossible to describe, without suspicion of exaggeration, how thickly they used to surround us'.

Typically, battlefields were characterised by corpses, both animal and human, cookhouse waste and wrecked equipment, plus much other detritus. Consequently, a disciplined approach to living in the field was vital and most soldiers had to confront such hazards on active service, whether they served in combatant or non-combatant units.

Burial of the dead was a further important issue, both from a morale and hygiene perspective. General Sir David Fraser who fought with the Guards Armoured Division in Normandy noted, 'burials took place as convenient- often near the Regimental Aid Post, wherever that was established. Wooden crosses were carried in the medical vehicles, records were made, graves – sometimes, inevitably, multiple graves – were dug.' Lieutenant Colonel Sir Paul Bryan, who commanded an infantry battalion in Tunisia and Italy, observed:

In England during our training we never gave enough, or indeed any, thought to the burial of the dead. In North Africa we initially buried our casualties as soon as possible in the most convenient spot and marked the name on a rough wooden cross, but soon discovered that this was woefully inadequate when we came across German graves with their beautifully made and inscribed metal crosses. The troops felt very strongly about this and I got our pioneer platoon to design a wooden cross with the regimental crest of which we could all be proud.

Given the conditions wartime soldiers faced, religious faith had a resonance with many and helped them cope, along with the comradeship they enjoyed under fire. As a young officer in the NSRY, Stuart Hills recalled that their Padre was fond of preaching with the old adage 'there are no atheists in a slit trench'. Similarly, Private Stanley Whitehouse witnessed several of his comrades in his infantry battalion hold small prayer meetings before going into action. Although he had entered the army as a sixteen-year-old Sunday-school teacher, by the end of the war in Europe, his faith had weakened as he struggled to accept 'any God who could allow so much agony, so much death and misery throughout the world'.

Opportunities were taken by British troops to appropriate anything from civilian properties, that would either make their lives more comfortable in the field, or could be sent back home. This might seem less than charitable behaviour, and technically could have been punishable. When he encountered looting in Italy, Sir Michael Howard was initially shocked, but soon realised his men saw it as one of the 'perks of the job' after the stresses they had endured. Although it made him uneasy, he noted civilians faired far worse under the Germans. In Normandy and North-West Europe during 1944–45, Sergeant Trevor Greenwood also witnessed British troops partake in acts of looting on numerous occasions. These always appeared to go unpunished, although often they related to the ransacking of former German positions rather than civilian property. However, by no means did all soldiers resort to stealing, and throughout the war the army went to considerable lengths to support soldiers by providing comforts such as extra clothing and tobacco.

Welfare and Entertainment

A War Office booklet entitled *The Soldier's Welfare – Notes for Officers* stressed that the main aims of army welfare were to 'make men as happy as possible' and 'link officers and men together in a bond of mutual friendship'. Consequently, officers in all units were expected to put the welfare of their men ahead of their own needs. In addition during 1940 Local Army Welfare Officers (LAWOs) were appointed on a nation-wide basis in Britain, and a new Directorate of Welfare was established that centralised the issue of welfare provision.

However, for soldiers on active service, maintaining a basic level of comfort was one of the primary means by which they coped with the conditions they encountered and raised their morale. During August 1941, the Army Comforts Depot in Reading despatched 133,272 woollen articles, 782 items of sports gear, twenty wireless sets, 43,200 cigarettes and 1,600 ounces of tobacco to troops stationed abroad. Many regiments also established their own comfort funds in direct support of their battalions serving overseas.

With the approval of their Colonel of the Regiment, Major General W. N. Herbert, the RNF established a committee in October 1939, 'to collect and co-ordinate the distribution of comforts for battalions of the Regiment on service overseas'. The committee was ably supported by the wives of senior RNF officers, and numerous individuals and organisations in the Northumberland and Tyneside region, who formed themselves into teams of voluntary knitters using wool purchased at subsidised prices. Notably mittens, scarves, helmets (balaclavas), socks and handkerchiefs were required by the troops.

During the winter of 1939–40 the RNF Comforts Fund supplied 4,538 woollen items, and the following winter this was increased to 9,398. According to one officer serving in the Western Desert during 1941 the arrival of woollen garments gave great pleasure 'to the Fusilier in his strange hole in the rocks and dust' where it was cold at night.

As the war progressed the Fund also supplied toffees, chocolate, cigarettes, books and magazines, and a special Christmas parcel to Fusiliers overseas. For Christmas 1942 these were sent to 1st RNF in Libya, wrapped in green paper tied with red string accompanied by a card. Each contained:

- 1 leather pocket book.
- 1 coloured handkerchief.
- 1 white hemstitched handkerchief.
- 1 packet of best Swiss chocolate.
- 1 piece of best English soap.
- 1 packet of Woodbine cigarettes.
- 1 woollen item (e.g. scarf, mittens or gloves).

An officer who witnessed his men receive their parcels described the scene as follows:

If you can picture their arid lives, surrounded by sand, you can picture their pleasure. Their days are bounded by the sun – they get up when it is light, and go to bed when it is dark, and now the fighting is further away, there is nothing to relieve the monotony. However, they had a good Christmas dinner (first for three years) and the parcels from our Comforts Fund were a great addition.

The demand for comforts continued throughout the war. During November 1944, Major General Wilson, then a more junior RNF officer, wrote home from the freezing banks of the River Maas: 'Can you do all you can to get people to make woollies, gloves, scarves? Soldiers can get socks from the army and they wear well. But scarves are not issued … and only one pair of gloves and one pullover are issued to each man.' The following December he was able to write 'the comforts really are appreciated … The cold has been bitter with the hardest frost I think I can remember.'

Mail was another important link with home for soldiers fighting overseas, and was sorely missed when it proved difficult to deliver letters to the front line. While serving as an infantryman in North Africa, Bill Cheall recorded with joy the first time he received letters from home, 'it was a most pleasant feeling to think that those letters had come from England'. Many soldiers wished to send letters home. However, in keeping with security protocols they were prohibited from writing about the recent activities of their unit. As a precaution, officers had to censor their men's mail, and as Doctor Ian Campbell who served with the RAMC discovered, it taught him a lot about life.

To try and counter censorship some soldiers developed their own methods of alerting loved ones at home as to their movements. Wartime artillery officer Sir Robin Dunn explained the effective system he employed with his wife: 'We each had an identical map … When I wished to tell her where I was I would write a particular sentence in my letter, put the map over the corner of the note paper and stick a pin through the place where I was.' Back in Britain his wife would then place his letter over her map, and stick a pin through the hole so that it pierced the map and indicated her husband's location.

Alternatively, soldiers could employ 'the green envelope system' where they were allowed to send letters home at regular intervals without being subjected to the normal rules of censorship. However, if necessary these could still be opened by a censor, and an officer was required to sign a statement on the letter declaring that it did not reveal classified information.

Newspapers such as *Eighth Army News*, printed in North Africa and Italy, and *SEAC News* which was published by South East Asia Command (SEAC), provided another conduit to boost the morale of soldiers by reporting world events. *SEAC News Number 93* from 11 April 1944 had reports on the progress of the war including operations at Monte Cassino, Italy, and the Germans being driven out of Odessa by the Soviet Army, along with other news items including a report on a protest against a law in Cairo forbidding girls to drink with patrons at cabaret clubs, many of whom were British NCOs and other ranks.

Newspapers were also published at divisional and battalion level, including *The Polar Bear News*, a weekly publication by 49th (West Riding) Infantry Division, and *The Arctic Times*, both intended for military personnel stationed in Iceland. *The New Poacher* was produced in 1945 by 6th Lincolnshire Regiment and as the battalion's commanding officer Lieutenant Colonel A. H. Wenham observed, this was a successor to the typed newssheets published in North Africa and Italy and incorporated pictures. There was even a special Christmas edition produced in colour.

A corollary of newspapers was the prevalence of cartoons that boosted morale, such as *Jon's Two Types*, even published in a special Italian campaign volume by the British Army Newspaper Unit. These were two likable characters, or 'dapper Eighth Army types', who served in the campaigns in North Africa and the Mediterranean, and soldiers could routinely follow their adventures. According to Field Marshal Alexander they were 'old favourites' and 'typical of the spirit which made such a contribution towards the success' of those campaigns.

Films and broadcasts provided soldiers with further relief from active service and contact with home. At a staging camp in Taranto, Italy, Lieutenant Colonel Wenham was pleased to discover there were cinemas that 'provided all ranks with much needed relaxation'. Army broadcasting services also produced programmes such as *Cairo Calling* and *Calling Blighty* for which soldiers could record messages for their families back in Britain.

For many soldiers reading material was prized, and the large trouser side pocket in Battledress uniforms, which was designed to carry field dressings, proved perfect for containing contemporary Penguin books. George Macdonald Fraser was starved of reading matter while serving in Burma, and on leave in Calcutta made full use of the local booksellers. 'They had a simple system: you bought a book for ten rupees and when you had read it they bought it back for seven.'

Keeping pets provided another pleasure to some troops. During his service in Italy with 5th RTR, Sergeant Jake Wardrop 'picked up a big dog' that kept his tank crew company. This was far from an isolated incident. One armoured brigade serving in the Middle East was compelled to issue special instructions relating to dogs:

While it is realised that troops find relaxation and pleasure in adopting dogs, it must be remembered that the dog tick is the vector of serious disease.

It is therefore advised that dogs be limited and constant supervision be exercised to prevent infestation and re-infestation.

In picking ticks off dogs, on no account will the ticks be squashed between finger and nail.

Games and sports provided further entertainment and relaxation for soldiers, and helped them to cope with front-line service. After D-Day some troops were issued with a sports pack, containing football cases and bladders, sets of draughts, dominos and cribbage, together with a dartboard, books, packs of cards and the ubiquitous army game of Lotto, better known as Bingo. Similarly, off-duty soldiers from 10th and 11th DLI based in Iceland during 1940–41 were entertained by spelling bees, mock trials and mock parliaments organised by their officers. Lieutenant Colonel Michael Lowry of 1st Queen's Royal Regiment recorded that within his unit in Burma, an individual poetry completion was held. Although there were only a few entrants, 'it caused great amusement as the poems were passed round for all the soldiers to read'.

Many soldiers were fond of sports, notably football, but boxing, rugby, basketball, hockey and cricket also proved popular. An officer from the NSRY in Normandy had the foresight to pack with him a cricket bat, ball and pads so that impromptu games were organised between officers and men when the opportunity offered.

Similarly, in the Middle East an off-duty officer from the RNF commented:

A glance between the tent flaps shows two games of football and one of hockey in progress. They are watched by some 50 or 60 men, not to mention a flock of sheep, 8 donkeys, 3 camels, and some local Arabs.

Ideally as many men as possible were encouraged to partake in team sports, as this would help keep them fit and provide off-duty enjoyment. However, there was a deal of kudos to be garnered if a unit was able to field a successful team in army competitions, and individual soldiers even if they were not on the team were understandably proud as this reflected well on their entire unit. In the Middle East a football team from the RNF boasted an impressive record: played 13, won 11, and lost 2 matches, scoring 60 goals and conceding 18. This included a 7–3 victory over a team from a battalion of the Rifle Brigade, and a 5–1 win against a team from the Queen's Royal Regiment.

Music, like sport, was a comfort to many soldiers, given the conditions they encountered, and could take a variety of forms. In late 1941 a dance orchestra, 'The Northern Lights', was established in Iceland to entertain troops stationed there, and comprised a number of personnel from the Lincolnshire Regiment and other army units, plus RAF. Robert Woollcombe, an officer with the KOSB. recalled that during 1944–45 in Holland, his unit were accompanied by a local lad who played the accordion for hours with them, including performing a stirring rendition of the Second World War soldier's favourite 'Lili Marlene'. Soldiers from the Border Regiment in Burma enjoyed an old Indian military song 'Deolali Sahib', and most units had their fair share of bawdy marching songs that helped raise morale. In Italy during 1944–45 many troops enjoyed singing a poignant song 'We're the D-Day Dodgers' to the tune of 'Lili Marlene', which had several different sets of lyrics, some more polite than others. As Lieutenant Colonel Colin Mitchell explained there were a variety of versions, 'but they all expressed the same bitterness' as troops in Italy felt their efforts were unappreciated at home, given that since D-Day the main focus had been on the advance towards Germany.

Soldiers on leave in Naples were able to enjoy performances by the distinguished San Carlo Opera Company which received official support from the British government. As a young liaison officer Major General Wilson remembered, 'during my first evening I saw Aida and the following day attended a performance of Rigoletto'. Denis Healey recounted that he and his commanding officer, a fellow music-lover, 'sought out the decrepit conductor of the San Carlo Opera orchestra … and persuaded him to form a string quartet to give concerts for the forces'.

Similarly, troops in North Africa and Italy in particular, were encouraged to enjoy appreciating the culture of those areas by visiting museums and archaeological sites when off duty. This served not only to benefit them educationally, but acted as a further reminder of what the Allies were fighting for – to preserve civilisation from the clutches of Fascism.

Overseas and at home, soldiers also came into contact with the official Entertainments National Service Association (ENSA), often dubbed 'Every Night Something Awful'. This was comprised of professional performers who agreed to put on shows for the troops, and although they were volunteers they received a small fee. This enabled troops to see the stars of the day such as comedian George Formby, singer Gracie Fields, and jazz musician Nat Gonella. The playwright and performer Noel Coward famously toured the Middle East during 1943 and sometimes found the troops 'bloody minded' although they livened up by the end of his shows.

Equally, under the auspices of ENSA, soldiers were offered entertainment by lesser-known performers, the quality of whose shows varied. Major Denis Forman recalled his unit witnessed an ENSA show in Italy entitled 'Stars in Battledress' which 'featured transvestite activities of the most outrageous kind, breasts made of balloons popping like fireworks, skirts lifted until they almost revealed incongruous male organs, and double entendres so thick in the air'. Similarly, ahead of the Rhine crossing in March 1945, Ian Hammerton, who by then was serving as an officer with 22nd Dragoons, endured an ENSA performance that was not very enjoyable in his opinion because it was full of bawdy jokes, what he termed 'a brothel show'. Trooper Leslie Blackie from 43rd RTR, who served in Britain and India, found some ENSA shows were good, but others 'stink as they usually have two or three blokes which can do anything except act and a few old "bags" which probably only come to see what they can get out of the officers'.

Food, Cooking and Rations

It is difficult not to overstate the importance of food to soldiers, particularly as a morale booster to those in the front line, where it formed part of their routine and was something to look forward to. In July 1944 during the thick of the fighting in Normandy, Sergeant Charles Murrell commented 'next to mail from home, tea and food and our issue of seven cigarettes, are the only events, the only things to look forward to'. Similarly, Terrence Dillon, a regular officer with 1st Battalion Gloucestershire Regiment during the 1942 campaign in Burma, observed how fatigued men were revived by 'a good hot breakfast'.

During the early years of the war complaints about messing arrangements and the quality of food were common amongst soldiers and featured in contemporary morale reports. While stationed in Lincolnshire during 1939, Trooper Ray Ellis found that the food was badly cooked and had to be transported several miles from the cookhouse in open containers on the back of a truck. Consequently, 'it was always cold and congealed and it was usually covered in dust'. The diet seldom varied either: 'Porridge, bacon and beans for breakfast, bully beef sandwiches at mid–day and greasy stew at night.' He recalled that the cooks appeared to be selected from the grubbiest and most illiterate men in his battery. This was typified by one 'filthy man with a pair of greasy mittens on his hands, dipping his mug into a dixie of cooling mutton stew and of him pouring the congealing mess onto my enamel plate'.

However, as the war progressed and the army expanded, it attempted to improve the situation, as evident by the formation of the Army Catering Corps in 1941. Typically, British soldiers were reasonably fed when out of the front line, even if the army diet could prove stodgy and monotonous. Infantryman Bill Cheall recorded that ahead of an overseas deployment in 1942, the food at his camp in Britain, was 'usually very good and wholesome … I don't ever remember going hungry'. Breakfast usually included strong tea, porridge, sausages, eggs and bacon and large amounts of bread. Evening meals comprised 'sardines, and a seven pound tin of jam on the table, always plenty of bread and margarine with tea'.

Monica Jackson served with the ATS as part of a mixed anti-aircraft battery during 1944 and recalled, that to break up the routine her commanding officer allowed men and women to hold concerts and tea parties at weekends. They were given permission to wear civilian clothes and when the ATS girls 'sent home for party dresses and shoes … we found to our horror that army rations had put pounds on our hips and waistlines'.

Most units, even on active service, attempted to maintain officers' and sergeants' messes where a degree of luxury could be experienced along with foodstuffs that made a change from basic rations. For example, 'A' Squadron Nottinghamshire Sherwood Rangers Yeomanry ran an officers' mess in the

Western Desert from the back of a 3-ton army truck. It provided wine, cigars, cocoa, cherries, chocolate, meat rolls, ersatz coffee and even cherry tarts.

Under some circumstances mobile cookhouses would support front-line troops and their presence could be conducive to maintaining morale. In his memoir *Lion Rampant*, Robert Woollcombe comments that when not in contact with the enemy, 'A' Company 6th KOSB relied on one. It was a 'rather grubby mobile temple, its altar a belching petrol cooker', that tirelessly and faithfully followed them from Normandy to the Baltic.

Peter White, an officer with 4th KOSB, recounted the delight he and his platoon experienced of being warmed up by the 'blowers' as his company's cooks established themselves in a German barn. From there they dispensed hot stew, tea, bread and jam, and spotted dick steam pudding with custard, to weary, hungry soldiers who had recently endured combat.

Another form of cooking many soldiers experienced was the use of 'Benghazi cookers', widely employed in the Western Desert. As Joan Bright, the regimental historian of the Northumberland Hussars explained:

Cooking was done over a an old four-gallon petrol can with holes punched in it for draught; a shovel full of sand was put in, petrol poured onto the sand and set alight and this resulted in an excellent steady flame. The same system was used to brew up tea … at every possible opportunity.

Despite the obvious dangers of using petrol, this form of cooking worked well and had the advantage of providing heat without too much smoke. It became employed in other theatres. Private Stanley Whitehouse who served in North-West Europe recalled that after an attack he relished being able to sit down and relax in front of the heat his unit's cooker provided.

If officially-issued petrol cookers were unavailable, soldiers manufactured their own by adapting jerry cans, biscuit tins or other suitable containers. Christopher Bulteel, an officer with the Coldstream Guards in Tunisia, recalled 'every vehicle in the desert would carry these two half-flimsies [petrol cans fashioned into stoves], rattling on the tailboard. They were more familiar than the vehicles themselves'. As Lieutenant Bryan Harpur who served during the Italian campaign observed, 'wherever there was necessity there was plenty of invention', particularly regarding cooking and improving a soldier's basic comfort.

Some tank crews developed a strap to hold a billycan of water and a tin of food against the exhaust pipe vents on the backs of their tanks. Later when in leaguer after action they had a hot meal readily available. Infantrymen found it possible to heat ration tins, such as those containing steak and kidney puddings, on the exhaust manifold of trucks or other TCVs. An even more unusual form of cooking was encountered by Trooper Hugh Patterson in Greece. To his amusement and that of his comrades their cook had used a pair of army underpants as the cloth in a 'Spotted Dick' pudding, baked in a crude field oven.

An advantage of small units cooking and eating together was that it tended to maintain their morale on active service. The regimental historian of the Northumberland Hussars observed that 'each gun crew was a family party and its members lived together, messed together, fought together, and had their existence together'. Likewise, infantry platoons or sections would eat together using their 'Benghazi cookers', when not relying on a mobile cookhouse, which helped reinforce *esprit de corps*.

Tank and other vehicle crews similarly messed together, typically forming self-supporting units which carried most of their own supplies. As Joan Bright, also regimental historian of the 9th Queen's Royal Lancers commented, tanks in that unit during the North African campaign, were routinely festooned with 'the sort of property contained on a tinker's cart', including bed rolls and water cans, plus washing and cooking equipment.

Initially rations on active service comprised such staples as bully beef, hard biscuits, tea, sugar, tinned milk, jam and margarine and sometimes bread. Even with such basic fare it was possible for soldiers to demonstrate considerable ingenuity in producing different meals. Keith Douglas, who fought with the NSRY in the desert, recalled 'every meal was a competition between the various tank crews' and 'the triumph of menus was endless'. They made porridge by 'smashing the biscuits to powder with a hammer, soaking them overnight and boiling the result for breakfast'. This proved surprisingly filling, especially with sugar and condensed milk added. Cakes and puddings were made from their biscuit ration as well, to which they added jam. These were 'well browned on the outside and doughy in the middle' and could be 'fried in the fat of American tinned bacon'. Tank crews also enjoyed stews of tinned meat and vegetables, often with Worcester sauce, onions and tinned potatoes. Alternatively, bully beef could be fried with potatoes to produce a comparatively appetising dish. If there were a flour issue, Keith Douglas recounted 'we had bully fritters, in batter, or fritters of dried fruit, or batter dumplings, or meat, jam, or treacle pies and pastries', assisted by normally having plenty of margarine.

Not all soldiers shared Keith Douglas's enthusiasm for the food they experienced. During the siege of Tobruk Trooper Ray Ellis's unit received meals from a kitchen close to the gun lines which were 'boringly repetitive and consisted mainly of corned beef served cold or as bully stew'. Unlike Keith Douglas he found the biscuit-based porridge, often termed burgoo by soldiers, highly unappetising. Other soldiers likened it to pigswill. By contrast, Michael Lowry, an infantry officer who served in Burma, recounted that sometimes his company had 'a most glorious biscuit dough' for their evening meal 'made out of nuts and raisins, powdered milk, sugar, army biscuits, rice and boiling water. It was grand!'

As the war progressed various ration packs became available, notably composite or compo rations issued in time for the Tunisian campaign of February–May 1943. These were packed into a wooden box and easily carried in a vehicle or on a mule. They contained enough food for three meals for fourteen men for one day, or alternatively could provide one man with three meals per day for fourteen days. As tank gunner Ken Tout of the Northamptonshire Yeomanry remarked, this could prove problematic:

> The army is not able to supply rations for the normal five-man tank crew, nor the four-tank troop. The army appears to only cater for seven men who eat six rashers of bacon between them every two days, or who in the same time consume seven and three-quarters hard biscuits each. So representatives of the four crews sit on the grass and barter for the odds and ends that are not divisible by four.

Another challenge was providing a decent meal from compo rations under front-line conditions, even though the tins contained a variety of ready-cooked foods. Artillery officer A.M. Cheetham lived on them in the mountains of

Italy, and complained that 'despite the assorted foodstuffs ... opportunities to prepare a hot meal were limited'. Some soldiers developed what they termed 'compo sickness', after relying on tinned food for prolonged periods. This was characterised by stomach disorders and a general feeling of being unwell owing to vitamin deficiency and the absence of fresh food.

However, many soldiers welcomed compo rations because if they could be prepared properly, they afforded some variety to the diet of front-line personnel. Brian Harpur experienced them as an infantry officer in Italy during 1944–45 and explained:

> There were three or four kinds of compo boxes having a variation of contents so the diet did not become too monotonous. They all had tea, chocolate, biscuits, sweet tinned milk and tinned rashers of bacon ... but the tinned meats and puddings varied. The latter included an absolutely delicious creamed rice and creamy sultana roll for which I used to trade my bully beef, or even my precious cigarettes.

Unsurprisingly, throughout the war individual soldiers and regimental cooks in all theatres sought to supplement rations when possible with produce obtained locally. Often this was done by bartering their rations with the local population. Richmond Gorle served as an artillery officer in North Africa, and recalled trying to vary the menu by purchasing several small eggs from the Arabs who only accepted tea as currency. British troops in Normandy discovered the local countryside offered a plentiful supply of eggs, apples and dairy produce, including Camenbert cheese. However, not all soldiers appreciated the latter, and when one well-meaning platoon commander distributed several amongst his men these were roundly rejected as 'officer's food'.

Soldiers resorted to pilfering when the opportunity arose. As infantry officer Peter White explained, 'having seen the trails of slaughter, looting and destruction left by the enemy in the Low Countries' he was disinclined to punish his men when on one occasion they stole a pig from a German farmer to provide a decent meal. Robert Boscawen, a junior officer with Guards Armoured Division, commented in his diary that in the war-torn suburbs of Caen, Normandy, his soldiers 'rounded up and captured for the pot all sorts of stray ducks and tame rabbits that were wandering about the deserted rubble'. Major Stuart Hamilton from 8th RTR remembered encountering an abandoned British supply dump in the Western Desert, 'the tank crews were, quite naturally, helping themselves to everything on hand'.

Fresh meat, fruit and vegetables were always highly prized if they could be procured. Soldiers from 3rd Battalion Coldstream Guards in Tunisia established one position within a farmyard, where they enjoyed picking tomatoes, apples and figs, although the latter had to be picked in full view of a German sniper who routinely loosed off a few shots. In Burma Lieutenant Colonel Michael Lowry observed, 'organised scrounging parties' would descend into local villages to bring back potatoes, beans, fruit, rice, eggs and perhaps a chicken or cow for fresh meat. Similarly, in North-West Europe personnel from Number 1 Independent Machine Gun Company (Royal Northumberland Fusiliers) were delighted to discover, on one occasion that the Germans had left behind 'pigs, chickens, bacon, hams and even bottled asparagus … in abundance'.

In addition to food, a clean, plentiful water supply was vital in all theatres. This had particular resonance during desert warfare, when supplies were frequently limited and of poor quality. The regimental history of the King's Dragoon Guards commented:

> Water was always short in the desert, and strictly rationed – normally three quarters of a gallon per man per day, sometimes reduced to half a gallon … Most men soon learnt the meaning of thirst, but realised sips from a water bottle at odd hours did not quench it. The best way was to drink as many mugs of tea at regular intervals as the ration permitted.

Major Stuart Hamilton explained it was needed for topping up vehicle's radiators, 'drinking, cooking, washing of self and then clothes and that was the order of preference'. According to another desert veteran, Rifleman Victor Gregg, they seldom seemed to operate where the water supply appeared very fresh.

During the Tunisian campaign, Lieutenant Christopher Bulteel remembered 'the condensed milk which went into the tea. The water was so foul that tinned milk would not dissolve, but lay on the surface in circular oily globules. Shaving soap would not lather either.' He went on to observe how a small issue of alcohol provided 'a wonderful change from the brackish water which had been our lot recently'.

Similarly, Private Stanley Whitehouse discovered in Normandy that shortly after D-Day, drinking water was scarce amongst front-line troops as it was required by hospitals near the beach-head. Consequently, 'we resorted to quaffing pints of calvados, the local brew made from apples, to slake our thirst, and for shaving and washing we had been using dirty canal water'.

Water was also necessary for making tea, a perennial favourite beverage among British troops that played a significant part in maintaining morale. Troop Driver Roy Close (RASC) recalled arriving back in Britain having been evacuated from Dunkirk. He was confronted by 'lovely looking Women's Voluntary Service [WVS] ladies dispensing mugs of hot tea' that were extremely welcome. Most soldiers carried a small solid-fuel burner as part of their kit, which allowed them to brew up at a moment's notice. Lieutenant Colonel Lowry stated 'It always amazes me how the troops can put on tea at the drop of a hat. As long as the tactical situation permits they will brew up tea all day long.' Historian John Ellis even highlights tea was so important that from 1942 the British Government sought to buy the world's entire crop, and routinely at least thirty million tons were stored in Britain.

Smoking was another great morale-booster for many soldiers, and even non-smokers were often able to barter their tobacco ration for other items. Some ration packs included as many as fifty cigarettes, or one ounce of tobacco, so it was relatively easy for young soldiers to become addicted. However, smoking, even using the much derided Victory 'V' brand rumoured to be manufactured from dried camel dung, provided many soldiers with a temporary release from the stresses associated with front-line service.

A significant source of comforts was the Navy, Army and Air Force Institutes (NAAFI) or Expeditionary Forces Institutes (EFI) as it was designated overseas. This non-profitmaking corporation provided service personnel with ration packs, ran canteen facilities and sold items including newspapers, chocolate, toiletries, tobacco, and alcohol. Near to the front line, mobile NAAFI canteens could often be found operating in most theatres.

Alternatively, they would frequently be established in buildings that were accessible to troops on leaving the front line.

Private Bill Titchmarsh experienced extensive action as an infantryman during the Italian campaign in 1944. During a lull in operations he was fortunate to be granted permission by an officer to visit a NAAFI at Fienza on behalf of his unit and this proved a tremendous fillip to their morale.

> I got a lift up by tank. Lovely NAAFI there was in a converted dance hall. I had a sack and I got the lot pipe tobacco, cakes, toffees, sweets, writing materials. On the way back there was a diversion, but I managed to get on a carrier [small tracked armoured vehicle] going back. The lads were thrilled when I arrived and showed them what I had managed to get our company. You should have seen the joy on their faces after we'd been in thick of it.

Drinking and Drunkenness

As historians Richard Holmes and John Ellis observed in their studies of battlefield behaviour, soldiers have traditionally resorted to alcohol for four main reasons. Many overwrought soldiers found that it helped them to sleep and so possessed a medicinal value in limited quantities. In both peace and war it has enabled the drudgery of garrison life to become more bearable, especially amongst soldiers separated for long periods from their loved ones. Communal drinking and celebrating has also facilitated the bonding of small units, such as infantry sections and consequently aided their performance on active service. Above all, alcohol has been widely relied upon to alleviate the stresses and strains of combat. This particular usage tends to be overlooked by much of the literature dealing with warfare, including much of that covering the Second World War.

During the war rum was issued usually under the watchful eye of a unit's Medical Officer or senior NCOs, but only under certain circumstances such as before an attack, or to warm men up when they came off duty in cold weather. Lieutenant Colonel Michael Lowry noted that in Burma under monsoon conditions, when men became soaking wet, a tot of rum was most welcome at last light and at dawn. It was termed a 'drop of morale' by the second-in-command of his unit.

Under the pressures of war there were occasions when the system went awry and men became drunk, or the ration was divided unequally. Stan Scott fought as an infantryman before volunteering for the Commandos and was involved in crossing the Rhine during March 1945. Ahead of that operation he was issued with the rum ration for six men but 'when I got back no one wanted it. I couldn't just throw it away.' After being taunted by his comrades, he drank it so as not to appear unmanly, and was 'the happiest man on the crossing that night'.

Beer was issued, but often in insufficient quantity to satisfy the troops. Wartime morale reports from SEAC, for example, observed that the beer ration of three bottles per man per month was widely considered inadequate. Vital shipping space could not be given over to bottled beer, and so the NAAFI sought the means of brewing beer abroad at local breweries, or ingeniously producing it in dehydrated and jellied form that could be more easily transported overseas. Supplies were also obtained from other countries including Canada and Australia. However, troops posted overseas typically missed the taste of British bitter, and were not overly fond of the lager issued in its place.

It was often easier to obtain spirits such as whisky, which was normally only issued to officers. In his diary Lieutenant Colonel Michael Lowry remarked 'Having a drop of whisky in the evening [in the Far East] is a grand tonic, especially for me, as I still have malaria in my system.' Sister Marjorie Pringle served as a British Army nurse in India, and noted that owing to the heat, which put a severe strain on medical staff, they were encouraged to have a glass of whisky every evening to 'raise blood sugar levels'.

Typically, spirits such as whisky and gin were available at officer's messes, even when on active service. Although as in the case of 1st Gloucestershire Regiment during 1942, supplies were sometimes limited and carefully rationed out by the Mess Sergeant. Ordinary soldiers on the other hand had to supplement their limited beer and rum ration with local alcoholic beverages or supplies captured from the enemy. On Malta off-duty troops from the DLI imbibed a local wine they christened 'Stuka juice', after the infamous Luftwaffe dive bomber.

During the fighting in North Africa soldiers from 5th RTR, part of 7th Armoured Division, filled the water cans on their tanks with Muscat siphoned off from a local supply. In North-West Europe a squadron from 3rd RTR were excited to discover a stash of brandy, champagne, wine and liqueurs assembled by the Wehrmacht, and hastily liberated it by hiding the various crates on the backs of their tanks.

Private Bill Titchmarsh, who fought with 2/6th Queen's Royal Regiment in Italy, obtained several bottles of Marsala from a house his platoon investigated during operations near the River Senio in 1944. Shortly afterwards he was accosted by his commanding officer who asked what he was carrying. Thinking quickly he replied 'Something for the officer's mess, sir' and regretfully handed them over but managed to avoid getting into trouble.

During the 'Phoney War', before the German invasion of France and the Low Countries, soldiers from the BEF found that alcohol of all types was inexpensive and readily available to all ranks. In March 1940 Sergeant Charles Murrell of 1st Welsh Guards commented in his diary 'we are certainly becoming hard and heavy boozers'. Likewise, Major General Dare Wilson who fought as a junior officer with the Royal Northumberland Fusiliers during the French campaign, recalled that during off duty periods there was 'unlimited champagne at 5/- [25 pence] a bottle'.

Equally, in Britain it was possible, particularly for officers, to enjoy what Richard Carr-Gomm called 'a picture of wartime gaiety'. During weekend leave as a junior officer with 4th Coldstream Guards, part of 6th Guards Tank Brigade, he stayed in the smartest hotels in London, replete with breakfast parties and champagne after dancing the night away in a club. Similarly, most British units, wherever they were posted, usually attempted to celebrate Christmas and Boxing Day with an appropriate ration of food and drink.

Alcohol, obtained both officially and unofficially, frequently helped soldiers of all ranks cope with the stress of battle. Many units hoarded their ration at company or platoon level or the equivalent, so that men on a few days break from the front line could enjoy what one junior officer termed 'a monumental piss-up' as relief from the conditions. When Lieutenant Colonel Colin Mitchell went into action for the first time as a young platoon commander with 8th Argyll and Sutherland Highlanders, he was perturbed to discover many of his men had become heavily intoxicated on vermouth taken from Italian farmhouses. However, his platoon sergeant calmed him: 'Don't worry, sir. They'll be sick on the way up and then they'll be alright.' Bill Bellamy, a junior officer with 8th King's Royal Irish Hussars commented that during the campaign in North-West Europe in 1944–45, he and fellow young officers partook in 'bouts of happy drinking' when there was a suitable opportunity. In Normandy during 1944 tank crews from the NSRY routinely laced their NAAFI-issue beer with liberal amounts of the local calvados. Similarly, Sergeant Jake Wardrop from 5th RTR recorded numerous drinking sessions in his diary. Usually these occurred during a lull in operations. One morning in Italy he and a comrade started sipping from a bottle of rum which had been stashed in their tank, intending only to keep the cold at bay. Soon they were joined by their sergeant major with a bottle of Marsala and 'passed a pleasant few hours' drinking.

Alcohol was also used to celebrate momentous phases of particular campaigns. To mark the fall of Tunis the poet and wartime tank commander Keith Douglas recounted that together with Tunisian French officers 'toasts were drunk amid a good deal of badinage, in brandy' before sharing three bottles of Canadian whisky.

Given the widespread availability of alcohol, drunkenness was a potential threat to discipline in most theatres. However, depending on the circumstances soldiers who became drunk might not necessarily be punished, particularly if inebriation did not prevent them from performing their duty. Sergeant Charles Murrell recorded that in Normandy during 1944 two soldiers from his battalion managed to steal the officer's whisky and were found 'blind drunk at stand to' and put under close arrest before facing a court martial.

By contrast, a sergeant from 8th RTR was fortunate not to be placed on a charge for self-inflicted injuries in the Middle East. Having become intoxicated in the mess tent when celebrating the award of his Military Medal, he stumbled outside into a cactus patch. This resulted in him being hospitalised with blood poisoning caused by over ninety cactus needles which had pierced his body.

Peter White, an officer with 4th KOSB, fought in North-West Europe and observed that many soldiers in his unit indulged in heavy drinking when supplies of captured alcohol were available. Once this tendency rendered around 35 per cent of his platoon ineffective which could have proved catastrophic had they been in contact with the Germans at that moment. He was deeply ashamed of his soldier's behaviour but observed:

> The whole battalion was incessantly faced with this problem of drink in which unfortunately some of the officers did not always show the example they should. What punishment could one awe a chap with to whom death and mutilation were constant companions in prospect or in fact week in, week out?

Conversely, away from the front line it was often more practicable to punish drunken behaviour when it constituted a problem. Jacky Burgess served with the ATS and recalled being aboard a troopship transporting 2,000 men and 200 women destined for Cairo. ATS personnel were only allowed to chat to officers on the boat deck and fraternising with the other ranks was forbidden. One night a group of male soldiers became drunk and threatened to break into the girls' cabins, which caused a riot. The offenders had to be arrested and taken off the ship at Durban.

Love, Romance and Sex

American historian Mary Louise Roberts noted that issues of romantic relationships and sex tend to be glossed over in military histories. Yet these were as much a part of many soldier's wartime experiences as their military duties. Amidst the chaos of wartime life it was natural for men and women to seek friendships when the opportunity arose, not least so as to provide an outlet away from army routine.

Many unmarried soldiers enjoyed brief romantic attachments with girls which enlivened their war service and provided a degree of emotional security. While stationed in Lincolnshire, Trooper Ray Ellis of the South Nottinghamshire Hussars spent several pleasant hours off duty in the company of a local farmer's daughter chatting with her in front of a blazing fire at her parent's house. Before joining the Coldstream Guards, Richard Carr-Gomm enlisted in the ranks of a Young Soldiers Battalion of the Royal Berkshire Regiment based in Oxfordshire, where he enjoyed 'a great walk-out with the local greengrocer's daughter'. As he recalled their 'affair never got beyond late-night hot chocolate together' but he remembers it as an extremely happy period for them both.

Equally, under wartime conditions some females, like their male counterparts, sought out friendships and romantic interludes with men. Battery Sergeant-Major P. G. Dowdall, first experienced action in France during 1940 with the Lincolnshire Regiment. He remarked 'quite a lot of the chaps got to know French ladies' after they had made the first move as was French custom. Vernon Scannell recounts how he was approached by a Scots ATS girl in a canteen attracted by his Gordon Highlander's cap badge, and even though he was a Sassenach they soon began to meet up regularly.

When a soldier was wounded badly enough to be hospitalised this typically brought him into contact with female nurses, which under wartime conditions could spark friendships and romances. After being wounded with the Green Howards in Normandy, Bill Cheall and the nurse who had cared for him back in Britain fell in love. However, as he sadly explained this posed a dilemma '... although I loved her, we had not known each other long enough to commit ourselves to a relationship'. He also feared he would soon be sent back to the front line and possibly be killed.

Undoubtedly, under wartime conditions many married couples drew enormous strength from each other. However, for some it imposed an unmanageable strain on their relationship, particularly when a soldier was posted overseas, uncertain when or even whether he would ever see home again. According to historian Jeremy Crang, one of the major challenges facing army welfare organisations was dealing with matrimonial disputes, particularly where soldiers' wives unable to cope with prolonged separation were alleged to have been unfaithful. As a senior army medical officer, Lieutenant Colonel J. C. Watt became aware of this problem, particularly from the perspective of married soldiers serving abroad. According to him some women thought 'there was nothing wrong in going out with other men whilst their husbands were overseas, but when propinquity led to the inevitable misconduct, they were not sufficiently adjusted to realise that the affair was a passing impulse' and had to romanticise it by stating it was 'the love of their lives' and their marriage a mistake. Consequently, instead of keeping it secret and try and make amends, some chose to write to their husbands 'confessing their misdeeds and demanding divorces'. A scheme instigated during 1942 attempted to mediate between couples, where necessary with the support of a soldier's commanding officer, and prevent family break-ups. However, an anonymous Fusilier cited by historian Pete Grafton, hints that unfaithful behaviour was relatively common in some quarters:

> I slept with a couple of women when their men were abroad. They were getting their money every week, buying the booze with it – all that stuff. There was not really a great deal of loyalty.

Other marriages survived the turmoil of war and gave tremendous strength to both parties during enforced separation. In October 1941 Sir Robin Dunn, an artillery officer and veteran of the French campaign, was posted to the Middle East shortly after getting married. He recalled writing to his wife every day from his troopship and posting her a long letter whenever they reached a port. En route in South Africa a thrilling reply from his wife awaited him announcing that their first child was expected the following June.

By contrast, for some troops sex, like smoking and alcohol, offered relief from the pressure of combat and boredom associated with military service. Access to sex, according to historian Ray Kaushik, was even a factor in determining the state of morale amongst British and Commonwealth soldiers posted to the Far East. Richard Holmes remarks in *Firing Line* (1985) that traditionally military uniform has 'enhanced male sexuality'. How far this applied to the British soldier of the Second World War is open to question. Academic and former wartime American infantry officer Paul Fussell noted, that when compared with the dapper American GI, the average British soldier with his hobnailed boots and 'coarse wool battle-dress jacket with working class collar, looked like a slob'. Likewise, ATS personnel often referred to their unappealing uniforms in disparaging terms, especially the army-issue underwear known as 'passion killers' or 'man catchers'.

Throughout the war efforts were made to educate soldiers and ATS personnel about the threat of sexually transmitted diseases and promote sexual hygiene, including issuing condoms. Former infantry officer and author Eric Taylor remarked, condoms or 'French Letters' as they were known during the war, were issued free to soldiers 'not so much for safeguarding women against pregnancy as for protecting themselves from VD'. As historian John Ellis stated the authorities were correct to take the issue seriously, as VD proved a significant drain on manpower, often leading to more hospital admissions than those caused through combat. In addition a barrage of films, illustrated lectures, posters and inspections by medical staff aimed at discouraging military personnel from having illicit or promiscuous sexual relations.

For old older family men in the ranks and hardened regular soldiers with pre-war experience policing the British Empire, such measures might have had limited value. In India for example, where the British had a long-standing military presence, it was widely accepted that significant numbers of servicemen would visit prostitutes who established themselves near most camps. However, the message appears to have made a significant impact on some younger, less-experienced soldiers. George MacDonald Fraser, a nineteen-year-old infantryman in Burma, found films regarding VD 'terrifyingly explicit'.

Similarly, ATS personnel often lived in fear of VD owing to army educational campaigns, and many young women in the 1940s were comparatively naïve about sexual matters by modern standards. Any ATS woman who became pregnant regardless of her rank also faced an automatic discharge, and for some this may have acted as a deterrent against illicit sex. However, for others pregnancy offered a means of avoiding further military service. Captain Geoffrey Picot began his army career with the Pay Corps in Britain and served alongside several ATS women. One evening he was approached by one of them who said '"I want to get out of the army. I can only get my release if I am pregnant." I looked at her, turned tail and ran for my life.'

Frequently in the course of their military service, ATS women had also to learn methods of avoiding the unwanted attentions of male soldiers. Dorothy Calvert who served in a mixed anti-aircraft battery remembered that after a few dates some men suffered from 'the wandering hand disease' and had to be slapped in the face. Ambulance driver Pat Hall, who served in North Africa and Italy, found some men 'like a dangerous corner, so obvious that you went slowly'. However, soldiers could at other times behave highly courteously to women. Troop Driver John Crawford observed that at Tobruk there were nine nurses who 'were treated with a respect far beyond anything seen at home'.

Society, church and family in the 1940s tended to discouraged casual sexual behaviour and disproved of related issues such as unmarried mothers. Even so, commanders including Field Marshal Montgomery realised that some troops would always seek what he termed 'horizontal entertainment'. As early as October 1939 while commanding 3rd Division in the BEF he strove to promote sexual hygiene by making sure soldiers had access to condoms and extolling the virtues of the more acceptable brothels in Lille. He also issued an order advising every soldier to use their 'common sense and take the necessary precautions against infection – otherwise he becomes a casualty by his own neglect, and this is helping the enemy'. His stance was highly controversial at the time, but did represent a pragmatic attempt to deal with soldiers who chose to use prostitutes, especially as he discovered some had been subsidising country girls for favours on local farms.

By late 1944, when the British Army had returned to the Continent, the introduction of penicillin made it possible to treat most VD cases within a matter of days rather than weeks as had previously been the case. However, troops continued to be cautioned on the dangers of illicit sex throughout the war. *Instructions for British Servicemen in France 1944* issued to troops ahead of serving in Normandy, claimed that syphilis was particularly prevalent in areas where there had been large German garrisons – 'may be as many as one in eight of the population.' Similarly, *Instructions for British Servicemen in Germany 1944* quoted a German expert as saying 'Venereal Diseases strike at every fourth person between the ages of 15 and 41'. Even if these official booklets exaggerated the figures for effect, soldiers were well advised to steer clear of loose women, or women desperate to sell their bodies in exchange for food.

The potential health risk that use of prostitutes posed to troops, particularly if they refrained from using contraception, was brought home to Doctor Ian Campbell who served with Number 2 Field Dressing Station and landed on Juno Beach during D-Day. Amid the turmoil he recorded that same evening a couple of French ladies established a makeshift brothel in an abandoned landing craft and had to be arrested.

If a soldier wanted to avail himself of a prostitute he would ideally visit a licenced brothel, rather than take advantage of amateurs. The latter were women and girls who were forced to sell their bodies because they were starving, as frequently occurred in war-torn Italy, where it proved especially difficult to regulate prostitution. At a licenced brothel numerous precautions would be taken including the provision of condoms, and prostitutes routinely checked for any signs of infection. Ablution rooms enabled soldiers to apply disinfectants, such as potassium permanganate and perchloride of mercury, to their genitals after intercourse under the watchful eye of attendants as a further health measure. While this caused moral indignation in some quarters, many military commanders realised it offered a practical solution to dealing with the issue of VD.

Sergeant Charles Murrell recorded being stationed at Arras in 1940 where he would share a drink with a comrade who had his 'regular girl at Number 4'. By contrast, Hugh Patterson served with the Northumberland Hussars and recalled entering a brothel in Cairo: 'I was revolted and did not take part in proceedings, but could now understand why we were obliged to have regular short-arm inspections [inspections of a soldier's penis by medical staff in order to check for signs of sexually-transmitted diseases] by the Medical Officer.' Some Medical Officers encouraged men to practice abstinence or advised soldiers to stick to masturbation. This was particularly pertinent in operational theatres like the Western Desert where few women were present.

For many soldiers and ATS women their war service provided them with an education in matters of sex and relationships. This was during a period when sex was largely deemed a taboo subject by society, and related issues regarding hygiene and bodily functions were not necessarily readily discussed. For example, it was not uncommon for some young women to join the ATS never having heard of sanitary towels.

According to Spike Milligan, who served with the Royal Artillery in North Africa and Italy, 'discussions on sex took up large portions of gunners' working hours'. It wasn't only sex-starved men who talked about it. John Costello in *Love, Sex and War* noted that for some ATS personnel the barrack room provided an ideal opportunity to discuss men. Equally, within some camps toilet-block graffiti was deployed to pass on information of a sexual nature from one woman to another.

As well as the threat of sexually-transmitted diseases, xenophobia and racial prejudices discouraged soldiers from having illicit sex. Vernon Scannell served with an infantry battalion in North Africa and noted that the prostitutes in Tripoli were rumoured to behave 'like animals' who slept with up to sixty or seventy men per day. In the Far East George Macdonald Fraser cautioned that 'the average Indian and Eurasian prostitute was not notable for her charm or beauty'. When on leave in India, he and his comrades, despite having been deprived of female company for months, were content to simply eat, drink beer, chat up and dance with servicewomen and wander the local bazaars.

During the war the army recognised the importance of good discipline and that it underpinned morale. Accordingly, it went to some lengths to improve conditions for combat and non-combatant personnel, both at home and overseas. It was recognised that soldiers on active service in particular encountered a high level of stress, and this could be eased by better conditions, including improved welfare arrangements, sexual hygiene, rations and access to recreational pursuits, such as sports and music. Even those of an ad hoc nature, such as the cricket matches organised by tank crews from the NSRY in Normandy were valuable in boosting morale. The regimental system remained important too, but was frequently reflected by the close comradeship cultivated amongst small groups of soldiers, rather than by grand traditions harking back to previous conflicts. All these factors that helped soldiers endure active service, were to an extent lost once troops were captured and became a POW, and their plight forms the subject of the next chapter.

Chapter 4

Prisoner of War Experiences

Most British soldiers who became POWs were captured early in the war when it was going badly on all fronts for Britain. The capitulation of France and the Low Countries in May/June 1940 yielded 34,000 POWs from the British Army alone. Subsequently, thousands more British soldiers were captured during the fighting in North Africa in 1940–43, most of whom became inmates of POW camps in Italy or Germany. The Germans also captured smaller numbers of British troops during operations in Norway in 1940, and Greece in 1940–41. Around 90,000 British troops became prisoners of the Imperial Japanese Army (IJA) during the fall of Singapore in February 1942, to add to those captured in Hong Kong.

The Hague Convention of 1907 and the Geneva Convention of 1929 set out rules governing the treatment of POWs. These documents included statements that all prisoners except officers could be employed as labour, but only of a non-military nature, such as agricultural work. POWs should be paid the same rate as soldiers of the nation holding them captive. They were to be protected from acts of violence, and freedom of religious worship was to be allowed. However, any POW who escaped and was re-captured was liable to face disciplinary punishment.

Typically, British soldiers held captive in Europe by the Germans and Italians endured a tough existence behind the wire, uncertain about when they might be liberated. Life was dominated by hunger, poor living conditions, monotonous routine and the misery of being beholden to the will of their captors.

As this chapter will demonstrate, to maintain their sanity and boost morale many POWs avidly pursued artistic and intellectual interests. It was even arranged for men to sit examinations in professional and academic subjects, with papers being distributed via the Red Cross and returned to Britain by them for marking. Music, theatre and sporting activities flourished in many camps, even if POWs could not always participate for lengthy periods owing to their physical weakness. Alternatively, acts of sabotage and escapes offered a direct means by which POWs could strike back against the Germans and Italians. However, if caught, men engaged in such activities potentially faced severe punishment.

Unlike the other Axis Powers, Japan never ratified the Geneva Convention, although she was a signatory. Japanese troops were indoctrinated with a warped sense of Bushido (the way of the warrior), central to which was the belief that it was better to die with honour than surrender. As General Hideki Tojo commented in *Instructions for the Military*, 'Don't survive shamefully as a prisoner; die, and thus escape ignominy.' This attitude was transferred into how the IJA treated prisoners, as well as its own soldiers. Effectively the Japanese flouted all the main aspects of the Geneva Convention, and considered prisoners as expendable, and unworthy of their respect because they had allowed themselves to be captured.

Race was another important issue during the war in the Far East. The IJA saw itself as a victorious force over the despised 'white' imperial races, who they perceived as oppressors. Consequently, many Japanese, Korean and even Indian Nationalists who were employed as guards proved capable of the utmost brutality. Yet, as the chapter illustrates there were times when guards were less inclined towards acts of violence, and could even demonstrate a limited degree of kindness towards prisoners.

Similarly, for the British race was a significant issue in the Far East. Prior to the fall of Malaya and Singapore, the British Army encouraged personnel of all ranks to believe that the Japanese were militarily and racially inferior, and they were even likened to 'monkeys' by some soldiers.

Far East Prisoners of War (FEPOWs) experienced similar feelings of demoralisation and humiliation as their counterparts held prisoner in Europe. However, these were compounded further by extremely harsh living conditions, sadistic guards, and levels of starvation caused by a diet dominated by small rations of rice. The tropical climate and constant threat of disease added to their woes. Conditions in many camps were horrific, but in others they were more bearable, especially those situated away from the infamous Thai–Burma railway.

Many FEPOWS discovered that, when practicable, activities such as sport and the theatre played a significant role in maintaining their morale. Although escapes did occur, the nature of the jungle terrain encountered in the Far East, coupled with uncertainties about the loyalties of local populations and the physical state of most prisoners, made such ventures less viable than they were in Europe.

Capture on the Battlefield

Typically, soldiers surrendered when exhausted, and with little or no remaining ammunition and rations, so that further resistance was futile. Having formally laid down their arms under such circumstances, and had their surrender accepted, troops hoped to be treated honourably as POWs under the terms of the Geneva Convention.

The action by Number 8 Platoon 'A' Company 2nd Gloucestershire Regiment at Cassel, France during late May 1940 provides a case in point. Here the Battalion occupied a significant position in the Dunkirk perimeter protecting a vital road junction. Under Second Lieutenant R. W. Cresswell, who was awarded the Military Cross, 8 Platoon were specifically tasked with occupying a blockhouse to help delay the German's advance. They held on for four days against concerted attacks by German infantry and armoured units, during which time the building caught fire, and for three of the days they were without rations. Eventually, the Platoon as the regimental history of the Gloucestershire Regiment observed, 'were so closely surrounded that escape was hopeless, and the survivors were taken prisoner'.

However, soldiers who tried to surrender were not necessarily guaranteed to be taken prisoner. In the heat and confusion of close combat troops on all sides sometimes shot or bayoneted enemy personnel attempting to surrender. Bloodlust, described by wartime infantry officer John Randle, as the 'animalistic-like desire to kill', could also lead to soldiers being killed, when under different circumstances they might have been captured. It tended to occur during especially tense situations in battle, and troops gripped by it invariably ignored pleas by their officers to take prisoners as they embarked on an orgy of killing.

Infantry on all sides sometimes killed captured personnel who were especially feared, such as snipers, machine-gunners, and flamethrower and mortar operators, despite this being against the conventions of war. Prisoners might even be killed simply because there was no escort available to take them safely to the rear. These were the harsh realities of warfare in the industrial age, and it would be naïve to think such actions did not occur during the Second World War.

The speed, mobility and intensity of the French campaign in May/June 1940 caught many British troops by surprise, and this contributed towards the sizeable numbers that went 'into the bag'. Soldiers in the BEF in 1940 joked that every campaign started with a retreat, and like their predecessors in August 1914, they rapidly became engaged in fighting a series of withdrawals. The regimental history of the Gloucestershire Regiment described it as a 'nightmare campaign'. For ordinary British soldiers it was dominated by a lack of information, weary marches along roads crowded with refugees under attack from the Luftwaffe and resolutely-mounted rearguard actions, culminating in the evacuation at Dunkirk.

On 20 May 1940 Territorial Army units had a particularly tough time, as although their morale tended to be good, most troops lacked training. Surviving elements of 5th Buffs (Royal East Kent Regiment), part of 36th Brigade from 12th (Eastern) Division, attempted to evade the Germans and ended up in woodland near Doullens. Increasingly demoralised, fatigued and low on ammunition they were eventually surrounded. Private Alfred Bryant who took part in the action, recalled that they were ordered to throw down their arms, leave the cover of the trees with their hands up, and be searched by German soldiers, one of whom really did say: 'For you the war is over!'

When captured, fear of the unknown was an immediate concern for many troops, particularly as they were likely to be fatigued and disorientated after experiencing combat. Near Arras on 20 May part of 23rd (Northumbrian) Division, including 11th DLI, were caught in the open by reconnaissance units and tanks from the 6th and 8th Panzer Divisions. There were heavy casualties. John Bell from 11th DLI, who was wounded and captured, immediately took out a photograph of his wife and children and kissed it, uncertain when he would ever see them again.

Some soldiers felt a sense of relief when captured, because although they were now a POW, they had experienced active service and survived. While serving as a despatch rider with the Royal Army Service Corps, Leslie Barter was wounded in the stomach near St-Valery on 29 May 1940. He felt thrilled to still be alive when he awoke on a stretcher in a barn with other British wounded, even though they had been taken prisoner by the Germans.

For personnel from non-combatant units the moment of capture could be less traumatic than that experienced by combatants. As an army surgeon, Philip Newman had stayed behind with 12th Casualty Clearing Station near Dunkirk, in order to treat those soldiers who were too seriously wounded to be evacuated. He was awarded the Distinguished Service Order for his actions, and recorded the moment the Germans initially arrived at 12th CSS:

It was a peaceful scene. No bombs, no guns, no bullets, no planes, no more diving for cover and splitting ear drums, but the bright sunshine highlighted the agony and devastation of total war. Enacted before our eyes was the background horror and spontaneous reaction of sympathy and friendship. The conquering troops were already bringing hot soup to the wounded and producing photographs out of well squashed wallets.

The campaigns in North Africa during 1940–43 yielded significant numbers of POWs for both sides. Warfare in the desert terrain of Egypt and Libya has often been portrayed as a comparatively chivalrous venture, but in fact it was as brutal as other theatres. Likewise, the campaign in Tunisia witnessed much bitter fighting over awkward terrain, before the Germans finally surrendered on 12 May 1943.

While the Germans generally treated British POWs well on capture, the Italians who subsequently took charge of them sometimes proved antagonistic and sadistic. During heavy fighting in July 1942, Trooper Ray Ellis was captured and while being held at a transit camp in Libya he witnessed an Italian guard beat another British POW to death with a stick. He also saw Italian guards taunted thirsty, bedraggled and demoralised British POWs by emptying buckets of water in front of them into the sand, having first pretended they were going to offer them a drink.

Trooper Hugh Patterson served with the Northumberland Hussars which became 102nd Light Anti-Aircraft and Anti-Tank Regiment Royal Artillery. He was deployed to Egypt, before taking part in the British intervention in Greece during 1941, and was fortunate to be amongst those soldiers evacuated safely from Crete. On returning to the Western Desert, Hugh Patterson was captured under bewildering circumstances that typified the ebb and flow of the North African campaign as experienced by ordinary soldiers. Having been ordered to drive his commanding officer to 4th Armoured Brigade HQ, he was left guarding their truck when:

> All hell broke loose, all sorts of action erupting in our midst. 'A great line of tanks are coming!' was yelled. There were fifty of them. After a few minutes another cry went up, 'It's all right chaps, they're ours!' We relaxed. Very shortly after, intense firing broke out. Our anti-tank guns began firing as it became obvious that the tanks were definitely NOT ours. As confusion developed, every sort of noise and command was evident. The smell of cordite was strong. I had no weapon, was standing in the open, so I ducked down under the HQ van. One of the 'B' Battery men was wounded, then we became aware of the ring of tanks surrounding us.

Similarly, on the Gazala Line during 1942 British troops fell into enemy hands, often under confusing circumstances. On 8 April a mobile patrol, known as 'Roscol' after its commander Major Ross Mclaren, was launched by 'D' Company 8th DLI supported by artillery and other units. The patrol encountered German armour and was heavily shelled. Although the order to withdraw was given, unfortunately not all elements of the patrol understood it. Consequently, many troops were left unprotected when faced by the German tanks, and thirty soldiers, including all of 'D' Company's officers, were captured.

Major Ian English, an officer from 8th DLI, was taken prisoner in March 1943 at the Mareth Line, Tunisia, which witnessed extremely heavy fighting. While attempting to liaise with the company on his flank, he encountered a party of Panzer Grenadiers: outnumbered and outgunned he had no option but to surrender. He later commented 'it was perhaps the most depressing walk of my life', surrounded by the dead from both sides and all the detritus of war, such as knocked-out British Valentine tanks and discarded personal kit.

Another North African veteran, Major Pumphrey of the Northumberland Hussars, was captured when his vehicle column was overrun by the enemy. He remembered that the German NCO in charge 'behaved very well to us, and asked if he could do anything before he handed us over to the Italians [knowing the Italians were unlikely to treat them so well]. I said that none of us had eaten that day … and he came back with armfuls of loaves.'

Kenneth Stalder served with Number 189 Field Ambulance Royal Army Medical Corps, and like Hugh Patterson was amongst those British troops serving in Greece during 1941. He was captured with a small party of other British soldiers by an airborne unit during the German invasion of Crete. It was a surprise to be approached by a friendly young German paratrooper offering them cigarettes who spoke perfect English with a London accent, and it transpired that he had been a shopkeeper in Tottenham before the war.

However, British soldiers were not always treated so well by their captors, particularly if they had offered stiff resistance. Although massacres were rare, they did occur. Some of the worst atrocities in the West were perpetrated by the Waffen SS, rather than conventional German units. During the French campaign at La Paradis on 27 May 1940, a company-sized force (approximately eighty men) from 2nd Royal Norfolk Regiment surrendered to 2nd Infantry Regiment SS 'Totenkopf' Division, having conducted a resolute defence in a large farm house. They were marched into a barn, where machine-gun teams opened fire on them and the survivors were bayoneted or shot with small arms.

The following day at Wormhoudt troops from 2nd Royal Warwickshire Regiment who had held up the German advance were massacred under similar circumstances by soldiers from the SS Leibstandarte Division. After surrendering, the prisoners were herded into a barn, where SS troops threw grenades at them and opened fire with machine guns. Only a few men survived and were treated by a passing German medical unit before becoming POWs.

Similarly, in the Far East during 1941–45 British troops encountered an enemy who was noted for his barbarity. Reginald Burton was an acting company commander with 4th Royal Norfolk Regiment when taken prisoner by the Japanese. During the fighting in defence of Singapore in February 1942, one of his fellow officers was beheaded with a Samurai sword: 'This was perhaps our first stark indication of the Japs' barbaric lust for killing.' Writing after the war, he explained that with regard to prisoners, Japanese aggression and brutality was frequently 'a thing of the moment, born of savagery of temper. The man who beat you up one day was quite capable of offering you a cigarette the next.'

At the Alexandra Military Hospital, Singapore, Japanese troops killed an estimated 200 patients and staff in retaliation for retreating Allied soldiers who they claimed had fired on them from the hospital grounds. Gunner Fergus Anckorn served with 118th Field Regiment Royal Artillery, and was posted to the Far East where he was wounded when attacked by Japanese aircraft. Having been sent to Alexandra Hospital he miraculously survived the massacre.

> The assumption is that, when the Japs came to my bed and found blood all over my chest and down on the floor and my face covered – like a corpse – they must have thought me dead already and passed me by.

Another soldier who served during the fall of Singapore was Alfred Allbury, who was frantically involved in ferrying ammunition from a dump to an artillery unit. On Sunday 15 February 1942 he heard they were to surrender, and a ceasefire had been arranged for later in the day. As the guns fell silent, like most British soldiers who fought in the disastrous campaign he was exhausted, and found himself listening to an ominous 'barbaric and discordant dirge: the victory song of the triumphant Japanese'.

Eric Lomax, a junior officer in the Royal Corps of Signals, was equally fatigued when he heard news of the surrender. Having served in Malaya and retreated to Singapore, he ended up working at General A. E. Percival's HQ in Fort Canning.

> In the signals rooms everyone went to sleep, depression and exhaustion flooding in, as we collapsed on old mattresses laid on top of cables and land lines. The spring of tension that had kept us going for weeks had been broken.

Having been conscripted early in the war, and posted to 2nd Gordon Highlanders, Alastair Urquhart also served at Fort Canning. He recalled the moment he came face to face with some of the conquering Japanese soldiers: 'Their eyes looked filled with fury and hate. Yammering and screaming in Japanese, they began jabbing their bayonets in our chests. It was so petrifying.' Subsequently, the full 'gut-wrenching realisation' hit him that he had become a prisoner, with no idea when his ordeal might end.

Many soldiers felt a sense of shame at the magnitude of the defeat in the Far East, and the fact they had played a part in it. In particular members of 18th Division were bitter, as they perceived that they had been needlessly deployed at Singapore. Prior to his capture, Captain Ronald M. Horner was a supply officer with 292nd Supply Company Royal Army Service Corps, and confided in his diary that it seemed scandalous to 'sacrifice a complete division to virtually a lost cause'.

The division had only embarked for the Far East in October 1941, and as the soldier and historian Brigadier C. N. Barclay commented, it lacked 'the high level of staff work and battle-craft' and 'lavish supplies of modern equipment which characterised the campaigns of 1944–45'. Neither had personnel from 18th Division sufficient time to adapt to tropical conditions, or previous experience of the techniques required in jungle warfare. On hearing of the surrender Reginald Burton, whose battalion was part of 18th Division, confessed he was 'was overwhelmed with despair and with apprehension, not just for myself but for all the men who'd served under me during the last hours of the fight'.

Transit to the Camps

Capture was often a stressful and confusing ordeal during which soldiers experienced a range of emotions. Sometimes the full realisation that they had been captured did not sink in until they were at POW collection point, or makeshift transit camp. Having witnessed the guns of his regiment (South Nottinghamshire Hussars) being overrun by the Germans in the Western Desert, Ray Ellis recalled, feeling 'dazed and disorientated' and was initially totally unaware he had been captured.

Similarly, when captured in France during May 1940, soldiers from the BEF often still felt the effects of battle and experienced confusion, fear and fatigue. Douglas Nelson, who served with 10th DLI, was still reeling from witnessing a French girl being mown down by machine-gun fire from a German tank as she ran from shelter screaming for her mother. After his capture, Sergeant L. D. Pexton was led to a field with other POWs. Here they initially feared they might all be lined up and shot, but in fact they were being assembled ahead of facing a long and arduous march to camps in Germany and Eastern Europe.

Rapidly all soldiers had to undergo a period of mental readjustment and recognise that they had become a prisoner. As Alfred Allbury explained in the Far East this could prove difficult: 'It was not easy in the first place to adjust ourselves to the hard fact that we were now complete prisoners.' For some soldiers the process of mental realignment was rapid, even if they were wounded or traumatised by recent combat. Shortly after his capture, Ray Ellis was ferried on the back of German tank to a POW collection point established in the desert. Here he witnessed a British officer being shot simply because he would not hand over his field glasses to the Germans. The incident had a sobering effect, and made him realise he had passed from being a combatant to a POW, whose life potentially had little value.

Ken Adams served with the Royal Army Medical Corps in Singapore, and the reality of being a prisoner hit him abruptly a few days after his capture. He was taken by a small group of Japanese soldiers who led him away from Alexandra Hospital.

Our guards were surly little monsters grunting, growling and kicking blokes or hurrying them along with their rifle butts. That image brought home to me that we were no longer proud British soldiers, lords of all we surveyed, but the flotsam and jetsam of a defeated army.

The magnitude of the defeat in Singapore was encapsulated by Bill Moylon. He had been posted there with the Royal Army Ordnance Corps, and ordered to fight as an infantryman during the desperate weeks leading up to the surrender. The troops were 'despondent, exhausted and bedraggled and we were gathered up by the Japanese and marched 16 miles across the island to Changi to a POW concentration area'.

This was in accordance with a Japanese order of 17 February 1942 that decreed all captured European troops would be housed at Changi, where there was a jail and a purpose-built barracks complex. As Eric Lomax recounted much of Singapore became filled with columns converging on Changi, 'jostling overloaded men trying to keep good order and dignity. This was the British Army marching to its humiliation.'

At Changi FEPOWs soon had to wire themselves in with barbed wire, and could only leave their compounds if they carried one of the few flags issued by the IJA. They tended to see very little of the Japanese, and instead were commanded and administered via British channels. Initially men survived on what rations they had been able to bring with them. According to Lieutenant Colonel H. S. Flower, who assumed command of 9th Royal Northumberland Fusiliers (9th RNF) on 14 February 1942, rations were pooled, and there was a lack of water, electricity and cooking equipment, and many other useful items such as blankets and mosquito nets were taken by the Japanese.

On 24 February prisoners at Changi received their first Japanese rations consisting of 12 ounces of rice, $1\frac{3}{4}$ ounces of meat, and $\frac{1}{6}$ ounces of tea per man per day. Like many FEPOWs, Alfred Allbury discovered that the near-starvation diet gave you blackouts: 'We had to lean against the wall until the mists and blackness cleared sufficiently for us to face yet another day of work and hungry longing.'

Prisoners were soon subjected to brutal discipline. According to Colonel Flower, 'all POW ranks had to salute sentries whether they were Japanese or Sikh [these were Indian Nationalists who opted to fight for the Japanese] and if the salute was not smart enough the sentry was allowed to administer punishment on the spot'. Usually this amounted to some form of beating, such as heavy slaps around the face which were degrading and painful.

It was from Changi that FEPOWs were detailed to form work parties, operating from other smaller camps around Singapore, tasked with cleaning up the island after the Japanese invasion. As Alfred Allbury found, this included salvaging by hand military and civilian vehicles for the IJA. Any resistance or hesitation on the prisoner's part normally resulted in 'a savage clout' or 'a clubbing with whatever lay to hand'. Men were also soon taken from Changi to act as labourers establishing transit camps for prisoners working on the Thai-Burma or 'Death' Railway. Three months after the surrender, Bill Moylon was picked for one of these, and travelled for five days by rail to Bang Pong, Thailand. Each railway truck was crammed with thirty-six men and despite the tropical heat little food or water was provided. 'We took it in turns to squat on the floor and relieve ourselves by hanging our backsides out of the train door.'

Other FEPOWs were chosen to be transported in 'hell ships' to provide slave labour in Japan, or territories within the Japanese sphere of influence. These were merchant ships in which the prisoners were crammed into the holds, often together with consignments of scrap metal and other materials destined for Japan. They had to endure appalling conditions with high temperatures, a lack of fresh air, limited sanitation and overcrowding. Many prisoners were already seriously weakened by disease and their diet prior to travelling on a 'hell ship'. In 1940 Jack Booth was called-up and joined 5th Searchlight Regiment Royal Artillery. After his training he was posted to Singapore and captured in February 1942 before becoming one of the first British FEPOWs to experience a 'hell ship', the SS *Bessar* destined for Saigon. He remembered that the Japanese reluctantly agreed with British officers to allow small groups of prisoners up on deck for ten minutes of fresh air per day. Otherwise they spent the voyage confined to the overcrowded, dark and fetid hold. There was always a danger that these 'hell ships' might be target by Allied navies, unaware of the exact nature of their cargos. In September 1944 the *Kachidoki Maru*, which was transporting approximately 1,000 British prisoners, was tragically torpedoed by the submarine USS *Pampanito*, and a third of the FEPOWs drowned in the ensuing chaos.

In other theatres POWs initial experience of capture usually incorporated some form of journey as they were taken to a permanent camp. Members of the BEF were marched via back roads across France and the Low Countries, so as to allow the Wehrmacht freedom of manoeuvre. They slept along the route in villages and fields, before eventually reaching camps in Germany and Eastern Europe.

Typically, little food and water was available despite the relentless sun, and there was limited opportunity for wounds to be treated. POWs were handed over to second-line personnel, many of whom proved willing to use force if necessary to maintain discipline and encourage stragglers to keep up with their column. Douglas Nelson recalled his feet were bleeding with the marching across France, and on many occasions he thought he was going to collapse and be unable to continue.

Troops captured in the Western Desert similarly faced a lengthy journey to POW camps in Italy and Germany. Typically, they were crammed into Italian trucks at bayonet-point and transported to Tripoli via numerous squalid transit camps established across Libya. One of the first POW cages that Ray Ellis experienced merely consisted of a rectangular area of desert enclosed by barbed wire. The ground was 'covered in human excrement' and there was 'no place to stand and certainly no clean spot to lie' or seek shade from the sun.

The conditions at the transit camp in Derna were little better as large numbers of POWs were herded into a dirty compound, and some soon developed dysentery. As Ray Ellis observed there was a lack of organisation, no sanitation, insufficient rations and water and an absence of transportation to move prisoners rapidly to better accommodation. Another camp at Benghazi was 'a misery of hunger and filth', and at Tarhuna there were only fifteen toilets for around 1,000 POWs and these had ceased working.

Having endured these conditions, during which many became increasingly weak and demoralised, POWs were crammed onto merchant vessels for transportation to the Italian mainland. According to Ray Ellis his was 'a journey full of foreboding, of hunger, of acute discomfort, with the ever present stink of excrement'. Like the 'hell ships' in the Far East there was always a danger that these merchant men would tragically fall victim to attacks by Allied aircraft or naval activity in the Mediterranean. On 14 November 1942 the Royal Navy submarine *P212* (*Sahib*) attacked and sank the SS *Scillin*, with the death of 783 POWs, forty-six of whom came from the DLI.

Alternatively, POWs were flown from North Africa to Italy. Private George Bateman was captured after the fall of Tobruk, and put on board a Savoia bomber employed as a transport aircraft. The flight from Benghazi to Lecce lasted around six hours, during which time the POWs desperately hoped they would not be shot down by the RAF.

Typically, in the Far East officers and other ranks remained together, but in Europe they were usually split up after capture. However, this did not necessarily ensure that officers, owing to their rank, were accorded better treatment. Captain Petre Norton of the Northumberland Hussars was captured on Crete during the summer of 1941, and flown to Athens before eventually being taken to Salonika. Here together with around 500 other Allied officers he endured six weeks' captivity in extremely torrid conditions.

The buildings that served as a transit camp were riddled with vermin and at night 'a lighted match would show bed bugs issuing from the walls and deploying across the floor'. Consequently, most POWs elected to sleep outside, although bullets often whistled through the air as the German guards would shoot at anyone who moved. Sometimes the corpses of those who had been shot were displayed by the guards during morning roll call, or left hanging on the wire as a warning to the other prisoners.

Days were usually spent lying in the dust trying to avoid the full glare of the sun and numerous flies. Men became progressively weaker as their rations comprised a pint of soup per day per man, made from rotten vegetables and mildewed barley with the odd scrap of horsemeat. Water was available, but the supply was deemed unfit to drink by the Germans. The only other food was one loaf of bread between nine men, and three biscuits to be shared amongst four POWs.

Eventually, Captain Norton and the other POWs were ferried by rail to a camp at Lubeck on the Baltic. The week-long journey was a horrendous ordeal, as up to thirty-six men remained permanently enclosed in goods wagons, in the heat of a European summer with no sanitary arrangements. He recalled that they were 'naked but for filthy shorts – standing, sitting, lying or squatting on the squalid floor, with sweat trickling down their grimy bodies, oozing from their matted hair, and covering their faces, unshaven and pinched by starvation'.

Conditions in the Camps

Most POWs in Europe arrived at permanent camps or work camps in a weakened and demoralised state, and in some cases were infested with lice, bugs and fleas as well as exhibiting signs of diseases such as dysentery. The

Germans in particular were paranoid about the risk of typhus and typhoid fever, both of which were spread by lice. Consequently, to contain this threat, when new POWs were registered they had their uniforms put into an industrial dry-cleaning machine and had all their body hair shaved off. Similarly, Hugh Patterson, who after his capture was shipped to Italy via Greece, was initially interned in what he described as a 'Disinfestation Camp'.

By contrast, unless they were sick or wounded at the time of their capture in the Far East, most soldiers were initially relatively healthy. For a time at Changi Reginald Burton served as hygiene officer and was able to construct a home-made washing machine in which the prisoner's uniforms could be deloused. However, the condition of most FEPOWs rapidly deteriorated under the Japanese regime with its starvation diet, and in the tropical climate. As Captain Horner noted they had to become 'used to being in a permanently bitten state as everything that flies or crawls seems to bite'. This included bed bugs 'the size of a lady bird' that were transparent until they had a 'belly full of blood'.

Men from non-combatant units that were captured when rear areas were overrun often had time to pack clothing and personal effects with them. Whereas combat personnel who became POWs wore the remains of the uniforms they were wearing when captured. Those captured in the Western Desert faired particularly badly, as they usually only had khaki-drill shirts and shorts to wear. Ray Ellis remembered that amongst his group of POWs 'our shirts and shorts were hanging in ribbons' by the time they arrived in Italy, and since being captured they had no opportunity to wash their clothes. Similarly, Hugh Patterson recorded that while at Campo PG 65 at Gravina, Italy they were issued with ill-fitting Italian uniforms, and life was 'dominated by keeping the wolf from the door'.

Douglas Nelson, who was captured in France during 1940, was issued with a distinctly mixed assortment of military attire to wear as his POW uniform. This included a shirt, French Army tunic, Belgian Army trousers, blue Dutch Army coat, and Dutch wooden clogs that were extremely difficult and painful to wear without socks. Similarly, Jimmy Langley who served as junior officer with the Coldstream Guards, and was wounded and captured near Dunkirk, 'acquired the top half of a Belgian despatch rider's uniform, a pair of battledress trousers and some felt slippers'.

In the Far East men were even worse off, as when it came time to replace their uniforms many resorted to wearing what they termed a 'Jap-happy'. Essentially this was a sort of home-made loincloth where a length of material with a tape around the waist, was pulled up between the legs and tucked into the waistband. Similarly, as Bill Moylon recounted, 'we had to improvise and make our own sandals' because in the tropics army boots simply rotted away.

Typically, in Europe the conditions experienced by POWs differed depending on which camp they were sent to, and what rank they held. Castles, monasteries and converted barracks all served as POW camps, alongside purpose-built structures with rows of huts and barbed-wire fences that have become familiar images from literature and films on the Second World War. Historian Adrian Gilbert provides a graphic impression of what it was like for new inmates to enter one of these huts: 'To walk into a crowded barrack block for the first time was to endure an assault on the senses. New prisoners were overwhelmed by the smell from unwashed bodies and night latrines.'

The Germans and Italians segregated officers from other ranks, although the former tended to be more efficient at achieving this than the latter. A number of other ranks also ended up serving in officers' camps as orderlies. This included Hugh Patterson who spent some of his captivity at Campo PG 21 near Chieti, Italy, which was purposely established as an Anglo-American officers' camp.

British Army surgeon Phillip Newman was for a time held at the officers' camp Oflag IX A/H at Spangenberg in Hesse, and found conditions were comparatively good. According to another inmate Airey Neave, who served as an officer with the Royal Engineers and Royal Artillery, the camp's 'arched doorways and clock tower reminds me of school [he was an old Etonian] ... we have our same sad possessions, packed away. Our Red Cross chocolate and carefully hoarded delicacies are guarded like a school-boy's tuck box.'

Oflag IX A/H was one of the oldest POW camps in Germany, and consisted of a castle, similar to the famous Colditz, situated on a crag encircled by a 30-foot deep dry moat. It was thought that its rock foundations and thick walls would act as a deterrent to any would be escapee thinking of digging a tunnel. Alongside the castle was a lower camp in the village of Spangenberg, consisting of an 'L'-shaped building, surrounded by barbed wire. Both parts of the camp were intended to house around 200 officers each. However, prisoners were able to use a local sports field twice a week, and had access to libraries, reading rooms, canteens and medical facilities.

By contrast, other ranks tended to experience less comfortable conditions, particularly if they were held at a work camp. Private Stanley Doughty (12th Royal Lancers) was incarcerated at Campo PG 52 in Chiavari, Italy, where the accommodation consisted of wooden huts with bunk beds and primitive washing facilities consisting of a trough filled with cold water by standpipes. The latrines were a deep trench in the ground over which soldiers had to squat while making sure they didn't fall in. Frederick Bedlington, a soldier from 11th DLI captured in France during 1940, was held prisoner at Fort 15 Stalag XXA. During the course of his captivity he worked on the construction of an autobahn, cleared ground for German barracks to be built, helped convert a hospital into a VD centre, and was employed as both a factory and agricultural labourer.

As a by-product of such work, prisoners were often able to hit back at the enemy by sabotaging machinery and steal materials for their camp. Frederick Bedlington recalled piercing small holes in tins of meat destined for German troops fighting on the Eastern Front so that it was rotten by the time it arrived. In this way POWs were still able to contribute to the war effort.

In the Far East conditions also varied between camps, and typically the Japanese were far less concerned about the rank held by their captives. Officers were forbidden from wearing British Army insignia and badges of rank, and instead initially were compelled to wear a single star on their left breast. Relatively speaking, Changi and the other camps in Singapore tended to be more bearable than those on the Thai–Burma Railway. Colonel Flower recorded in his diary, compiled after the war, that Keppel Harbour Camp, Singapore, where he and approximately 1,000 other FEPOWs were held from May–October 1942, had electric lighting, and running water which enabled washing facilities to be established. Unusually for the Far East the camp was also comparatively free of flies and mosquitoes.

By contrast, at Chungkai Camp on the Thai–Burma Railway, Colonel Flower came across the sort of accommodation that typified many Japanese camps. There were lines of bamboo huts about 100 yards long, 6 yards wide and 12ft high at the ridge. The roofs were thatched with 'Attap palm leaves side by side, bent double, and stitched over a stick making a tile that was lashed to the rafters'. Often there were no walls, or just matting hung down the sides of the hut, and the floor was bare earth. In each hut there was a central passage six feet wide, and each side there was 'a platform of bamboo 18 inches from the floor and 6 inches wide, divided at intervals by one or two cross gangways'. Consequently, each soldier had approximately '20 inches of lying space', and these huts had to be used for every aspect of the prisoner's existence, even serving as makeshift hospitals with improvised equipment.

The Thai-Burma Railway was a nightmarish venture covering 258 miles of inhospitable jungle terrain. The plan to link the Thai and Burmese rail systems had been investigated by British engineers and surveyors in the early 1900s, but shelved as being too difficult a project owing to the topography of the region. However, with their shipping increasingly falling foul of Allied submarines in the Straits of Malacca and Andaman Sea, the Japanese saw this proposed route as the answer to their logistical problems. Construction began in June 1942, and relied on British FEPOWs and other prisoners being employed as slave labour, thousands of whom were worked and starved to death.

As Alfred Allbury discovered, virtually no man was considered too weak or sick to work on the railway. Even, 'those dying of malaria and dysentery were made to labour on the railway track 12 or 14 hours a day'. Eric Lomax, who was brutally tortured by the Japanese for his part in maintaining a secret radio set, considered that the track-laying gangs had one of the worst jobs. Any slackening of the pace on their part was met with violence or verbal abuse, and the men were perpetually hungry and exhausted.

A flat-bottomed steel rail weighed about 70 pounds per yard, and usually came in 24-foot lengths. A rail therefore is a massive thing for hungry men to lift and manoeuvre into position, and one rail followed another relentlessly on this criminal folly of a line. The steel rails were spiked directly to the wooden sleepers by hammering in big steel nails. This is brutally heavy work.

Fergus Anckorn, another prisoner employed on the railway, recorded that, 'we were being shoved, punched, butted, kicked, and bashed with sticks, even while working. Black humour was our only defence'. As he stressed prisoners had to develop methods of coping with these beatings, and his was never to react, except to keep affirming to himself mentally that he would survive no matter what the Japanese did to him.

Any prisoner who displeased the Japanese, such as by allegedly threatening a sentry or attempting to sell materials to the locals, received special punishments. These included water torture where a victim's belly was filled with water by a hose pipe, and he was then tied up with barbed wire before being kicked and beaten. Another form of water torture was akin to what has now become known as 'water-boarding' (simulated drowning). Eric Lomax endured this at the hands of the Kempetai (Japanese Secret Police, equivalent to the Gestapo), and described how his torturer 'directed the full flow of the now gushing pipe on to my nostrils and mouth at a distance of only a few inches. Water poured down my windpipe and throat and filled my lungs and stomach. The torrent was unimaginably choking.'

Other punishments involved forcing men to kneel for a number of hours on sharp sticks while holding a heavy rock that they were forbidden to drop. Alternatively, men might be suspended from the branch of a tree by their thumbs, with only their toes touching the ground. One of the more senior FEPOWs, Lieutenant Colonel Phillip Toosey of the Royal Artillery stated, 'nowhere in the world was sadism practised with greater efficiency than in the Japanese Army'.

Food and Rations

Food played a substantial part in the life of all prisoners of war, whether in Europe or the Far East, not least because they seldom had enough. As historian Adrian Gilbert observed, with all POWs 'the absence of food was constant … hunger was not the vaguely unpleasant sensation of a missed meal and a grumbling stomach. Their hunger was an ache that dominated thought and conversation' which over time wore them down both physically and psychologically.

The routine at Campo PG 75 at Bari provides a typical example of the sort of 'meals' prisoners experienced in Italy. At 06.30 hours they had an egg cup full of Ersatz coffee and this was followed at 10.30 hours by a bread ration of four small loaves between five men. Normally the bread was of poor quality, and if POWs were lucky they might have been given a little cheese with it. At noon soup was issued and this was again served up at 16.00 hours with either one tomato or green fig added, or perhaps a chilli and some anchovies. On Sundays a small piece of meat was handed out as well, although it was often mostly gristle. Ray Ellis who was held at Campo PG 53 near Sforzacosta, and found that this type of diet did 'little to satisfy the hunger of young men, in fact it was barely enough to keep us alive'.

Prisoners held by the Germans often fared little better. When he came out of hospital in 1946, after having endured four long years of captivity during the war, Kenneth Stalder weighed only 5½ stone. In most camps Ersatz coffee was issued which was made from crushed acorns or barley and tasted unpleasant. Soup, or 'Skilly' as it was often known, was a constant feature in the diet of most POWs. As Alfred Bryant who was held at Stalag XXA, Thorn discovered, this usually consisted of some form of rotting vegetable matter floating in greasy water. Occasionally scraps of meat would be added to bulk it out. Prisoners were sometimes given limited amounts of bread or potatoes, although normally the quality of both was poor.

Officers also endured the hardship of hunger, although their basic ration was a marginal improvement on that issued in Stalags. Lieutenant William Bompas of the Royal Artillery who was held at Oflag VIIIF recorded, that breakfasts normally comprised tea or coffee, sardines or meat roll, plus prunes, bread and jam. Lunch was soup or 'Skilly', and the evening meal frequently consisted of bully beef and potatoes.

In the Far East the Japanese typically issued two small portions of rice per day and their standard ration for men engaged in hard labour was 790 grams of rice per day. In reality most prisoners received less than this. Starving men were forced into taking desperate measures to try and sustain themselves, and combat their vitamin-deficient diet which reduced many to living skeletons. At Changi sparrows become something of a delicacy, while men at the work camps in Thailand discovered it was frequently possible to capture local monkeys to be chopped up, cooked and eaten. Reginald Burton recorded that he experimented with cooking snails to supplement the rice, although this wasn't 'entirely satisfactory'. Unsurprisingly, many FEPOWs began to despise the sight of rice, and as Captain Horner recalled ingenious methods were employed to make it more palatable, including disguising it as biscuits, buns, porridge, duffs and even pasties and pies.

The Red Cross issued food parcels that were supposed to supplement what prisoners were fed in the camps. In reality many POWs in Europe came to rely on them, and their arrival was eagerly anticipated. Hugh Patterson received his first Red Cross parcel while a prisoner in Italy during April 1942. It contained tins of meat and vegetable stew, apple pudding, fish paste, plus margarine, strawberry jam, lemon curd, meat roll, cheese, army biscuits, tea, milk, sugar and soap. This enabled him for a time to be in a position to barter with other prisoners, so as to improve his conditions, and to share materials with comrades. However, camp authorities would frequently spike the tins with bayonets to prevent their use in escape attempts, which forced prisoners into consuming the contents quickly.

Although Red Cross parcels were sent to the Far East, they were often looted by Japanese guards, who either kept the contents or attempted to sell items to prisoners at vastly-inflated prices. Alternatively, Red Cross parcels were issued on a much reduced basis. Captain Horner recalled that at Changi in late March 1945, a 'normal fortnightly parcel' for one man was split between twenty prisoners and contained small amounts of dried milk, jam, butter, bully beef, biscuits, sugar, coffee, cheese, chocolate, raisins and prunes.

Another form of assistance came via regimental comfort funds established in Britain. For example, in the autumn of 1940 the Royal Northumberland Fusiliers POW Fund was founded to 'help next of kin exercise rights to send POW relatives a quarterly parcel and ensure parcels contained articles most needed'. By the end of the war the ladies overseeing the packing centres in Tyneside and Northumberland had managed to send thousands of parcels to captive Fusiliers, mainly in Europe. Similarly, the Duke of Wellington's Regiment POW and Comforts Fund was able to despatch over 3,000 parcels to POWs during 1940–45, including 200 cigarettes or the equivalent to each man per month. Typically, these type of funds enabled entire communities to take part and support their local regiments, either financially through fundraising efforts such as holding dinner-dances, or by sending appropriate goods.

Coping with Captivity

There were numerous ways in which POWs in all theatres attempted to improve their conditions and cope with life in captivity. Many found life more bearable if they were able to team up with a close comrade from their unit, or with another prisoner with whom they had a particular affinity.

Alfred Allbury was captured by the IJA along with his comrade Vic, and they supported one another in Singapore, until the latter was tragically sent to work on the Thai–Burma Railway, from which he never returned. Soon after being captured in North Africa, Ray Ellis met another resourceful soldier nicknamed 'Buster', who had previously been awarded the Military Medal. In the squalid conditions of their transit camp, the two of them attempted to maintain a soldierly bearing and look after themselves as best as possible, while simultaneously attempting to encourage their fellow prisoners, many of whom were extremely demoralised.

Similarly, the regimental system helped some POWs cope with their ordeal, particularly when several men from the same unit were held together in captivity. In the Far East Reginald Burton noted how a large contingent from 5th Royal Norfolk Regiment was sent to Serangoon Road Camp. This included several NCOs, warrant officers and officers, as well as other ranks. Consequently, it was relatively straightforward to maintain morale and enforce British Army disciplinary standards amongst prisoners. Although some soldiers complained it was 'Bloody Aldershot Serangoon', complete with bugle calls and parades, it was no coincidence that because of the disciplined atmosphere the camp had a good health record.

Letters, when they arrived, provided a means for prisoners to keep in touch with loved ones and the outside world. Under the Geneva Convention other ranks were entitled to send two letters and four postcards per month. For officers the allocation was more generous, and comprised either four or six letters per month depending on their seniority. Hugh Patterson observed that writing and receiving letters while captive in Italy did much to relieve the boredom associated with camp routine, although frustratingly it took fifty days for post to reach him from Britain. Historian Adrian Gilbert comments that the volume of mail in Europe was often huge, and during a single month at one POW camp in Germany over 8,000 letters were sent and over 5,000 received.

In the Far East the postal system was fairly haphazard. Captain Horner was delighted to receive a batch of letters from home during August 1944, although these were months old by this time, one even dating from April 1943. Typically, most FEPOWs were worse off than their counterparts held by the Germans and Italians, and only received a handful of letters during their entire captivity. Similarly, the basic postcards that the Japanese allowed prisoners to send to their families, that had boxes to tick that indicated issues such as the state of their health, often never reached their destinations in Britain.

Reading was a tangible way in which prisoners of all ranks could occupy themselves whilst in captivity, and even take their minds off their plight. Reginald Burton while recovering from illness at Tamarakand Bridge Camp, helped out on the tropical ulcer ward by becoming a book reader in extremely distressing circumstances. He remembered doggedly ploughing through a beaten-up copy of Agatha Christie's *Murder on the Blue Train*, to patients amid 'sights ... too ghastly for my stomach and the revolting stench'. Books were prized by prisoners of all ranks both in Europe and the Far East. According to one estimate approximately one million books were left behind when POW camps were liberated in Germany during 1945. Predominantly these had originated from welfare organisations such as the YMCA and the British Red Cross.

A logical corollary of this enthusiasm for literature and reading was that many camps in both Europe and the Far East set up libraries and 'universities' which kept men's minds active, aroused their intellectual curiosity, and even furthered their education. With the help of the Red Cross it proved possible in many camps for prisoners to study for academic or vocational qualifications and sit the relevant examinations. While at PG 49 Fontanellato, Italy, Major Ian English of the DLI continued to study agriculture, which enabled him to complete his degree at Cambridge after the war and later obtain employment with an agricultural merchant.

Clubs and societies were another means by which POWs, particularly in Europe, attempted to improve their lives and cope with their predicament. Stalag 383 at Hohenfels, Germany was a positive hive of prisoner activity that included its own bee-keeping group, the 'Captive Drones', established with the help of the Red Cross who provided the equipment. According to Joan Bright, the regimental historian of the Northumberland Hussars, POWs dabbled 'as amateurs in almost every trade, occupation and profession in existence'. This included playing sports, gambling, giving or attending lectures, debating, bird-watching, knitting, embroidery, making music, and even constructing 'models of miraculous accuracy out of the minimum of material'. Bill Davidson, a doctor with the RAMC who was captured in France during 1940, spent many hours meticulously carving a set of chessmen out of pieces of hardwood he had been able to scavenge in captivity. This was termed by his fellow prisoners as 'flogging the bishop'.

With the help of the YMCA and Red Cross who provided the instruments, many POWs in Germany and Italy were able to put together small orchestras or bands. Theatrical pursuits provided a further outlet for many men in both Europe and the Far East, to as Captain Horner put it 'forget for a couple of hours that they were POWs'. This entailed not only being actors or the audience, but making scenery and costumes, so potentially prisoners were able to develop an array of talents. At Changi POW Camp in Singapore 'The New Windmill Theatre' was able to create a 'pukka theatre atmosphere' according to Captain Horner, and staged numerous plays and variety acts by prisoners that lifted their comrade's spirits. During a production of *I Killed the Count* in September 1942 'laughter was so prolonged as sometimes to hold up the show'. These endeavours were ably assisted by the artist and cartoonist Ronald Searle, an officer with the Royal Engineers captured at Singapore, who helped make the scenery. Similarly, at Oflag VII D at Tittmoning, officer POWs staged an impressive production of Hamlet that even had support from the Munich Opera House which provided the costumes and make-up.

Sports also helped soldiers cope with captivity, and in many cases welfare organisations donated equipment. According to historian Adrian Gilbert, in 1943 over 10,000 footballs and 6,900 pairs of boxing gloves were shipped to camps in Germany. At PG 73 Carpi, Italy no less than fifty-four football teams were established, all fielding different home-made strips. They played on a field near the camp, that was surrounded by a high barbed-wire fence under the watchful eye of their Italian guards. However, the prisoners were so weakened by their diet that they could only play matches of ten minutes each way. Rugby, football and cricket were also popular amongst prisoners in both Europe and the Far East. Colonel Harold Sell of the DLI was held at PG 21, and observed there was basketball, baseball and cricket with leagues organised with registered players and bookies to help prisoners bet on matches. Cricket at Changi in particular allowed many FEPOWs to renew Anglo–Australian rivalries. Lieutenant Bompas, who was held captive in Europe, recalled that it was common for officers in his camp to either have a game of rugger or read in the afternoon. More sedentary games were pursued in some camps as well, including darts, with homemade boards being fabricated from the packaging of Red Cross parcels.

Smoking provided a great relief for prisoners in all camps. Sometimes starving men would even forgo their meagre food rations and sell them in order to obtain cigarettes and satisfy their nicotine craving. Captain Horner noted in his diary that he smoked Malayan tobacco and made it 'go further by mixing it with cheroot butts'. When stocks were running low he would mix in dried cherry leaves to try and obtain something that he could reasonably smoke. The materials necessary for smoking were often bartered between prisoners as well. Although books were valued for reading, to desperate men they provided much-needed cigarette papers, especially in the Far East. According to distinguished journalist and author Brian MacArthur, one enterprising soldier captured by the Japanese, was even able to profit by selling pages from his copy of Jane Austin's *Pride and Prejudice* at three sheets for ten cents for use as cigarette papers.

For soldiers captured in Europe and North Africa who were sent to work camps it sometimes proved possible to establish relationships with women because they were able to mix with local German workers and slave labourers. Jim Witte served with 414 Battery Essex Yeomanry and was captured in the Western Desert during spring 1941. Subsequently, he was transferred from Italy to Germany and went on numerous work parties or *Arbeitskommando* which enabled him to conduct numerous affairs, including with a Belgian woman and later a Russian girl.

However, for many prisoners this was not possible, and those in the Far East in particular tended to be so weakened by their ordeal that they had little or no interest in sex. In the close confines of prison camps there was also the possibility that men might find an outlet for homosexual tendencies, even though this was illegal and frowned upon in the 1940s. Historian Adrian

Gilbert makes the point that the men who dressed as females during various theatrical productions in POW camps in Europe often became objects of lust. It would also have been possible for like-minded men to show affection for one another during some of the artistic pursuits engaged in during captivity such as dancing.

Escape and Evasion

Escape represented a bold means by which any POW could hit back at the enemy. Even if they weren't successful they still might perform a valuable function by tying down enemy troops forming search parties. However, escape was easier to contemplate in some theatres than others. Ideally soon after capture was a good time to attempt to break free, because in the confusion a soldier was initially unlikely to be well known to the enemy. The route to the camps also presented opportunities for escape that seldom existed once a man was incarcerated in a permanent camp.

Typically, in the Far East escape was an unrealistic option, although attempts were made, and many FEPOWs mulled over the possibility during their captivity. As Colonel Flower observed, it was relatively easy for men to walk off into the jungle as there were no wire fences, but equipped with nothing more than an ordinary atlas they had limited chance of escaping safely in the hostile terrain. In Siam (Thailand) the coast lay around eighty miles to the west, and northwards lay Burma, thick jungle and rivers hindering movement in both directions. Another possibility was to try and aim for Bangkok then head northwards towards China. 'In every case we were Europeans with no knowledge of the language or outside contacts, our presence would literally smell ahead of us, and the Siamese [Thai] or Burmese would have been quick to rob us and then hand us over to the Japanese for further reward.'

An escape mounted during March 1943 bears this out. Sergeant E. Reay, Fusilier T. Kenneally (both 9th RNF), Private J. Fitzgerald (RAOC Light Aid Detachment attached 9th RNF), and Sergeant F. Kelly (RAMC) walked out of Tarkilen Camp into the jungle armed with a few provisions, a blanket, limited amount of cash, compass, field glasses and a sketch map based on a school atlas. On 28 March they were seen handcuffed and recognised by other prisoners at Tarso Camp, around twenty miles away. They were recognised again at Chungkai Camp, but nobody among the prisoner population was able to reach them and they were subsequently led into the jungle and shot.

By contrast, evasion was a more practicable proposition during the early phases of the campaign in the Far East. On 13 February 1942, two days before the eventually surrender of Singapore, units from 18th Division were ordered to provide volunteers who were to assemble at Britannia Docks. Around 500 men from various units congregated at the docks, believing they might become involved in some mission against the Japanese. The plan was for the Royal Navy to evacuate these men, and presumably they would have formed the nucleus for reconstituting their units when Singapore fell. However, the arrangements for a naval evacuation broke down, and soldiers were given the option of either returning to their units or making an individual effort to escape Singapore. A party from 9th RNF under the command of Major B. J. Leech, who were later joined by personnel from other units, commandeered an 18-foot rowing boat they christened the 'Pushme-Pullu'. This was because, as an article in the *St. George's Gazette* commented, she had 'no keel or centre board, and that a broken oar served as a rudder … her progress is deceptive, and more sideways than forwards'.

Even so, these soldiers turned sailors managed to evade capture and reached Padang on the west coast of Sumatra (Indonesia) on 1 March 1942. Here they were fortunate to meet with Royal Navy ships refuelling which took them to Colombo in Sri Lanka. On their daring journey they successfully evaded Japanese aircraft by appearing like a native Malay craft with a homemade sail. They also drew confidence from carrying an array of small arms and ammunition. Owing to the difficulties of navigation and tides they only travelled in daylight, and were fortunate in being able to bring numerous stores from the YMCA in Singapore, as well as acquire food and drinking water along their route.

In Europe both escape and evasion were more viable options. After the fall of France in May/June 1940 Lieutenant (later Lieutenant Colonel) Richard Broad and seven other ranks from the Seaforth Highlanders determinedly avoided being captured by the Germans, and managed to escape through occupied France and into Spain, from where they eventually reached Britain. They relied on sympathetic locals to assist them, but even so conditions were tough and at one stage the soldiers were reduced to trying to survive on redcurrants that were flourishing in an abandoned garden. They had received no specific escape and evasion training which further added to their difficulties.

Although a significant challenge, it was still easier for British soldiers to blend in with the local population on the Continent than it was in the Far East. An *Army Training Memorandum* issued in July 1940 advised escapers and evaders to try and adopt French habits, never march in military fashion, obtain a bicycle, carry watches in pockets not on the wrist, use a beret for disguise, obtain local shoes instead of army boots, never use a walking stick as it was a British custom, and be prepared to seek help from locals, particularly village priests.

However, most escapees from permanent POW camps relied on a considerable degree of luck, first in breaking out successfully, and subsequently in evading recapture. Ian Reid served as an officer in the Black Watch and was wounded and captured in North Africa in April 1943 and sent to a POW camp in Italy. Five months later he managed to escape when the Italians pulled out of the war. He described the moment he and other escapees narrowly avoided being re-captured by the Germans:

As we entered the piazza we noticed a group of men gossiping outside a house. I was about to address them, when we heard the sound of a motor bike approaching from behind. We darted hastily up a side alley. I glanced over my shoulder and saw the motor cyclist ride into the piazza and dismount. He was dressed in German uniform, with a rifle slung across his back. We took refuge in a pig-sty.

Planning was another important ingredient in escapes and in some camps teams of prisoners supported escapees by helping providing items such as tools, forged documents, fake enemy uniforms or civilian disguises. Many prisoners also became actively engaged in goading their guards, a practice known as 'goon baiting'. Some soldiers found this juvenile, but obstructive behaviour such as deliberately holding up the twice-daily roll calls had a serious purpose in providing cover for other prisoners attempting to escape.

As the war progressed, British Intelligence fostered escape activity by supplying parcels via the Red Cross that contained escape aids, such as a screwdriver concealed in the handle of a cricket bat or a hacksaw blade hidden in a comb. Escape lines were established that enabled soldiers evading capture after Dunkirk or escaped POWs to negotiate their way across Occupied and Vichy France via various safe houses and cross the Pyrenees into neutral Spain.

One of the best-known was the PAT Line, run by a Belgian Army medic who joined the Royal Navy under the assumed name of Patrick O'Leary, and it was estimated to have helped around 600 servicemen successfully evade the German authorities. Army surgeon Philip Newman experienced the PAT line and found crossing the Pyrenees a gruelling ordeal, but it was a 'revelation' to witness the twinkling lights of Spain after 'nearly three years of black-out had become a natural phenomenon. It was an exciting ghost of peace.'

Distinguished politician and much-decorated wartime officer Airey Neave was extremely escape-minded, and discovered that his British service dress cap could be readily converted to appear like a German officer's cap. He used this as part of a cunningly-fabricated disguise to make him appear like a German officer, in an escape attempt that saw him become the first British officer to successfully break out from Oflag IVC Colditz. The brim and sides of the cap were bent to stand high above the peak in German style, and the whole covered in Dutch uniform material. The insignia including the familiar eagle's wings and swastika were cut from linoleum and the cap finished off with white piping being sewn on the edge of the brim. As he put it 'with such a uniform I could face the arc lights once more with confidence'.

As historian Adrian Gilbert observed, escapes tended to conform to three main types. First there was the over-the-wire effort as exemplified by Philip Newman. He described the blissful feelings he and a comrade experienced at Sotteville, near Rouen, after getting over the wire fencing of their camp unobserved using wooden planks obtained from one of their huts. 'Suddenly there we both were outside the cage free as the wind. It was a wonderful feeling. We gave each other a bear hug and sped the field to the nearest hedge.' However, this was normally extremely risky as any POW seen trying to climb over the fences was liable to be shot.

Secondly, there were attempts that went through the gates of camps, relying on some method of subterfuge. Airey Neave's successful break out from Colditz was a classic example of this type. Together with a Dutch officer who spoke good German, he was able to walk out off the front gate disguised as a German officer. Subsequently, the pair posed as Dutch electrical workers employed in Nazi-occupied Europe, complete with the appropriate forged paperwork. Eventually they managed to make it to Switzerland by train and walking.

Finally, there were escape efforts that went under fences or walls via tunnelling. These had the drawback that it was not necessarily easy to dispose of the soil from excavations, or find the necessary digging materials, and they were liable to be slow and arduous affairs. Major Pat Reid, who had an engineering background, was put in charge of tunnelling efforts at Colditz, much aided by British Intelligence having been able to provide a plan of the castle that had been archived with the British Museum. An officer from the Northumberland Hussars, held prisoner at Veano near Piacenza similarly noted that 'one very satisfactory tunnel was dug'. However, tunnelling could be dangerous as Hugh Patterson observed, at Campo PG 21 near Chieti where a tunnel from a cookhouse broke into a sewer and one of the 'digger's lamps ignited the gas leaving him burnt, blackened and shocked'.

It wasn't just officers who mounted daring escape efforts. Gunner William Surtees was captured on Crete in 1941. From there he was taken to a camp at Klagenfurt, Austria, comparatively close to both the Yugoslavian and Italian borders. Together with another soldier, Private Lock who had served as a driver, they prepared for escape during late 1942. The plan was for Private Lock to disguise himself as a girl, so he grew his hair long, and Gunner Surtees would take on the role of 'her' boyfriend. They fabricated hiking clothes in secret, and toughened themselves up by running and playing sports in their camp.

In May 1943 they made their bid for freedom. Having left a work party, they hid in a hole, quickly donned their disguises and 'emerged hand in hand, a young couple very much in love'. They succeeded in joining a band of Yugoslav partisans and hoped to be able to establish contact with British forces in Italy. However, frustratingly after seven weeks on the run they were recaptured by an Italian patrol, and eventually handed over to the Germans after languishing for several unpleasant weeks in Italian prisons.

Contrary to the impression conveyed in popular literature and films that deal largely with escapes at the expense of other aspects of POW life, there was nothing romantic about being held captive by the Axis powers during the Second World War. Clive Dunn, who famously portrayed the aged Corporal Jones in the popular BBC comedy series *Dad's Army*, spent much of his war as a POW in Europe. With a heavy degree of understatement he later commented: 'Those years weren't much fun.' Even when liberation seemed close at hand, many POWs continued to suffer. During January–February 1945 the Germans, desperate to hold onto their prisoners, force marched those from camps in Eastern Europe westwards, so as to escape the advancing Soviet Army. At least 3,000 Allied POWs died on these forced marches conducted under appalling conditions.

Other POWs found that when they first encountered Allied forces they were not necessarily made to feel welcome. Having escaped his camp, Ray Ellis spent a lengthy period hiding in the Italian countryside and fought with a partisan unit. He eventually made contact with a British unit, only to discover they refused to feed or cloth him because he was not on their ration strength.

Surviving POWs in Europe were gathered during the spring of 1945, and under Operation Exodus flown to specialist reception centres located across Southern England. Here they were issued with new uniforms, documentation and fed, before in many cases seeing out their remainder of their army service, prior to being demobbed and able to embark on new lives as a civilian. Similarly, in the Far East during late 1945 arrangements were made to meet the complex task of gathering, caring for, and shipping home former prisoners of the Japanese. Bill Moylon remembered arriving back in Southampton aboard the *Orion*, before making it back to his home in Newport, where he was overwhelmed by the welcome he received. Like many FEPOWs he required extensive hospital treatment before he was able to embark on a civilian career in post-war Britain.

Many men, particularly those held by the Japanese, could never easily forget their experiences, even if they seldom talked about them during the post-war years once they had returned to civilian employment. If they were fortunate enough to marry and have a family, or return to love ones, this may have helped some come to terms with their wartime experiences. Even so, writing in 2010 Alistair Urquhart, who had been captured at Singapore, confessed he continued in old age to have difficulties: 'both physically and mentally ... Even after I married, life could be hell. To this day I suffer pain and the nightmares can be so bad that I fight sleep for fear of the dreams that come with it.'

Chapter 5

Casualties and Medical Matters

The British Army went to war in 1939 with one of the most advanced systems of medical support in the world. As historian Mark Harrison highlighted it was the only army with a fully-functioning blood transfusion service, and this was improved during the war. There was also a strong cadre of medical officers trained in military surgery, and by the late 1930s the importance of preventative medicine had been widely acknowledged. In its approach to hygiene the army sought not merely to prevent disease, but also to promote health within the ranks.

The contribution of the Royal Army Medical Corps (RAMC) towards the eventual Allied victory was immense, and can be gauged by the following statistics. Over 1,000 medical units were mobilised during the war, including 148 field and general hospitals overseas, plus eighty-eight in Britain. Nearer the front lines thirty-six Casualty Clearing Stations (CCSs) and 141 Field Ambulance Units (FAUs) operated. Casualty evacuation was covered by forty-nine ambulance trains and thirty-four hospital ships, and as the war progressed increasing efforts were made to employ aircraft in this role as well. The RAMC also provided fifty Field Surgical Units (FSUs), thirty-six blood transfusion teams, sixty-four Field Dressing Stations (FDSs), 122 Field Hygiene Units (FHUs), seventy-one specialist anti-malaria units and twenty-seven convalescent depots.

Such an effort was highly dependent on the dedication and devotion to duty of the doctors and other personnel of the RAMC, who often had to work under awkward conditions particularly in forward areas. During the war members of the RAMC were awarded 322 Military Crosses and 254 Military Medals, along with numerous other decorations, and 2,463 were killed. Similarly, the army relied on the women of the Queen Alexandra's Imperial Military Nursing Service (affectionately known as the QAs). As the author Nicola Tyrer observed 236 QAs lost their lives during the war, and typically their story was one of 'guts, self-sacrifice, inspirational leadership and dogged good humour in the face of suffering, privation and death'.

This chapter outlines the medical challenges that faced the army during the war, and the arrangements that were made to counter them. In doing so it highlights both the experiences of individual medical staff in a variety of theatres, and those of soldiers who were wounded, or became sick and required treatment. As many wartime medical staff discovered there were occasions when they were required to treat non-combatants as well, and enemy personnel who had become casualties and been captured.

Battle Casualties

Casualties could have a profound impact upon combat units. As historian John Ellis noted, throughout the campaign in North-West Europe in 1944–45, 50th (Northumbrian) Division suffered 452 officer casualties and 6,002 from other ranks. If it is 'assumed that 90 per cent of these casualties were in the nine rifle battalions, and that the division as a whole had an 80 per cent replacement rate, then slightly over 49 per cent of all men who served in these battalions throughout the campaign became casualties'.

Similarly, the Tunisian campaign (February–May 1943) witnessed some particularly bloody encounters for men in the infantry. Lieutenant Colonel Sir Paul Bryan who commanded 6th Battalion Royal West Kent Regiment (6th RWK), recalled that the fighting near Djebel Azzag and Djebel Ajred, known as Green Hill and Bald Hill by the troops, cost his unit eleven officers and 150 other ranks either killed, wounded or missing. This equated to roughly a quarter of 6th RWK's total strength. Later he confessed 'I was new to casualties on this scale and kept on thinking of the tragic news soon to be delivered to wives and mothers in towns and villages all over Kent'.

Typically, as leaders, officers' chances of survival were even worse than those for other ranks. When 6th RWK returned from France in 1940 only four officers remained from the original complement of thirty who had gone out with the battalion to join the BEF. Lieutenant–Colonel Martin Lindsay commanded 1st Gordon Highlanders in North-West Europe, and calculated that between D-Day (6 June 1944) and the end of March 1945, a total of 102 officers had eventually served with his unit. Of these 53 per cent were wounded, 24 per cent killed or died of wounds, 15 per cent were invalided out of the army, and only 5 per cent remained with the unit.

Despite these chilling statistics, for some soldiers the prospect of becoming wounded, provided it did not prove fatal, was welcomed because it ensured that they might be removed from the front line. Vernon Scannell fought as an infantryman in North Africa and Normandy, and during the latter campaign noted men who were being evacuated to a CCS in the beachhead were considered 'lucky bastards'. However, as he explained after the war, 'it's a funny old world where you call somebody lucky because they've had their foot blown off'.

Wound agents came in many different forms. Official statistics cited by historian John Ellis reveal that during the entire war 75 per cent of British casualties were caused by mortars, grenades, aerial bombardments or shelling, whereas only 10 per cent resulted from bullets or anti-tank shells, and a further 10 per cent were caused by land mines and booby traps. The remaining 5 per cent of casualties were due primarily to blast injuries, or soldiers being crushed by falling debris, and chemical agents, notably phosphorous. This supports the observations made in Chapter 2 that mortars and artillery were one of the principle threats to Second World War soldiers, and tended to be the weapons that were most feared. This was especially the case in wooded terrain, where as Lieutenant Colonel Lindsay explained, when a shell exploded on hitting a tree, 'it causes more casualties than when it bursts on the ground' as wooden splinters acted as additional projectiles.

If a soldier was not killed by the explosive force of a shell or mortar bomb, he was liable to be in a state of shock, and initially may not have appreciated he had been hit by shell splinters. These tended to become embedded in soldier's bodies, often causing large and irregular entry wounds. Bill Cheall was wounded while serving as an infantryman in Normandy. He recalled that he could not hear the shell which landed near him coming, but was suddenly thrown into the air by the blast. When he landed blood was pouring down his leg from a gash near the top of his inner left thigh. Later after surgery a medical orderly handed him a fragment from a German 88mm shell 'about one-and-a-half inches long and a quarter of an inch thick' that had been recovered from his wound.

Similarly, wartime artillery officer Sir Robin Dunn was working as a Forward Observation Officer (FOO) directing artillery fire in support of infantry at Lebisey Wood, Normandy, when a German shell exploded close by. 'I remember an explosion … and falling to the ground. I found I could not speak [he had been wounded in the head affecting his speech], although I could think, and wrote a fire order on a message pad for transmission to the guns. I felt no pain.' As a junior officer with 2nd Coldstream Guards in France 1940, Jimmy Langley was wounded by a shell which hit the roof of the house he was using as a sniping position against the Germans. 'There was a long silence and I heard a small voice saying "I've been hit", which I suddenly realised was mine.' He felt no pain but his left arm had been badly injured and there was 'blood all over my battle-dress'.

Coming under aerial bombardment was another harrowing ordeal faced by soldiers, and could result in similar injuries to those caused by shell fire. Gunner Fergus Anckorn was driving a lorry on 13 February 1942, when he came under attack from Japanese aircraft. He actually saw a bomb 'coming down less than 10 feet away', so close he could even make out the Japanese lettering on it. The blast was deafening and he was 'engulfed in what sounded like metal hailstones from what must have been an anti-personnel bomb. I knew I was getting wounded but it didn't seem to hurt.'

Compared to wounds from mortars, shells or bombs, bullets, which hit soldiers at greater velocity, tended to cause smaller entry and larger exit wounds. As the historians Sir John Keegan and John Laffin observed, they usually resulted in numerous internal injuries as well. This could result from bullets being made to tumble inside the body when they hit bone. According to Keegan, 'the effects of a tumble … were enhanced by the bone's splintering under the impact, its own fragments then becoming secondary projectiles which produced massive damage to tissues round about'. Wounds from small arms were also troublesome, because as wartime army surgeon Lieutenant Colonel J. C. Watts explained, bullets travelled faster than the speed of sound so were 'preceded by a pressure wave, and it is this that macerates any tensed tissues, such as muscle, although the tough and elastic skin stretches and recoils, leaving the small exit wound concealing the extensive damage underneath'. When bullets hit the human body, soldiers sometimes describe hearing a 'dull thwack'. Vernon Scannell was hit by small-arms fire during a skirmish with a German patrol in Normandy. Under such confusing circumstances he attempted to fire as he rose from a kneeling position, but found that his own weapon had jammed. Suddenly, he heard a crack from behind and a 'frantic metal jabbering ahead'. Then he felt 'a blow like a kick from a heavy boot knock one leg from under him' as bullets hit him, and he fell into a ditch, unable to move without his comrades dragging him along.

Grenades, booby traps and mines resulted in various injuries, mostly from their explosive blast and from metal fragments or flakes which caused multiple wounds, as soldiers caught by these weapons tended to be hit more than once. Writing in *RAMC* (1944) Major Anthony Cotterell noted, that in Eritrea a majority of wounds were caused by 'tiny Italian hand grenades which burst into a shower of aluminium fragments and spattered the skin but did not penetrate deeply', Whereas in Normandy Sergeant Trevor Greenwood of 9th Royal Tank Regiment observed, that 'Jerry sappers [military engineers] seem to spend their lives devising new and devilish methods of slaughter'. This included constructing booby traps by suspending hand grenades inconspicuously from trees that exploded 'upon the slightest touch'.

Depending on their type, mines could be particularly awkward to deal with, and were feared because of their potential lethality. Christopher Bulteel, a junior officer with 3rd Coldstream Guards, recorded that in North Africa the Germans and Italians deployed several sorts of mines, many of which were booby-trapped so that 'there were enough fragments of metal, from ball bearings to rusty nails, to cut legs to smithereens, even to kill'. Mines of the right type could be equally devastating against armoured and soft skinned vehicles. Battery Sergeant Major Ernest Powdrill recalled an incident in Holland during late 1944, where a Universal Carrier from his unit was blown up on a mine. The driver 'was killed instantly, his left leg torn off at the thigh' and the young officer travelling with him received a severe injury, with metal fragments remaining in his head long after the war.

Compared with infantry, crews of armoured vehicles tended to receive more burns because of the dangers of exploding ammunition, and petrol igniting when tanks were hit. Multiple wounds were also more common amongst armoured personnel because explosions in confined spaces (such as the inside of a tank) gave rise to concentrated fragmentation, and often pieces of armour plate broke off when a tank was hit, forming an additional hazard to the crew inside. The German Panzerfaust, a hand-held anti-tank weapon that fired a hollow-charge projectile, was widely employed by the Germans during 1944–45. At close ranges it could punch through the armour on most British tanks, badly wounding or killing the crewmen inside. However, as Stuart Hills, an officer with the Nottinghamshire Sherwood Rangers Yeomanry, recounted one of the most feared weapons by British tank crewmen were specialist anti-tank guns, such as the various 88mm models employed by the Germans. If the shot from one of these penetrated the hull of a tank its 'white hot nose would ricochet about inside, burning and destroying whatever it touched' and ignited fuel and ammunition it contacted. Those crewmen not killed by the initial impact, had a few precious seconds in which to escape their tank, but even then they were likely to 'suffer disfiguring burns or worse'.

Tragically, friendly fire also accounted for deaths and injuries among British soldiers, particularly when cases of mistaken identity occurred, and when artillery or aerial bombardments missed their objectives. Under these conditions the wounds inflicted on troops were the same as those resulting from enemy action. Ken Tout, a Sherman tank gunner with the Northamptonshire Yeomanry, witnessed an unfortunate incident in Normandy during late July 1944. A British M-10, a tank-like vehicle with an open turret mounting a powerful anti-tank gun, had become lost and was seen approaching a well-camouflaged tank from Ken's unit, whose commander assumed it must be a German tank. At this time none of the soldiers in the Northamptonshire Yeomanry had seen an M-10 because they were not in widespread service, which partly accounted for the confusion. Consequently, it was engaged by the tank from the Northamptonshire Yeomanry, and the M-10's crew returned fire convinced they had been targeted by a German tank lying in ambush. Eventually, both vehicles 'went up in flames', and although some crewmen escaped, at least one was killed in the 'flurry of shots ... that reduced both vehicles to burning wreckage'.

Non-Battle Casualties

Typically, disease accounted for large numbers of British casualties during the Second World War. As historian John Ellis commented, 'in every theatre more men fell victim to microbes and viruses than to enemy action'. Ultimately, soldiering on active service could be arduous and dangerous, even when not in contact with the enemy. As Chapter 2 demonstrated, combat personnel in particular often had to spend long periods living in the open, which exposed them to numerous health threats.

Common diseases and ailments in the dust and heat of the Middle East included skin conditions, VD, disorders of the digestive system, dysentery, inflammation of the tonsils, sand fly fever and malaria. According to John Ellis during the Italian campaign in 1943, more soldiers were put out of action by VD, skin diseases, malaria, tonsillitis, pharyngitis and respiratory problems than through enemy action. In the mud and damp conditions of North-West Europe during 1944–45, significant casualties resulted from all of the above conditions, plus muscular complaints and conditions affecting the ears, nose, and throat. By contrast, in the Far East during 1941–45, personnel were exposed to the risk of numerous tropical diseases, notably various strains of malaria, plus typhus, small pox, dysentery, and eliminate-related conditions such as heat exhaustion.

Sister Marjorie Pringle spent much of her war service as a QA at British military hospitals in India. She recalled having to nurse patients with typhoid, cerebral malaria and black-water fever, and faced two cholera epidemics. However, one of the greatest challenges the army faced in the Far East was in containing the threat posed by malaria. According to Major Anthony Cotterell, writing in 1944, 'the Bengal-Burma frontier is one of the worst malarial districts in the world ... and it is nothing out of the ordinary for units to lose 25 per cent of their men per month'. Sir Charles Evans, a medical officer who served in the Far East, remembered he had one British soldier with malaria, 'who lost consciousness at 1300 and was dead at 1530', having only first exhibited symptoms the previous day.

To combat malaria, mepacrin tablets started to be issued mid-way through the war. This required strict discipline to ensure soldiers took their regular dose, and it was a military offence for them not to take their tablets. Even so, rumours abounded that mepacrin caused impotence, and it turned soldiers' skin a yellowish hue which made the tablets unpopular. Neither were they a certain guarantee that a soldier would not contract malaria. As an infantryman in Burma, George Macdonald Fraser succumbed to 'a touch of malaria' and was accused by his battalion's medical officer of not taking his mepacrin. He pointed out that he 'was a rich yellow in colour from swallowing the bloody things' and the MO reluctantly admitted 'they were not an infallible prophylactic'.

Malaria was also a serious threat for troops serving in North Africa and the Mediterranean. Private Bill Titchmarsh contracted the disease in August 1944, while serving with 2/6th Queen's Regiment in Italy, despite having taken the precautions encouraged by the army. As he remembered 'I had … turned myself yellow with mepacrin tablets, and used cream and rolled my sleeves down at night. At about 2 am I woke up with a blinding headache and staggered out of my tent and fell over the guy rope.' The next day 'an order was given for the Battalion to march ten miles and we had to carry all our own kit, as 78th Division had commandeered our transport'. By then he was in a bad state, 'somehow my mates dragged me along. I couldn't open my eyes and I still had a blinding headache. I don't know how I got there but I eventually ended up at 66th General Hospital.'

As well as mosquitos, flies were another vector of disease, particularly in the Middle East and Far East. As army surgeon Major John Baty noted, 'flies were our constant companions' and at mealtimes 'they decorated the slices of bully beef and rather dampened the appetite'. He found that in Burma the maggots of the Arakan house fly (equivalent to a bluebottle) were an effective agent in cleaning up wounds as they ate only dead flesh, whereas other flies would attack both living and dead tissue so that patients required more serious surgery than had initially been envisaged. The minute 'so-called mango fly' which flourished during the pre-monsoon season, was another serious pest, as it laid 'its eggs within the eyelids, the result being a troublesome conjunctivitis' which could develop into 'corneal erosions and permanent impairment of vision'.

Other common ailments in hot climates included various types of sores, and foot trouble, which if not treated could develop into more serious conditions. In the Far East soldiers often suffered from a form of foot rot, where their feet felt unpleasantly hot and spongey. Similarly, many suffered jungle sores, and even the slightest nick or graze could become septic under tropical conditions. The monsoon was a particularly unpleasant, and as George Macdonald Fraser discovered it 'puckered the skin in a revoltingly puffy fashion, and brought forth a great plague of jungle sores on wrists and ankles'. Even worse were the so-called 'Naga sores' that resulted when inexperienced soldiers ripped off leeches leaving their heads buried in their flesh, which caused a saucer-sized ulcer to develop that reeked of putrefying flesh.

Many troops captured in the Far East also developed tropical ulcers, not helped by their starvation diet and the climatic conditions they experienced. The worst cases often had to undergo primitive surgery in appalling conditions in order to amputate a limb. As a medical orderly captured by the Japanese, Ken Adams continued to help care for patients in captivity, and recorded 'around half of amputees eventually died from a combination of shock and general weakness from dysentery, malaria and avitaminosis diseases or perhaps from other complications'. Other amputees were more fortunate. Fusilier Andrew Woodcock served with 9th Royal Northumberland Fusiliers at Dunkirk, and was later captured during the fall of Singapore. While in captivity he developed a huge ulcer on one leg and had to undergo an amputation with a butcher's saw, via what soldiers christened 'fork and knife surgery' which gave him a 'most lovely feeling' of freedom as the poison drained out of the abscess on his stump.

Troops in the Middle East often developed what were known as desert sores, which resulted from flea bites or minor injuries that had become infected. Soldier's diets were also thought to have contributed to the problem, especially a lack of fresh fruit and vegetables. Although not usually life-threatening, in some cases, as the historian Mark Harrison observed, sores became infected with diphtheria germs that could be fatal.

Rifleman Henry Taylor observed that old hands advised younger, inexperienced soldiers to wear trousers rather than shorts in the desert. These same veterans 'were plagued by these sores; any exposed area which you knocked was soon covered by weeping sores' and when they rested near the coast these 'blokes would go for a swim in the sea and let the salt disinfect the sores and the fish nip the tops from the scabs'.

By contrast, in wetter, colder climates, trench-foot was a significant threat, particularly to soldiers operating in waterlogged conditions for prolonged periods where it was difficult to properly dry out. In the worst cases soldiers' feet would go numb and turn purple or black as nerves died and gangrene developed, requiring the amputation of toes or even an entire foot.

To counter this threat troops were encouraged to routinely dry their feet, apply foot powder, and change into a dry pair of socks. However, this could be difficult to achieve under battlefield conditions. Recalling his service as a junior officer with 2nd Field Regiment Royal Artillery in the mountains of Italy, A. M. Cheetham remarked, one of the chief problems they faced was 'to avoid getting trench feet' after standing in gun positions 'for days in cold wet boots'. As they lacked suitable waterproof footwear the solution was 'to take off one's boots every day, massage a bit of life back into the toes, put on dry socks and hope to survive. The wet pair of socks was then put inside one's battle dress blouse and gradually dried out by body heat.'

Accidents were another major cause of non-battle casualties in all theatres, and often more troops were put out of action owing to these than wounds sustained in battle. Even experienced soldiers could become careless when handling small arms, priming hand grenades, or dealing with other weaponry. Lieutenant Colonel Watts experienced extensive service as a surgeon with the RAMC during the campaigns in North Africa, Italy, Normandy and North-West Europe in 1940–45: 'the number of … unnecessary tragedies, was a serious reflection on the careless handling of small arms that went on'.

Fractures and head injuries resulted from traffic accidents caused by careless or tired drivers and poor roads. Likewise, burns were frequently caused when soldiers became careless in the use of petrol for lighting their stoves, and as Major Cotterell observed this was just as effective at putting them in hospital as enemy action. A. M. Cheetham discovered that although it was potentially dangerous, unused sticks of cordite were commonly used by soldiers in artillery units as a 'form of accelerated cooking'. Usually one stick at a time was carefully fed onto a fire, which resulted in water being boiled extremely quickly for cooking. At one gun position in Italy 'we had hardly arrived when a signaller appeared, very badly burnt' after having been engaged in such a practice.

Many other forms of injury occurred owing to accidents while on active service that produced further non-battle casualties for the medical system to treat. In many theatres soldiers caught fish to supplement their diets by tossing a hand grenade into a river and collecting fish that rose to the surface after the explosion. The army surgeon Major Baty noted the tragic case of a young officer from the King's Own Scottish Borderers in the Far East, who was an explosives expert and opted to employ a more powerful charge in this role. This exploded prematurely, and he was brought to Baty with multiple injuries including 'loss of the right hand, blindness, deafness, blast-injury to the chest and abdomen together with skin loss from thighs, penis and scrotum'. The unfortunate officer died within a week, despite being carefully nursed.

Stanley Whitehouse, who fought as an infantryman in Normandy and North-West Europe, witnessed a comrade pierce his eyeball on the aerial of a radio set. The soldier had only left his slit trench to urinate, but as he jumped back into it he collided with the extended aerial and had to be taken off by the battalion's cooks to receive urgent medical treatment, and was never seen again.

Accidents could be deeply traumatic for all of those concerned. Guardsmen D. J. Kennedy served with 4th Grenadier Guards, part of 6th Guards Tank Brigade, and witnessed a horrendous incident in Holland during April 1945, by which stage the war in Europe was nearly over. The Churchill tanks from his unit were preparing for the night when at:

Last parade on tanks, i.e. fill with petrol, oil and water, re-stock with ammunition. We parked in lines close together. Corporal B was standing and bending over the back turret bin, removing blankets etc. for the night when, in the tank behind his, a sergeant getting into the turret accidentally trod on the foot trigger for the 75mm gun, there was a shell in the breech and no safety catch on. The shell was an APBC [armoured piercing ballistic cap]. The shell on hitting the bin exploded, blowing Corporal B off the tank and shattering both his legs. Everyone dropped to the floor, thinking for a second we were being shelled [by the Germans]. Corporal B lay on the floor in agony, moaning – his legs, from his knees down, were like jelly. The shell went into the back of the turret and stuck with the point of the shell inside the tank in line with the gunner who was in the turret. One guardsman had his hand on the muzzle of the gun when it fired, he lost two fingers. The sergeant who fired the shot is a bundle of nerves.

Casualty Evacuation

When a soldier received a wound either he, or a comrade, was supposed to apply a field dressing. Alternatively, medical personnel such as stretcher-bearers applied them when initially assisting a casualty. All soldiers were expected to carry field dressings and there was even a special pocket on the right-hand side of battledress trousers designed to hold them. The directions for use on a field dressing manufactured by Vernon & Co Ltd, Preston, November, 1943 read: 'Take the folded ends of the bandage in each hand, and keeping the bandage taut, apply the gauze pad to the wound and fix the bandage. One dressing to be used for each wound.' Soldiers had to avoid touching the gauze or wound, and if a casualty had a head injury and was wearing a gas mask care was required to ensure the gauze pad didn't interfere with the fit of the face-piece.

When Sir Robin Dunn was first wounded in Libya during 1942 he recorded, 'I took a bottle of whisky from my tank and drank half of it neat. The doctor then gave me a shot of morphia and dressed my leg and put me in the ambulance.' Similarly, Jimmy Langley who sustained a serious arm injury as a platoon commander near Dunkirk, remembered that one of the first things to happen was 'a stretcher-bearer arrived and put a field dressing on my arm, removed my watch, which he later sent to my parents in England, and bandaged my head'.

If casualties could walk, they were expected to make their way to a Regimental Aid Post (RAP), otherwise they would be carried by stretcher-bearers. As Major Cotterell observed these were ordinary soldiers trained in basic first aid that sought out casualties on the battlefield, and were not expected to administer any form of complicated treatment. However, they were often determined and undertook their duties in difficult conditions, not helped by the fact wounded troops often didn't relax when carried by stretcher which made them even more difficult to evacuate. As Cotterell noted, stretcher-bearers knew 'that the further forward they advance the further they are likely to have to evacuate stretcher cases', and the greater the distance covered 'the higher the proportion of casualties who will relapse from walking to having to be carried on a stretcher'.

At an RAP emergency treatment was given to casualties if necessary by a unit's medical officer supported by his medical orderlies. Otherwise wounds were simply cleaned of debris such as mud and fragments of clothing so as to reduce the risk of infection. In this regard medical personnel were helped because soldiers were issued packets of sulphonamide powder that were tipped into wounds. By 1944 penicillin started to become more readily available as well, so that casualties in 21st Army Group in Normandy and North-West Europe could expect to receive an injection of this new 'wonder drug' shortly after being wounded. At RAPs any missiles were also removed from wounds if practicable, and fresh dressings applied.

However, for more complex treatment casualties had to be evacuated further along the medical chain. Dr Ian Campbell (RAMC) worked in the Normandy beachhead during summer 1944 at a Casualty Evacuation Point (CEP). As he stressed the onus was on receiving casualties, reviewing and treating them, and if necessary evacuating them away from the battlefront. On arrival at the CEP every patient was 'examined by a medical officer; given necessary treatment such as Penicillin or Sulphonamides, when due, and dressings and splints adjusted as required'.

As far as possible the army tried to provide treatment for wounded and sick soldiers throughout the evacuation process, and the basic medical organisation was adapted from one theatre to another to achieve this. Typically, FAUs operated near front lines and provided stretcher-bearers for removing casualties from RAPs or the equivalent, plus helped establish Advanced Dressing Stations (ADSs), where urgent treatment for conditions such as shock and fractures could be administered. From there casualties were often transferred to a Main Dressing Station (MDS) situated further back that provided urgent treatment if necessary, plus filled in documentation on patients. In forward areas FDSs were also frequently employed, notably to provide blood transfusions, and Advanced Surgical Centres (ASCs) set up for emergency operations.

Away from the front line, CCSs provided a wide range of treatments for patients evacuated through the system. Ultimately, depending on the seriousness of a soldier's condition, he was liable to be admitted to a General Hospital in a rear area, or even be evacuated back to a hospital in Britain, before spending time at a convalescence depot. Both General Hospitals and those in Britain offered a wide range of diagnostic techniques and treatments.

Lieutenant Colonel Watts observed that CCS during the North African Campaigns initially had a staff of thirteen officers and nearly 100 other ranks capable of handling 200 patients, and 'had all the facilities for surgical and medical treatment, including a portable X-ray set in a lorry'. However, while the organisation could be reinforced by other surgical teams, overall it was immobile. This was only rectified by deploying captured Italian transport that allowed self-contained surgical teams to attach themselves to any CCS, FDS or FAU and establish an ASC. Similarly, the evacuation of casualties in North Africa could be tortuous and uncomfortable. Sir Robin Dunn wrote of a 'nightmare drive' by motor ambulance to Tobruk, before ending up in a hospital at Mersa Matruh after the Battle of Knightsbridge in June 1942.

In Burma the conditions also made it awkward for medical personnel and the evacuation of casualties. Major Baty recorded that it was seldom possible to receive large numbers of casualties simultaneously. Typically, a wounded man was carried through the jungle by a friend before finding a stretcher-bearer unit which, 'in turn, invariably had a difficult journey before reaching an ADS for first measures. The next stage from ADS to MDS could mean further delay, caused by bad road conditions', so surgical units were usually able to deal with one lot of wounded before another arrived.

By contrast, in Normandy during 1944 it proved possible to evacuate casualties across the Channel in LSTs, which having delivered their cargo, were effectively turned into temporary hospital ships able to accommodate 350 stretcher cases. Lieutenant Eric Ashcroft, who served with 1st South Lancashire Regiment, was wounded on Sword Beach, and considered that the medical aspect of operations was extremely efficient, as it appeared that RAMC or naval medical personnel were able to carry out quite sophisticated procedures right from the beaches. Wounded soldiers were ferried by DUKWs (amphibious trucks) straight onto LSTs for evacuation to hospitals in Britain. Alternatively, British soldiers were evacuated by hospital ships that berthed at the floating Mulbery Harbour at Arromanches, or transported by air.

Richard Carr-Gomm was wounded in Normandy while commanding a troop of tanks with 4th Coldstream Guards in 6th Guards Tank Brigade. He was ordered to signal to a scout car behind his tank: 'As I put my head out of the top of the tank a large shell landed … I found myself at the bottom of the tank with a signaller shouting I had been hit. There was a lot of blood.' His crew got him out of the tank, applied a field dressing and he was rushed to the RAP and then an FDS. He was given tea at the first and morphine at the second, 'which eased the pain', and found himself waking up at a hospital in Cardiff, having been transported by air and train.

Triage, or the process of accessing casualties by their clinical needs and chances of surviving treatment, was another facet of the evacuation process. This could be emotionally disturbing for ordinary soldiers as well as medical personnel. During the heavy fighting he experienced at Anzio, Italy in 1944, Bill Titchmarsh and some of his comrades attempted to carry a wounded man to a RAP, after tragically being caught in a barrage laid down by their supporting artillery.

> There was injured lying all over the bloody place. Stretchers were mangled and had bits and pieces of wireless aerials, and branches from grape vines littered the place. I put this fellow on a stretcher and with two other soldiers we tried to carry him, and he had a hole the size of a tea cup in his back. He fell off that's how I noticed it. We got him back on and rushed him to where the doctor was, about 200 yards away, a herculean effort it was. And the doctor came up to me and said 'Get him out, get him out of here!' I said 'But he is still alive, Sir'. The doctor replied 'Well take him outside and let him rest'. So we took him outside and he died right there.

The evacuation process also dealt with sick as well as wounded personnel. When Christopher Bulteel contracted malaria in Italy during 1943 he was evacuated straight to a general hospital near Salerno. From there a hospital ship, the *Leinster*, took him to Philippeville in north-east Algeria, where the British had established a large base organisation that included reinforcement depots and medical facilities. There followed a 'nightmare journey' to another general hospital in Algiers by train in the depths of winter, where the lavatory for sick men with dysentery, malaria and other diseases comprised 'a hole in the floor of the cattle-trucks, where wind and snow would whistle up on to the squatting patients'. In February 1944 Bulteel was considered well enough to be transferred back to Britain via the hospital ship *Llandovery Castle*, for what he considered a long, dreary convalescence.

In all theatres the medical system had also to deal psychiatric casualties, who required assessment and evacuation if necessary. As early as 1939 the army realised that some soldiers might break down owing to the stress of battle or what had been termed shell shock in the First World War. During the French campaign in 1940 a 600-bed psychiatric hospital was established in theatre, and in Burma during 1944 a forward psychiatric centre treated soldiers who had experienced heavy fighting at Kohima and Imphal.

Major Cotterell observed that a soldier, who shall be known as Private X, was treated successfully for psychiatric problems while still in the front line. Private X was already a veteran of the Norwegian and French campaigns in 1940, by the time he was posted to East Africa. During one action two soldiers were killed near him simultaneously, and Private X broke cover and ran in a dazed state towards the enemy lines. He tripped and was brought back to British positions and 'given an immediate injection of morphine and after a few hours rest was able to return to normal duties'.

However, although many soldiers suffering from battle exhaustion, the catch-all term used for psychiatric conditions, were offered treatment in forward areas, large numbers still had to be evacuated to hospitals in the rear for effective treatment. Sister Meta Kelly served as a QA with 81st General Hospital in Normandy during 1944, and was deeply upset by the sight of soldiers whose nerves appeared shattered. She remembered that they lay apathetically in bed, but when gunfire started they behaved like terrified wild animals trying to claw their way into the ground with their bare hands, and had to be calmed down via a combination of talking and administering sedatives.

Treatments and Recuperation

Doctors and other military medical personnel were liable to have to deal with a wide variety of wounds and illnesses. For the uninitiated this was a daunting prospect. Sister Molly Budge served with the QAs in North Africa throughout 1940–43, and was initially shocked at the sight of the wounded men her unit received. These arrived fresh off the battlefield with horrific injuries from landmines and shelling, the like of which she had never seen before.

Similarly, in the Far East Ken Adams, who served as a medical orderly with 198th Field Ambulance RAMC, confessed that he wondered how he would cope when faced with badly injured and dead soldiers. On active service in Malaya and Singapore during 1942 he soon had to deal with badly-wounded men, including one who 'had a split in the side of his head and part of his brain was hanging out' and another with 'a large hole in his back'. He 'held a pad over the wound – it was oozing blood – and could feel the sucking movement of his lungs through my fingers as he struggled for breath'.

Arguably one of the most distressing and disturbing experiences that medical personnel endured during the entire war was when British forces liberated the concentration camp at Belsen. Thousands of emaciated corpses littered the area of those who had died from neglect, starvation, typhus, tuberculosis and dysentery. Those still alive required urgent medical attention, especially the administration of fluids, although it was doubtful how many would ultimately survive. On 4 May 1945, nine days after its liberation, Colonel Martin Herford, who commanded 163rd Field Ambulance RAMC, entered the camp at the head of his unit.

Although No. 32 CCS and No. 11 Light Field Ambulance had done magnificent work there in the previous ten days, it was still a distressing sight that can never be erased from memory. Piles of corpses lay everywhere naked and emaciated. Huge grave-pits were filled with thousands of bodies. Sub-human creatures prowled about apathetically with expressionless eyes. The huts were so crowded that it was impossible to tell the living from the dead. Yet miraculously, many had retained their magnanimity and humanity.

Sometimes there was little that could be done for the seriously injured, other than to make the patient as comfortable as possible, provide first aid and any necessary drugs. On D-Day (6 June 1944) Patrick Brown served as a medical orderly with 33rd Field Surgical Unit RAMC, dealing with casualties in the Normandy beachhead. The worst cases were give injections of morphine and he had to mark an 'M' on their foreheads, and note down the date, time and amount given. Brown also assisted in the operating theatre where numerous patients with gun-shot wounds and horrific injuries from mortars received emergency treatment. He hurriedly cut off clothing so that wounds were exposed for surgery, and assisted the anaesthetist with administering anaesthetic, plus ensured men's heads were kept up so they didn't swallow their tongues during surgery.

Another facet of the medical treatment given to soldiers was that under wartime conditions it was common to improvise. Major Baty recalled treating a soldier in Burma whose lower jaw, chin and lower lip had been shot away. This posed a significant problem as a patient in that condition could not swallow fluids and risked dying from dehydration during the lengthy, hot evacuation to India. The solution was to fashion a temporary jaw from 'dental "Stent", a compound which becomes malleable when soaked in boiling water and regains its rigidity when cooled'. With this in place the patient was able to drink fluids during evacuation, and survived to eventually undergo reconstructive surgery at a facio-maxillary unit using plastic surgery.

Army surgeons, as Brigadier Charles Donald (Deputy Director of Medical Services Eighth Army) observed, had to be physically fit, adaptable, of strong character and skilful if they were to provide effective treatment and work for long hours. During November 1941–February 1942 Brigadier Ralph Marnham served as a surgeon with a field surgical unit at Tobruk. The unit treated 5,497 battle casualties with only ninety deaths, or a mortality rate of 1.6 per cent. At one time surgeons performed an operation every twenty-four minutes, and several shifts in the operating theatre lasted well over twenty hours.

At Salerno in September 1943, Lieutenant Colonel Watts worked as surgeon with a CCS that received 512 casualties on its first day in action and was 'going full blast'. In another eight-hour shift in North Africa he recalled, dealing with a blood transfusion and leg amputation, a case of multiple wounds from a mortar bomb, severe petrol burns to a soldier's hands and legs, and a German soldier who had been shot through the knee before being captured. At times civilians were treated by army medics as well. In Burma Major Baty recalled a local man was admitted to his CCS, who had fallen from a bridge and suffered an 'intracranial haemorrhage from a meningeal artery' that required emergency surgery.

Similarly, Sister Mary English witnessed a wide variety of injuries while working at 67th British General Hospital in Philippeville, Algeria, including fracture cases, gunshot wounds and several soldiers who lost arms or legs via amputation as a result of gangrene. Typically, any patient requiring complex treatment was nursed until they were well enough to be evacuated to Britain or Gibraltar via a hospital ship.

The British Army was fortunate in being able to rely on blood transfusions, and techniques for doing this improved throughout the war, and helped in providing effective surgery to severely wounded troops. In the late 1930s a blood supply depot was established at a hospital in Bristol that stored blood from voluntary donors. As the war progressed blood and plasma were prepared here for sending to medical teams operating in the field. However, as Lieutenant Colonel Watts recalled, initially blood transfusions involved finding a donor and cross-matching his blood to ensure there was a match, then the blood was withdrawn into a complex apparatus before giving it to the patient. Although this worked, it was time-consuming and cumbersome in the field.

By 1943 'surgical teams had a field transfusion unit attached, with highly trained personnel and supplied with bottles of blood by air from the base transfusion unit'. Consequently, once a patient's needs had been assessed by a transfusion officer, a medical orderly would slip a needle into a vein in his/her arm, and within a matter of minutes they would be receiving blood. As Major Cotterell observed it became possible to offer three types of transfusion: whole blood 'directly from a comrade', or sent from 'the base in a bottle in a refrigerator', plasma, sent from Britain 'as a liquid, or in dried form, like powdered eggs, to which water must be added before use', and finally glucose-saline.

Another area in which medicine advanced during the war was in the treatment of fractures. The 'Tobruk Splint' was developed during the campaigns in North Africa where wounded troops faced an arduous evacuation, particularly if they were transported by road. As the historian

Mark Harrison commented it was 'a conventional Thomas splint [as employed during the First World War] reinforced by plaster of Paris to immobilize limbs without impeding circulation'. When Sir Robin Dunn was first wounded in the Western Desert in 1942, he experienced one of these splints as a patient. 'My left leg was encased in a "Tobruk splint" with metal rods on each side of the plaster to keep my leg rigid.' This made the drive from Tobruk to Mersa Matruh more bearable, in a rickety ambulance operated by Americans from the Society of Friends (Quakers).

Dealing with burns formed another important component of military medicine. Typically, these resulted from accidents owing to the wide spread use of petrol as cooking fuel, or when armoured vehicles were hit and caught fire. In the latter case they were often accompanied by other wounds from shrapnel and high explosives. As historian Mark Harrison observed such cases tended to have a profound impact on the medical staff that treated them. As an army nurse in Italy, Mary English treated some dreadful wounds, including a burns case where part of a man's uniform had melted into the wound, and this was difficult to clean and dress effectively. Often painkillers such as morphine were administered, and sulphonamide gauze and bandages applied over cotton wool, although later in the war penicillin gauze became available. Ultimately, patients with burns might require some form of plastic surgery, such as skin grafting, the techniques for which were refined during the war.

In hot climates heat stroke was a further issue that required consideration by the medical authorities. Mild cases could be dealt with by medical orderlies under the supervision of a doctor. However, more serious cases required urgent attention, or else a soldier's body heat-regulating mechanism would go askew, leading to an increased temperature and convulsions, causing him to lapse into a coma from which he would probably not recover. As Sister Molly Budge discovered in North Africa, one way of treating patients suffering from heat stroke was for them to lie naked under a sheet on a bed beneath an electric fan. Ice was then placed around the patient and they were regularly doused with cold water, and given a cold enema and intravenous transfusions of saline and glucose.

Whether a soldier was taken sick, or wounded via an accident or on the battlefield, he was eventually likely to face a period of recuperation. Often this was in Britain, having initially received treatment overseas. Depending on their condition, soldiers also faced the possibility that they might be medically downgraded, or even discharged from the army.

Fusilier William Close enlisted in the Royal Northumberland Fusiliers as a seventeen-year-old in 1933. By the outbreak of the Second World War he was a hardened regular soldier who had seen extensive service in the Middle East. In August 1941 he was wounded by shrapnel in the face at Tobruk and medically downgraded to Category 'B'. However, he persuaded his unit's Medical Officer to reclassify him as 'A.1' so that he could return to action. By May 1942 he had become a dispatch rider for his old platoon, but both his legs were fractured when he fell off his motorbike. After treatment in North Africa, he was returned to Britain and potentially faced being discharged, although after much pleading he was classed as Category 'C', and even though still on crutches was able to remain in the army, albeit unfit for front-line service.

A major aim of the recuperation process was to strengthen soldiers recovering from wounds or ill health, so that they could be returned to duty as rapidly as possible. Given that the British Army was running out of manpower by 1944–45, this was an important objective. In the final stage of a man's treatment he was liable to spend time at a convalescent depot. Despite their benign-sounding name these could be tough institutions. After being wounded in the knee and groin in Italy, and suffering a relapse of malaria, Bill Titchmarsh was eventually posted to a convalescent depot near Scarborough. It was 'full of warrant officers and sergeants slinging their lead with young lads just back from hospitals falling out on route marches and being threatened with a court martial'.

Health and Hygiene

Yet another important strand of RAMC work was preventative medicine, and promoting health and hygiene within the army. Soldiers joining the wartime army were, as historian Mark Harrison emphasised, effectively joining a 'citizen army'. As such they could expect their rights, including access to medical and dental care, to be respected. However, as responsible citizen soldiers they simultaneously had an obligation in return to maintain high standards of hygiene and personal turnout. As Sydney Jarry, a platoon commander in Normandy and North-West Europe remarked, his troops 'seldom went unshaven and never once did I have to reprimand a man for uncleanliness. Their personal standards avoided the lice which plagued the Germans.'

Inoculations were an important factor in countering the threat posed by disease. Troops posted to the Middle East received a vaccine that was proven against typhoid fever and paratyphoid. Similarly, typhus, spread by lice, was widely feared and troops in Egypt and Libya were educated about the danger it posed, and encouraged to routinely inspect their uniforms for lice eggs and to wash regularly. In the Far East tetanus was a serious threat to soldiers wounded in paddy fields, as the bacillus which caused it lived in the intestinal tract of domestic animals. According to Major Baty the low incidences of this condition under these circumstances, was because it became standard practice 'to provide injections of tetanus toxin' when soldiers 'received their TAB [anti-typhoid] inoculations'.

Throughout the war a concerted effort was mounted against malaria, especially in North Africa, the Mediterranean, and Far East. This included issuing mepacrine and encouraging troops to take practical precautions like using mosquito nets when they were sleeping. Historian John Ellis highlighted that within 14th Army in Burma, malaria was reduced from '628 cases per 1,000 men to only 128 per 1,000, in the last months of the war'. Part of the success in combating this disease in Burma was due to the employment of Malarial Forward Treatment Units (MFTU). As Major Baty explained these were 'bashas [huts] or tents a few miles behind the fighting lines', where 'the disease could be treated in its early stage and brought a cure within a few weeks'. This enabled soldiers to be returned to duty as quickly as possible, and significantly had less impact on the lines of communication in such an awkward theatre. Sir Charles Evans, who spent some time as a doctor with No. 7 Indian MFTU, noted, 'patients lay on rows of stretchers in tents accommodating about fifty men and were treated with Quinine, Mapacrine and Pamaquin for two to three weeks, after which they went to another camp to get fit'.

In all theatres basic hygiene measures were equally important in countering the spread of disease. Soldiers on active service were encouraged via their officers, films, broadcasts and leaflets to appreciate the link between hygiene and disease. As Rifleman Henry Taylor stressed, the British Army could also fall back on its experience of colonial warfare that had provided significant experience in hot climates of the need for good hygiene amongst troops. When he served in the Western Desert, Henry Taylor discovered that latrines often comprised 'a deep hole into which a bottomless empty petrol tin was placed vertically. Another was placed at an angle and this was frequently disinfected with chloride ... the frequency of disinfection did not vary as dysentery and other fly borne plagues' were constant dangers.

Specialist Field Hygiene Units were employed by the RAMC to assist in maintaining the health of front-line personnel, which included ensuring as higher standard of sanitary arrangements were maintained as possible. Similarly, Mobile Bath Units (MBU) offered an important means by which soldiers could wash, and have some respite from service at the front. Peter White served as an officer with 4th King's Own Scottish Borderers in North-West Europe during 1944–45, and described the joy brought by visit to a MBU and a change of uniform: 'A host of naked Jocks [term for other ranks in Scottish units] and officers, singing, shouting and popping in and out of' a cloud of steam. 'Soon the whole Battalion, rejuvenated, glowing, and re-clothed with fresh socks, shirts and underwear, was busily engaged on smartening up.'

Medical personnel also had numerous routine tasks that had to be addressed, along with promoting and maintaining health. Sir Charles Evans, who as well as combating malaria, spent periods as a Regimental Medical Officer in the Far East. 'My routine varied from day to day: a daily sick parade of some kind, a bit of administration and the treatment and evacuation of casualties when we were in action'. As a junior NCO with the RAMC, R. J. Meads experienced much routine medical work, particularly when posted as part of a medical team aboard the *Rangitata,* a New Zealand troopship. Chief amongst this was assisting the daily sick parade where once:

We had one man reported with advanced VD. Several came in needing stiches through fighting. Many with ear trouble. One cook who had scalded himself with hot soup. But our worst case was a Marine who was found to have advanced TB.

However, as Major Cotterell emphasised, medical officers also had to be wary of malingerers who tried to con them into pronouncing them unfit for duty at sick parades. Although he reckoned they were in minority, there were always 'old soldiers who have a convenient gammy leg for use when they want to dodge something' and those 'whose military career is a simple pilgrimage towards discharge, uninhibited by any of the normal restrictions of self-respect'. As Doctor Ian Campbell, who served as a medical officer in Normandy and North-West Europe during 1944–45, confessed, working as a wartime army medic had taught him a great deal, not just about medicine, but human nature as well.

The army's medical services played a crucial role in the eventual Allied victory. Whereas those of the Axis powers had by 1944 begun to disintegrate, the RAMC and other medical personnel continued to provide effective treatment, often under awkward conditions in forward areas. As the war progressed techniques of surgery and other forms of medicine relevant to the military were constantly adapted or improved. Consequently, British troops knew that if they were wounded or became sick, whatever the cause, they were likely to be well cared for, and this was a massive boost to their morale.

The Aftermath, c. 1945–1946

For many soldiers the cessation of hostilities during the spring and summer of 1945 brought with it a sense of weariness and dislocation, mixed with relief. On hearing the two-word message: 'HOSTILITIES ENDED' over his unit's wireless network, Richmond Gorle, an officer with 181st Field Regiment Royal Artillery in Germany, observed, 'there was no cheering or elation, just a kind of stunned feeling and an intense thankfulness that one had survived to hear those words'. Similarly, after serving overseas as a nurse with the QAs, Dorothea Chisholm returned to Britain and on being demobilised was dominated by an overpowering feeling of flatness and disappointment.

Such emotions could be even more pronounced amongst combat personnel. By May 1945 Major General Dare Wilson, who as a more junior officer had experienced action in France during 1940 and 1944, plus service in the Middle East, Italy, the Low Countries and Germany. On reflection he considered that 'a high proportion of those who had been closest to the action found the greatest sense of anti–climax in its ending'.

Thanksgiving services, such as those held by units from British Second Army that had fought from Normandy to the Baltic, went some way towards allaying such feelings. As Major General Wilson noted they were highly memorable and important events, 'with lusty singing' and 'many names to recall, associated with the gaps that had appeared in our ranks'.

Riotous victory celebrations provided a further tonic for many war weary soldiers, albeit their effect might have been short lived. On Victory in Europe Day (VE–Day, 8 May 1945) Philip Kenyon was working as duty driver with the Royal Engineers in Brussels, assigned to a Personal Utility van designed to carry four passengers plus cargo. 'I was boarded by a mass of squealing girls, those who couldn't get inside climbed on top, 13 at my last count. I drove along peering through legs dangling over the windscreen.' A veteran of the Italian campaign, Hardy Parkhurst ended his war as a major with 2nd Royal Northumberland Fusiliers, attempting to monitor the political situation in Greece. Towards midnight on VE-Day he remembered that where they were stationed:

> Alarms grew in crescendo. Finally it burst into full symphony, A/A [anti-aircraft] guns, rifles, ships' hooters, church bells, horns of vehicles … the whole town seemed to be singing. Soon we were down again in the mess, and we had an uproarious time. There was singing, dancing, drinking; we went quite crazy.

Likewise, as the regimental history of 11th Hussars testifies, men from that distinguished unit filled the 'skies of Holstien with every missile from a variegated armoury' as they waited for the unconditional surrender to be signed by the Germans. This included Schmeissers, Spandaus and Lugers, as well as British manufactured small arms. When the din had died down the troops gazed upon the early morning sky, and the full realisation that the war really had ended hit them.

In Germany, soldiers from British units rapidly had to readjust their outlook to appreciate that they had become part of an army of occupation, and were no longer on combat operations. This entailed numerous awkward tasks including providing security, maintaining law and order, offering medical assistance and acting as relief workers, plus helping deal with vast numbers of displaced persons and liberated POWs. As Major General Wilson remarked the entire system by which Germany had been governed had collapsed and 'virtually everything was in chaos'.

Initially a strict non-fraternisation or 'non frat' rule with the German population was enforced. According to Richmond Gorle, who spent a period in Germany immediately after the war, 'in spite of our aloofness, there was, I think, quite a father-son relationship. The Germans accepted the fact that it was a stern father, but knew that they were being treated fairly.' Bill Bellamy, who commanded a tank troop with 8th King's Royal Irish Hussars from 7th Armoured Division, found that it was difficult for his unit not to demonstrate the British soldier's traditional affection towards children and girls once on occupation duties in Germany. However, 'we kept stern faces and maintained our lofty pose of indifference by walking past them without acknowledging their presence in any way'.

Soldiers remaining on occupation duties in Germany were also confronted by a defeated nation, and all that this entailed from a human perspective. Towns and cities were destroyed, communications prostrate, food and fuel limited, hospitals overflowing, and provision for electricity, gas and water services virtually non-existent. Bill Bellamy found entering Hamburg in early May 1945 particularly disturbing. Rapidly he became aware of 'the agony of non-combatant death on a large scale', as he witnessed the full extent of the damage caused by the Allied air offensive that had involved fire bombing. The city appeared completely levelled and the 'roads were nothing but gaps in the mountains of rubble ... The whole place stank of death.'

Captain Geoffrey Picot was deployed with his infantry battalion as part of the British garrison in Berlin during autumn 1945:

It was horrible. More buildings were in rubble than were standing. The people were in abject distress. They were servile towards us, grovelling to be allowed to open the door or do any service. Many women, it was well known, would offer any sexual activity for a bar of chocolate.

Three months later, on 14 August 1945 Japan finally surrendered unconditionally, after Hiroshima and Nagasaki had been targeted by the Americans dropping atomic bombs. Nearly seventy years later it may seem callous, but at the time, many people including British soldiers, welcomed America's decision to deploy these weapons. Prior to his Berlin posting, Captain Geoffrey Picot had been earmarked for potential deployment to the Far East. He later commented 'the two atomic explosions killed something like 100,000 Japanese. Without them full-scale war would have raged on the mainland of Asia, in the Pacific and finally in Japan itself.' This would have claimed millions more Japanese and Allied service personnels' lives, not to mention those from civilian populations in the area. 'On simple arithmetic grounds the case for using the bombs was overwhelming.' Reflecting on news of the atomic bombs and VJ-Day, Robin Painter, an officer in the Royal Corps of Signals who had experienced extensive service in the Far East, expressed matters even more succinctly: 'At last this terrible war had come to an end.'

As with the defeat of Nazi Germany, the unconditional surrender of Japan was good reason for jubilation. Many troops embarked on celebrations when they heard the news, particularly in rear areas where conditions were more relaxed than in the front line. Major John Baty, an army surgeon recalled that while in India, he joined 'the widespread celebrations' on 15 August 1945 and even attended the wedding reception of a former anaesthetist who had served with him at a Mobile Surgical Unit.

However, joy at the end of the war in the Far East was not universal, in large part owing to the perceived attitudes of the Japanese. As Sir Charles Evans an army doctor explained, when news of the surrender was relayed to his unit 'the words did not sound like those of a people that had been beaten and were surrendering unconditionally', rather the Japanese appeared to think 'they had reached some sort of accommodation with us ... We did not like it.' Similarly, Brian Aldiss, a signalman in Burma wrote home on 20 August: 'There was no excitement on VJ-Day and very little celebrating.' Years later he considered that this had owed 'something to a puzzled distaste for the Japanese' amongst British soldiers.

Overseeing the surrender brought innumerable practical problems as Lieutenant Colonel Robin Painter identified. Chief amongst these was that in the jungles of Burma and Siam (Thailand) many Japanese troops would be unaware the war had ended owing to lack of communication with the outside world, and so continue to act as if undefeated. Others would, it was expected, reject the surrender outright and fight until killed, displaying the sort of fanaticism that had typified the Imperial Japanese Army during the war. The academic Louis Allen, who served as a wartime intelligence officer in South-East Asia, explained how the Allies tried to find a solution to these problems. All capitulating Japanese servicemen were to be classed as Japanese Surrendered Personnel (JSP), and remained under the command of their officers who were responsible for maintaining discipline. At the same time, looting from the Japanese was strictly prohibited.

As the Second World War ended numerous security threats emerged, that potentially required a military response from Britain. In Europe there were signs that the Red Army of the Soviet Union, a wartime ally, might become more hostile in its outlook towards the West. The Yugoslavs were trying to annex Venezia-Giulia, and in Greece the Communist EAM-ELAS threatened to topple the existing government. The clamour for independence from Britain was strong in India, coupled with the extensive scope for communal violence. Equally, there was political unrest in Egypt, and in Palestine where the Stern Gang and others attempted via terrorism to establish an independent Jewish state. British troops had been drawn into assisting with counter-insurgency operations against Indonesian nationalists in the Dutch East Indies.

It was against this backdrop that the Labour Party won 47.8 per cent of the vote in the July 1945 General Election. Many soldiers hoped this heralded a better future that had been worth fighting for, not least because Sir William Beveridge's 1942 report on the welfare state had inspired numerous servicemen and women throughout the latter war years. As historian Juliet Gardiner commented, Labour promised badly-needed new homes, and community facilities as 'part of a social services matrix that would also include improved education and free medical and welfare services'.

During the latter phase of his service with the Coldstream Guards, Sir Michael Howard worked as his battalion's education officer and recalled that resettlement courses were organised, designed to fit soldiers with skills for civilian life and as part of a conscious effort to prepare troops to act as responsible citizens, who could 'think seriously about the political, social and international problems that would confront them as voters'.

The demobilisation of the wartime army commenced during this period as well. In late 1944 Ernest Bevin, Minister of Labour in Winston Churchill's wartime coalition government, unveiled his demobilisation plan. Within this there were two categories of soldier: Class A and Class B. The latter contained men who had occupations vital to the reconstruction of Britain, including civil engineers and tradesmen, and these were supposed to be demobilised first, provided they went back into jobs working in the national interest.

Every serviceman and woman was issued a demob number, and could calculate their relevant release group via a chart in the official booklet on release and resettlement. For those in Class A this required their date of birth and the month when their war service began, with two months of service being equivalent to one year of age. Older soldiers with longer service were placed in lower numbered release groups, and under the system all personnel were theoretically treated equally regardless of their rank.

Even so, there was a degree of inherent unfairness within the system. A soldier who had spent years on active service overseas could find himself treated the same as one who had spent the entire war based in Britain and never fired a shot in anger. This was compounded by ordinary soldier's frustrations with the army's PYTHON system which intended to rotate troops back to Britain after a set period overseas. Initially this was six years, but by 1945 had been re-set at four years in Europe and the Middle East, and three years eight months for those in the Far East.

Wartime signalman Brian Aldiss, like many of his contemporaries in 14th Army (often dubbed the Forgotten Army), felt they had been shipped out to the Far East with little idea of when they would ever get back home. In his case after serving in India and Burma during August 1943–August 1945, he was re-mustered into 26th Indian Division and posted to Sumatra to face Indonesian nationalists in October 1945, before finally coming back to Britain in the summer of 1947.

With the war over demobilisation gathered pace, and according to *Demobilisation in Britain* (Central Office of Information, 1 May 1947), by December 1945 a total of 1,511,800 men and women had been demobbed from the British Armed Forces. For soldiers the demobilisation process was usually relatively straightforward. Rifleman Henry Taylor served in North Africa and Italy during 1942–45, and his battalion was disbanded in Egypt on 14 May 1946. He was swiftly returned home the following month and released from the army, although placed on the reserve list so he could potentially be called back to the Colours if required.

Major Hardy Parkhurst left the army during March 1946, and returned to Britain from Greece by sailing to Northern Italy, and then taking a train to Calais. During the journey he hardly dared think about the reunion with his family that had appeared 'remote and impossible' during the war. Having sailed into Dover he was taken to a dispersal unit at Aldershot, where as he put it soldiers were processed, 'which meant a lot of tearing out of pages of our release books, much stamping, and pamphlet distribution. In a kind of daze you went from table to table; there was a bang and a crash, the tearing of a page, and off you went to the next one.'

Subsequently, he was sent to a clothing depot at Woking, where he handed in his baggage and was herded into a waiting room. Eventually he was summoned to find himself a demob suit: 'choosing civilian clothing after six years in the army was a bit of a business, especially with such a galaxy of stuff to bewilder you, but at last it was all gathered up and packed for us'.

Typically, men were kitted out in a style suitable for what the authors Barry Turner and Tony Rennell described as, 'a middle class family man dressed for church'. This included:

- A hat.
- Suit (jacket, waistcoat and trousers) in a variety of styles, colours and sizes, or alternatively a sports jacket and flannel trousers.
- Shirt with two collars.
- Tie (these came in many different patterns).
- Two pairs of socks.
- One pair of shoes (black or brown).
- Raincoat (four styles offered, or mackintosh in two styles).
- Two studs.
- One pair of cuff links.

Some soldiers found it ironic that after years in khaki they were forced to opt for a brown suit, and similarly many quipped that you could have any colour of shoes you liked so long as it was black. From clothing depots the recently demobilised were usually taken to railway stations so they could finally return to their home areas. At Woking Station Major Hardy Parkhurst encountered a 'seething mass' of persons, all released from the forces like himself and desperate to get back home as quickly as possible.

The demobilisation of women from the ATS tended to be similarly efficient. However, unlike men they were issued with fifty-six clothing coupons, allowed to keep their underwear and granted a one-off payment, so they were spared having to go through clothing depots. Like most of her colleagues Vera Cole had been watching out for her demob number to appear on the notice board at her barracks. Suddenly it happened and 'I realized that my days in the ATS were fast coming to an end'. An officer bade her farewell and handed over her Conduct Sheet, on which was written 'Exemplary', and almost before she knew it she was aboard a train heading for a dispersal unit at Northampton. Here she handed in her kit, and was accosted by a corporal who asked for her name and number, and gave her a small jam-jar. 'This was not only my urine test but my medical exam as well ... I couldn't believe it; all the strict medicals to get into the ATS and there, without even being seen by a doctor, I was out, services no longer required.'

Most soldiers and ATS personnel hoped that their war experience and release documentation would be beneficial to them on demobilisation, especially the reference written by a senior officer. Elizabeth Waterhouse joined the ATS on the outbreak of war and was not released until August 1945, having attained the rank of sergeant. She mainly worked in an administrative capacity and her testimonial read: 'As NCO in charge of guardroom has vast experience in dealing with all types of auxiliaries. Would be good in supervisory position.'

Basil Levi enlisted in the Territorial Army in May 1939, and served in Britain during the war with a searchlight regiment that was part of the Royal Artillery. Subsequently, he was promoted bombardier, and posted to Norway from June–December 1945 as part of the Allied forces sent to garrison the country in the wake of the German capitulation. He was demobilised during the spring of 1946 and his release papers stated:

Bdr Levi is thoroughly recommended – he is hard working, trustworthy and very capable. His work in the stores and as ration NCO has called for plenty of initiative and hard work. Both these attributes he has in plenty. It is desired to give this NCO the highest recommendation to whoever may be fortunate enough to secure his services in civilian life.

Compared with the demobilisation process, the actual experience of entering civilian life after the war varied from soldier to soldier. Some found it comparatively easy to settle down, but others found it more difficult. Major Hardy Parkhurst painted an idyllic image of his homecoming to Sussex, spending time with his wife and young son 'in comfort and seclusion' and the 'wonderful sense of home – fires and a beautiful hot bath – clean clothes, primroses and daffodils and aubretia in the garden'.

By contrast, after four and a half years in the Middle East with the Rifle Brigade, Sergeant Jim Ford was demobbed and returned home to South London. He was shocked by how ravaged it looked after the Blitz, and his young wife who he had married in 1940 now seemed to be a mature woman with whom he had little affinity. Consequently, he initially remained distant and was discombobulated by the situation he found himself in.

He was not alone. Many soldiers on return to Britain found the lack of housing stock, food and clothing shortages difficult to contend with, after a comparatively secure environment in the army when compared with the civilian world. As Rifleman Victor Gregg discovered, it was easy for soldiers to become institutionalised because all their basic needs were met by the army, and they didn't really have to think for themselves. Bomb damage, particularly in larger cities like London, Liverpool and Coventry, was a shock to many as well, along with the general shabbiness encountered in much of Britain.

Despite the hope engendered by the 1945 General Election, troops discovered, as authors Barry Turner and Tony Rennell noted, that the 'bluebird over the white cliffs of Dover that they had for so long been promised in song turned out to be a scrawny sparrow, more dead than alive'.

As a result numerous husbands and wives, plus their children if they had any, found it difficult to acclimatise to post-war life together, and deal with the privations they faced. Matters were especially difficult if one or other partner had found somebody else during the war. Divorce petitions were up in England and Wales from 19,155 during 1944 to 34,443 by 1949. A corollary of this trend was that there were serious cases of violent crimes by jealous soldiers against unfaithful spouses. In the spring of 1945, not long before war ended in Europe, Jock Cairns, a sergeant in the Royal Engineers, returned home on leave from Italy. He discovered his wife had been having a relationship with a recently-demobbed airman. Tragically Cairns ended up shooting his wife before turning the gun on himself.

Another pressure facing demobbed soldiers was coming to terms with distressing events that they had experienced during their war service. This was particularly the case for men who had been POWs, or experienced combat and witnessed the death or mutilation of comrades at close hand. The travel writer Eric Newby served in the Black Watch and Special Boat Section during the war, and from 1942–45 was a POW in Germany. On his repatriation he recalled that at one camp he witnessed 'the SS stripping Yugoslav men and women, kicking them round the compound in the snow and later singing harmoniously together in their huts'.

By 1945 Bill Titchmarsh was a veteran of the Italian campaign and after being wounded had eventually been shipped back home. He had experienced war from an infantryman's perspective with the mixture of hardship, horror, boredom, close comradeship and exhilaration that this entailed. On return to Britain he had the difficult task of visiting the parents of a mate who had been decapitated by German shellfire when one night they had agreed to swapped sentry duties. 'I went into the cottage and spoke [to his mother] a homely woman she was. Believe me he [his mate] knew nothing about it he never ever felt anything.'

Even more emotionally wounding was his experience relating to another soldier in his battalion called Willie, a former music teacher. 'He should never have been a soldier as he was too old and his left eye automatically closed when you spoke to him, so you can imagine the trouble he got into when the sergeant addressed him!' At Anzio during February–March 1944 Bill Titchmarsh stuck by Willie and they often manned listening posts together. Tragically during one counter-attack they were ordered to advance, when they were caught by friendly artillery and Willie was seriously injured. After the war Bill Titchmarsh went to visit his comrade and was deeply shocked.

> He had his right leg off below the knee, the other one up above the knee, and his left arm off at the shoulder. I couldn't believe it. I stayed with him about half an hour and his wife comes up and says 'You will have to go now the nurses are coming to dress Willie'. Once I got to the door of their little cottage his wife thanked me for coming to see him but then said 'I would rather you not come again'.

This was typical of the sorts of traumas faced by countless former soldiers as they desperately tried to return to a normalised civilian life in the post-war years. Despite the army's resettlement courses, and support of welfare organisations like SSAFA and the Royal British Legion, this was a difficult task for many men and women who had served during the war.

In reviewing the experiences of British soldiers during the Second World War, it is difficult not to find sympathy with historian James Holland's sentiment that they came from an 'extraordinary generation'. This was all the more so when it is considered that with Britain's allies, they were part of a victorious force, and comparatively few were trained professional soldiers. Rather the bulk of the wartime army were either civilian volunteers, or conscripts, who did not necessarily have any natural aptitude for acquiring the necessary martial skills required to defeat the Axis powers.

Bibliography

Durham County Record Office

D/DLI 7/19/2, Divisional Routine Orders issued by OC 50th (Northumbrian) Division, c. August 1944 (within papers of Capt. Arnold, MT Officer 9th DLI).

D/DLI/13/4–11, German and British propaganda leaflets, Italy c. 1943–45.

D/DLI 2/10/8, 'All this (and Iceland too)' Review Christmas Entertainment, 1942.

D/DLI 2/10/9, *Polar Bear News* No. 6, November 1945.

D/DLI 2/11/1–2, *Current Report from Overseas* Numbers 54 & 55, Normandy (War Office, September, 1944).

D/DLI 2/9/257, Lessons from Sicily: Report by Lt. Col. J. R. Woods (OC 9th DLI), August 1943.

D/DLI 2/6/524, Account by Ernest Harvey regarding his service with 70th and 9th DLI, 1942–47.

D/DLI 2/9/342–344, Account of his war service with 70th DLI and the Parachute Regiment by Eric 'Bill' Sykes.

D/DLI 2/9/341, TS Memoir compiled by Jim Ratcliffe (9th DLI), July 1943–November 1946.

D/DLI 7/213/68, Papers regarding the History and Contribution of 9th DLI, compiled by Major R. Griffiths.

D/DLI 7/208/13, Capt. Michael Farr, MBE, 'War and Wine': TS autobiography regarding his war service and period as a POW, particularly at Colditz.

Lincolnshire Archives

Doc Box 3/399, Records for Pte. Leonard Dales (Lincs Regt).

——/470, Records for C.S. Naylor (6th Lincs Regt) Italy and Austria, 1944–46.

Doc Box 5/343, Records regarding release of Major Douglas Victory Skinner.

Doc Box 7/432, Papers and Diary regarding war service of Major Robert Darby Pullman.

——/392, Records Pte. John George Elliot (4th Lincs Regt, 1939–45).

Doc Box 11/163, Papers of Guy Bray (4th Lincs Regt First World War & RE Second World War).

Doc Box 12/854, 1st Lincolnshire Regt-Burma Campaign, SEAC Newspapers.

Doc Box 19/450, TS account: 'Of Polar Bears and Imps' compiled by Sgt. Tom Anderton (4th Lincs Regt).

Doc Box 32, Military Newspapers for servicemen stationed in Iceland, deposited by Cpl. L. T. Dobbs (Lincs Regt).

Doc Box 38, Derek Bonner Birch, 'My Life Story:' TS memoir regarding his wartime service with 6th Lincs Regt and RASC.

——, Records for Sgt. Reginald Cyril Greatorex (Royal Artillery), 1940–46.

Doc Box 42, 'Darby Hart Memories of Dunkirk and D-Day', typed by Major D. R. F. Houlton-Hart, undated.

——, Assault on Winnekendonk, TS account regarding role played by 2nd Lincs Regt as part of Operational Veritable, March 1945.

Northumberland Archives

NRO 08922/1, Army Release Book Robert William Watson (RAMC, 1945).

NRO 07937/3, Army Release Book Harry A. Brown (RNF, 1945).

NRO 07909/20, Army Release Book Cpl. J. J. Lee (RASC, 1946).

NRO 07937/1, 5 Postcards from Fus. Harry A. Brown to his wife while a Japanese POW.

NRO 06519/1–2, POW Newsletters Vol. 1 Numbers 7 and 8, November–December 1942.

NRO 07958/1/1, TS Notes by Col. Harold Sell, POW 1942–45.

NRO 08258/8, Obituary for Jim Bradley, former Far East POW & Escapee.

Oral History Interviews:

T/502, Jennie Warwick (ATS att RAPC).

T/593, Henry McCreath (officer 9th RNF & FEPOW, 1942–46).

T/594, William Brown (9th RNF & FEPOW).

Tyne & Wear Archives

DF.BL Accession Number 1181, Letters home from Trooper Leslie Blackie of Gateshead (43rd RTR), c. 1944–47.

DX889/1/4/4–6, Letters home from Sapper L. Crighton, Royal Engineers, Middle East, 1941–42.

DX1324/1, Army Book 64 Soldier's Service and Pay Book Pte. Alfred George Grey (Hertfordshire Regiment c. 1936–45).

DX 914/1–9, Papers regarding the war service of Captain Lawrence Cyril Ashford, MC (Scots Guards).

L/PA/1314, Booklet entitled 'Steady as a Rock' The DLI at War, 1939–45.

Lincoln Central Library

L355, Ex BSM P. G. 'Bill' Downdall, MBE, *Off to War and Back Again: My Dunkirk Story* (Privately published, undated).

L355, Major L. C. Gates, *The History of The First Battalion Lincolnshire Regiment in India, Arakan, Burma and Sumatra, September 1939–October 1946* (Privately published, Lincoln, 1946).

L355, Oliver Hardy, *The Seven Lean Years 1939–1946 (Incorporating The History of Sixth Battalion Lincolnshire Regiment 1939–1946)* (Privately published, undated).

L355, Lt. Col. A. H. Wenham, *The History of The Sixth Battalion Lincolnshire Regiment* (Lincolns Unit Printers, Obersteirische Printing Press, Leoben, Austria, 1946)

Newcastle City Library

L355 R888W, Papers of Matthew Waterhouse relating to military service in the Northumberland Fusiliers, 1924–43.

L355 R888F, Diary of Lt. Col. H. S. Flower (9th Battalion Royal Northumberland Fusiliers), 1941–45. Compiled by R. C. Fenwick (1986).

L355 R888M, Mather T. I., and Vander Gucht, H. B., *A History of No. 1 Independent Machine Gun Company (RNF) in the Campaign in North-West Europe, 1944–45.*

L355 R888P, Summary of the History and Traditions of "The Fifth" The Royal Northumberland Fusiliers, Compiled by Maj. R. M. Pratt OC Regt Depot, 1948–50.

L355 R888B, Lt. S. R. Barney (Middlesex Regiment) and Lt. E. J. Frary (Middlesex Regiment) (eds), *An Informal Record of 26 Machine Gun Training Centre* (W. H. Evans, Chester, 1946).

L355, *The St. George's Gazette* (Regimental Journal of the Royal Northumberland Fusiliers) Vols. c. 1939–45

Imperial War Museum (Online Oral History Interviews)

Andrews, Sidney

Avery, William

Barlow, Tom

Bellows, James

Best, Reg

Blake, John

Blanchard, Carlotta

Brooke, Albert

Brown, Harold

Brown, James

Case, Ronald

Clack, Ronald

Claxton, Edward

Crouch, Leslie

Daunt, Ivan

Dewar, Andrew

Donaldson, James

Ferguson, Stanley

Forbes, Ron

Gillham, Gwen

Gilmour, John

Gourd, Philip

Grogan, Ted

Grove, Stanley

Hammerton, Ian

Harwood, Herbert

Hart Richards, Malcolm

Hay, Helen

Lashbrook, Donald

Lock, Jack

McLane, Martin

Miller, Harry

Old, Douglas

Phillips, Richard

Radmore, Guy

Reeves, Joan

Rose, Donald

Russell, Helen

Sheppard, William
Simpson, Harry
Speelman, Edward
Stevens, Elizabeth
Vardy, Jack

Vickers, Lionel
Weightman, William
Wheeler, Eric
Whybro, George
Williams, Richard

Author's Collection

Papers of Basil Levi relating to his military service with the Royal Artillery, 1939–46.

Interview with Bob Taylor regarding his wartime service with the Commandos, Royal Hospital Chelsea, 18 August 2010.

Papers of Bill Titchmarsh relating to his military service with the Queen's Royal Regiment c. 1943–46, and interview at Royal Hospital Chelsea, 18 August 2010.

Papers of John Wray relating to his wartime military service with the Royal Electrical and Mechanical Engineers.

Interview with Bill Ness regarding his war service with the Parachute Regiment, Newcastle upon Tyne, 26 January 2015.

Papers of George Henderson relating to his war service with the Royal Navy aboard LST Number 8, and interview Newcastle upon Tyne, 23 January 2015.

Instructions for British Servicemen in France 1944 (Reproduced from the original prepared by The Political Warfare Executive and issued by The Foreign Office, London).

Instructions for British Servicemen in Germany 1944 (Reproduced from the original issued by The Foreign Office, London).

Notes From Theatres of War Number 13: North Africa-Algeria and Tunisia, November 1942–March 1943 (The War Office, May 1943).

Notes From Theatres of War Number 16: North Africa November 1942–May 1943 (The War Office, October 1943).

War Office Manual Code WO 7589, *Infantry Training Part VIII Fieldcraft, Battle Drill Section and Platoon Tactics*, 4 March 1944.

Secondary Sources

Adams, Ken, *Healing in Hell: The Memoirs of a Far Eastern POW Medic* (Pen & Sword Ltd, 2011).

Addison, Paul, and Calder, Angus (eds), *Time to Kill: The Soldier's Experience of War in the West 1939–45* (Pimlico, 1997).

Ahrenfeldt, Robert H., *Psychiatry in the British Army in the Second World War* (Routledge & Kegan Paul, 1958).

Aldiss, Brian, *The Twinkling of an Eye: My Life as an Englishman* (Little Brown, 1990).

Aldrich, Richard J., *Witness to War: Diaries of the Second World War in Europe and the Middle East* (Doubleday, 2004).

Allbury, Alfred, *Bamboo and Bushido* (Robert Hale Limited, 1955).

Allen, Louis, *Burma: The Longest War 1941–45* (Guild Publishing, 1984).

Allport, Alan, *Demobbed: Coming Home After the Second World War* (Yale University Press, 2010).

Anon, *Eyewitness to War: Personal Accounts of World War II* (The Publishing Corporation UK Ltd and Imperial War Museum, 1995).

Bailey, Roderick, *Forgotten Voices of D–Day: A New History of the Normandy Landings* (Ebury Press in association with the Imperial War Museum, 2010).

Barber, Neil (ed.), *Fighting With the Commandos: The Recollections of Stan Scott No. 3 Commando* (Pen & Sword Ltd, 2008).

Barclay, C. N., *The History of the Royal Northumberland Fusiliers* (William Clowes & Sons Ltd, 1952).

——, *The History of the Duke of Wellington's Regiment 1919–1952* (William Clowes & Sons Ltd, 1953).

Bartlett, Basil, *My First War: An Army Officer's Journal For May 1940 Through Belgium to Dunkirk* (Chatto & Windus, 1940).

Baty, John A., *Surgeon in the Jungle War* (William Kimber, 1979).

Beddington, W. R., *A History of The Queen's Bays (The 2nd Dragoon Guards) 1929–1945* (Warren & Son Ltd, 1954).

Bellamy, Bill, *Troop Leader: A Tank Commander's Story* (Sutton Publishing, 2007).

Bidwell, Shelford, *Gunners at War* (Arms & Armour Press, 1970).

——, *The Royal Horse Artillery* (Leo Cooper Ltd, 1973).

——, *The Women's Royal Army Corps* (Leo Cooper Ltd, 1977).

Bigland, Eileen, *Britain's Other Army: The Story of the ATS* (Nicholson & Watson, 1946).

Bogarde, Dirk, *Snakes and Ladders* (Triad Granada, 1979).

——, *Cleared for Take Off* (Penguin Books, 1996).

Borthwick, Alastair, *Battalion: A British Infantry Unit's actions from El Alamein to the Elbe, 1942–45* (Baton Wicks Publications, 1994).

Boscawen, Robert, *Armoured Guardsmen: A War Diary, June 1944–April 1945* (Leo Cooper Ltd, 2001).

Briant, Keith, *Fighting with the Guards* (Evans Brothers Ltd, 1960).

Bright, Joan, *The Ninth Queen's Royal Lancers 1936–45: The Story of an Armoured Regiment in Battle* (Gale & Polden, 1951).

——, *History of the Northumberland Hussars Yeomanry 1924–1949* (Mawson, Swan & Morgan, 1949).

Broad, Roger, *The Radical General: Sir Ronald Adam and Britain's New Model Army 1941–1946* (Spellmount, 2013).

Bruce, Colin John, *War on the Ground 1939–45* (Constable, 1995).

Bryan, Paul, *Wool, War and Westminster* (Tom Donovan Publishing, 1993).

Buckley, John, *British Armour in the Normandy Campaign 1944* (Frank Cass, 2004).

—— (ed), *The Normandy Campaign 1944: Sixty Years On* (Routledge, 2006).

——, *Monty's Men: The British Army and the Liberation of Europe* (Yale University Press, 2013).

Bulteel, Christopher, *Something about a Soldier* (Airlife Publishing Ltd, 2000).

Bungay, Stephen, *Alamein* (Aurum Press Ltd, 2003).

Burton, Reginald, *Railway of Hell: War Captivity and Forced Labour at the Hands of the Japanese* (Pen & Sword Ltd, 2010).

Carr-Gomm, Richard, *Push on the Door: An Autobiography* (Carr-Gomm Society Ltd, 1982).

Carew, Tim, *The Royal Norfolk Regiment* (Hamish Hamilton Ltd, 1967).

Carver, Michael, *Out of Step: The Memoirs of Field Marshal Lord Carver* (Hutchinson, 1989).

Chandler, David, and Beckett, Ian (eds), *The Oxford History of the British Army* (Oxford University Press, 1996).

Chaplin, H. D., *The Queen's Own Royal West Kent Regiment 1920–1950* (Michael Joseph Ltd, 1954).

Cheall, Bill, *Fighting Through from Dunkirk to Hamburg: A Green Howard's Wartime Memoir* (Pen & Sword Ltd, 2011).

Cheetham, A. M., *Ubique* (Freshfield Books, 1987).

Clarke, Dudley, *The Eleventh at War* (Michael Joseph, 1952).

Clayton, Tim, and Craig, Phil, *Finest Hour* (Coronet Books, 2001)

Close, Bill, *A View from the Turret: A History of The 3rd Royal Tank Regiment in the Second World War* (Dell & Bredon, 2002).

Close, Ray, *In Action with the SAS: A Soldier's Odyssey from Dunkirk to Belsen* (Pen & Sword Ltd, 2005).

Costello, John, *Love, Sex and War 1939–45* (Pan Books Ltd, 1986).

Cotterell, Anthony, *R.A.M.C.* (Hutchinson & Co Ltd, 1944).

Crang, Jeremy A., *The British Army and the People's War 1939–45* (Manchester University Press, 2000).

Crawford, Robert John, *'I was an Eighth Army Soldier'* (Victor Gollancz Ltd, 1944).

Daniell, David Scott, *Cap of Honour: The Story of The Gloucestershire Regiment (28th/61st Foot) 1694–1975* (White Lion Publishers Ltd, 1975).

Davy, G. M. O., *The Seventh and Three Enemies: The Story of World War II and the 7th Queen's Own Hussars* (W. Heffer & Sons Ltd, 1952).

Dear, Ian, *Escape and Evasion* (The History Press, 2010).

Delaforce, Patrick, *The Polar Bears: Monty's Left Flank from Normandy to the Relief of Holland with the 49th Division* (Chancellor Press, 1999).

——, *Monty's Marauders* (Chancellor Press, 2000).

——, *Monty's Highlanders: 51st Highland Division in World War Two* (Chancellor Press, 2000).

——, *The Black Bull: From Normandy to the Baltic with the 11th Armoured Division* (Chancellor Press, 2000).

——, *Monty's Iron Sides: From the Normandy Beaches to Bremen with the 3rd (British) Division* (Sutton Publishing Ltd, 2002).

——, *Churchill's Desert Rats: From Normandy to the Baltic with the 7th Armoured Division* (Sutton Publishing Ltd, 2003).

——, *Monty's Northern Legions: 50th Northumbrian and 15th Scottish Divisions at War 1939–45* (Sutton Publishing Ltd, 2004).

——, *Battles with Panzers: Monty's Tank Battalions 1 RTR & 2 RTR at War* (Amberley Publishing Plc, 2010).

——, *Taming the Panzers: Monty's Tank Battalions 3rd RTR at War* (Amberley Publishing Plc, 2010).

Dillon, Terence, *Rangoon to Kohima* (RHQ, The Gloucestershire Regiment, 1978).

Doherty, Richard, *Only The Enemy in Front: The Recce Corps at War 1940–46* (Spellmount Publishing, 2008).

Douglas, Keith, *Alamein to Zem Zem* (Faber & Faber Ltd, 1992).

Dunn, Robin, *Sword & Wig: Memoirs of a Lord Justice* (Quiller Press Ltd, 1993).

English, Ian R., and Moses, Harry, *For You the War is Over: The Experiences of the DLI Prisoners of War during World War II* (Business Education Pub. Ltd, 2006).

English, John A., *On Infantry* (Praeger, 1981).

Ellis, John, *The Sharp End: The Fighting Man in World War II* (Pimlico, 1990).

Ellis, L. F., *Welsh Guards at War* (Gale and Polden Ltd, 1946).

Ellis, Ray, *Once a Hussar: A Memoir of Battle, Capture and Escape in the Second World War* (Pen & Sword Ltd, 2013).

Evans, Charles, *A Doctor in XIVth Army Burma 1944–45* (Leo Cooper, 1998).

Evans, Roger, *The 5th Royal Inniskilling Dragoon Guards* (Gale & Polden Ltd, 1951).

Farrar-Hockley, A. R., *Infantry Tactics 1939–45* (Almark, 1976).

Feebery, David (ed.), *Guardsman and Commando: The War Memoirs of RSM Cyril Feebery, DCM* (Pen & Sword, 2008).

Fergusson, Bernard, *The Black Watch and the King's Enemies* (Collins, 1950).

Fennell, Jonathan, *Combat and Morale in the North African Campaign: The Eighth Army and the Path to El Alamein* (Cambridge University Press, 2011).

Fitzgerald, D. J. L., *History of the Irish Guards* (Gale & Polden Ltd, 1949).

Ford, Ken, *Battle Axe Division: From Africa to Italy with the 78th Division 1942–45* (Sutton Publishing Ltd, 2003).

——, *Mailed Fist: 6th Armoured Division at War, 1940–1945* (Sutton Publishing Ltd, 2005).

Forman, Denis, *To Reason Why* (Andre Deutsch, 1991).

Forty, George, *British Army Handbook 1939–45* (Sutton Publishing Ltd, 2002).

——, *Tanks Across the Desert: The War Diary of Jake Wardrop* (Sutton Publishing Ltd, 2003).

Fraser, David, *And We Shall Shock Them: The British Army in the Second World War* (Sceptre, 1988).

——, *Wars and Shadows: Memoirs of General Sir David Fraser* (Penguin Books, 2003).

Fraser, George MacDonald, *Quartered Safe Out Here* (Harper Collins, 2000).

French, David, *Raising Churchill's Army: The British Army and the War against Germany 1919–1945* (Oxford University Press, 2001).

——, *Military Identities: The Regimental System, the British Army, & the British People c. 1870–2000* (Oxford University Press, 2008).

Fussel, Paul, *Wartime: Understanding and Behaviour in the Second World War* (Oxford University Press, 1989).

——, *The Boys' Crusade American G.I.s in Europe: Chaos and Fear in World War Two* (Weidenfeld & Nicolson, 2004)

Fyans, Peter, *Captivity, Slavery and Survival as a Far East POW: The Conjuror on the Kwai* (Pen & Sword Ltd, 2012).

Gardiner, Juliet, *Wartime Britain 1939–45* (Review, 2005).

Gilbert, Adrian, *POW: Allied Prisoners in Europe 1939–45* (John Murray, 2007).

Gooch, John (ed.), *Decisive Campaigns of the Second World War* (Frank Cass, 1990).

Gorle, Richmond, *The Quiet Gunner at War: El Alamein to the Rhine with the Scottish Divisions* (Pen & Sword Ltd, 2011).

Goulty, James, *Second World War Lives: A Guide For Family Historians* (Pen & Sword Ltd, 2012).

Grafton, Pete, *You, You and You! The People Out of Step with World War II* (Pluto Press Ltd, 1981).

Graham, Dominick, and Bidwell, Shelford, *Tug of War: The Battle for Italy 1943–45* (Pen & Sword Ltd, 2004).

Greenwood, Trevor, *D-Day to Victory: The Diaries of a British Tank Commander* (Simon & Shuster Ltd, 2012).

Gregg, Victor, *Rifleman: A Front-line Life from Alamein and Dresden to the Fall of the Berlin Wall* (Bloomsbury Publishing Plc, 2011).

Griffith, Paddy, *Forward into Battle: Fighting Tactics from Waterloo to Vietnam* (Antony Bird Publications, 1981).

Gudgin, Peter, *'With the Churchills to War': 48th Battalion Royal Tank Regiment at War 1939–45* (Sutton Publishing, 1996).

Gunning, Hugh, *Borderers in Battle* (Martin's Printing, 1948).

Hall, Mathew, *A Doctor at War: The Story of Colonel Martin Herford, The Most Decorated Doctor of World War Two* (Images Publishing, 1995).

Hallam, John, *History of the Lancashire Fusiliers, 1939–45* (Alan Sutton, 1993).

Hamilton, Stuart, *Armoured Odyssey: 8th Royal Tank Regiment in the Western Desert 1941–1942 Palestine, Syria, Egypt 1943–44, Italy 1944–45* (Tom Donovan, 1995).

Harpur, Brian, *The Impossible Victory: A Personal Account of the Battle for the Po* (Coronet Books, 1988).

Hart, Stephen Ashley, *Colossal Cracks: Montgomery's 21st Army Group in North-West Europe, 1944–45* (Stackpole Books, 2007).

Harrison, Mark, *Medicine & Victory: British Military Medicine in the Second World War* (Oxford University Press, 2012).

Harrison Place, Timothy, *Military Training in the British Army, 1940–1944 from Dunkirk to D-Day* (Frank Cass, 2000).

Hastings, Max, *Das Reich: The March of the 2nd Panzer Division through France, June 1944* (Pan Books, 2009).

Healey, Denis, *The Time of My Life* (Penguin Books, 1990).

Heald, Tim, *Brian Johnston: the authorised biography* (Arrow Books, 1998)

Hills, Stuart, *By Tank into Normandy* (Cassell, 2003).

Holland, James, *Heroes: The Greatest Generation and the Second World War* (Harper Perennial, 2007).

Holmes, Richard, *Firing Line* (Jonathan Cape Ltd, 1985).

Howard, Michael, *Captain Professor: a life in war and peace* (Continuum, 2006).

Howard, M. E., and Sparrow, J., *The Coldstream Guards, 1920–1946* (Oxford University Press, 1951).

Hudson, John, *Sunset in the East: Fighting Against the Japanese Through the Siege of Imphal and Alongside them in Java 1943–1946* (Leo Cooper, 2002).

Jarry, Sydney, *18 Platoon* (Sydney Jarry Ltd, 1994).

Jones, John Philip, *Battles of a Gunner Officer: Tunisia, Sicily, Normandy and the Long Road to Germany* (Pen & Sword Ltd, 2014).

Keegan, John, *The Face of Battle: A Study of Agincourt, Waterloo and the Somme* (Pimlico, 1998).

Kennedy, D. J., *2623520 Gdsm. Kennedy, D. J. 6th Guards Tank Brigade Reminisces* (Privately published, undated).

Kenyon, Philip, *One Small Soldier* (Forces and Corporate Publishing Ltd, 2012).

Laffin, John, *Combat Surgeons* (Sutton Publishing Ltd, 1999).

Langley, J. M., *Fight Another Day* (Magnum Books, 1980).

Lewis, P. K., and English, I. R,. *8th Battalion The Durham Light Infantry, 1939–45* (J. and P. Bealls, 1949).

Lindsay, Martin, *So Few Got Through: The Personal Diary of Lt. Col. Martin Lindsay, DSO, MP, who served in the Gordon Highlanders in the 51st Highland Division from July, 1944, to May, 1945* (Collins, 1946).

Lomax, Eric, *The Railway Man* (Vintage Books, 1996).

Lowry, Michael, *Fighting Through to Kohima: A Memoir of War in India & Burma* (Leo Cooper, 2003).

Lyttelton, Humphrey, *It Just Occurred to Me … the reminiscences & thoughts of Chairman Humph* (Portico, 2009).

MacArthur, Brian, *Surviving the Sword: Prisoners of the Japanese 1942–45* (Abacus, 2007).

McCann, Graham, *Dad's Army: the story of a classic television show* (Fourth Estate, 2001).

McCorquodale, D., Hutchings, B. L. B., and Woozley, A. D., *A History of the King's Dragoon Guards, 1938–1945* (Privately printed for the Regiment, 1950) .

McEntee-Taylor, Carole, *A Battle Too Far: The True Story of Rifleman Henry Taylor* (Pen & Sword Ltd, 2013).

McManners, John, *Fusilier Recollections and Reflections 1939–45* (Michael Russell Ltd, 2002).

McQuaid, Sally Moore (ed.), *Singapore Diary: The Hidden Journal of Captain R. M. Horner* (Spellmount Ltd, 2007).

Meads, R. J., *A Reservist's War and the 252* (Merlin Books Ltd, 1988).

Minns, Raynes, *Bombers & Mash: The Domestic Front 1939–45* (Virago Press, 2012).

Miller, Harry, *Services to the Services: The Story of the NAAFI* (Newman Neame, 1971).

Milligan, Spike, *'Rommel?' 'Gunner Who?'* (Penguin Books, 1976).

——, *Mussolini, His Part in My Downfall* (Penguin Books, 1980).

Mills, John, *Up in the Clouds, Gentlemen Please* (Weidenfeld & Nicolson, 1980).

Mitchell, Colin, *Having Been a Soldier* (Hamish Hamilton, 1969).

Moore, William, *The Long Way Round: An Escape Through Occupied France* (Leo Cooper, 1986).

Moreman, T. R., *The Jungle, The Japanese and The British Commonwealth Armies at War 1941–45: Fighting Methods, Doctrine and Training for Jungle Warfare* (Frank Cass, 2005).

Moylon, Bill, *A Very Pleasant Journey Through Life: A Chelsea Pensioner Remembers* (Privately Published, 2009).

Murrell, Nick (ed.), *Dunkirk to the Rhineland: Diaries and Sketches of Sergeant C. S. Murrell, Welsh Guards* (Pen & Sword Ltd, 2011).

Neave, Airey, *They Have Their Exits* (Coronet Books, 1974).

——, *The Flames of Calais* (Grafton Books, 1989).

Newby, Eric, *Something Wholesale: My Life in the Rag Trade* (Picador, 1985).

Newman, Philip, *Over the Wire: A POW's Escape Story from the Second World War* (Pen & Sword Ltd, 2013).

Nicholson, Virginia, *Millions Like Us: Women's Lives During the Second World War* (Penguin Books, 2012).

Niven, David, *The Moon's A Balloon* (Coronet Books, 1975).

Noakes, Lucy, *Women and the British Army: War and the Gentle Sex, 1907–1948* (Routledge, 2006).

North, John, *North-west Europe 1944–45: The Achievement of 21st Army Group* (HMSO, 1953).

Painter, Robin, *A Signal Honour* (Leo Cooper, 1999).

Parkhurst, Hardy, *Diary of a Soldier* (The Pentland Press Ltd, 1993).

Patterson, Hugh, *'Geordie Hussar P.O.W'. Opportunity Sometimes Knocked* (Privately Published, 2000).

Picot, Geoffrey, *Accidental Warrior: In The Front Line From Normandy Till Victory* (Penguin Books, 1994).

Powdrill, Ernest, *In The Face Of The Enemy: A Battery Sergeant Major in Action in the Second World War* (Pen & Sword Ltd, 2008).

Randle, John, *Battle Tales from Burma* (Pen & Sword Ltd, 2004).

Reid, Howard, *Dad's War* (Bantam Books, 2004).

Risssik, David, *The DLI at War: The History of the Durham Light Infantry 1939–45* (Depot DLI, 1952).

Rogers, H. C. B., *Troopships and their History* (Seeley, Service & Co. Ltd, 1963).

Rollings, Charles, *POW: Voices from Behind the Wire in the Second World War* (Ebury Press, 2008).

Sadler, John, *Dunkirk to Belsen: The Soldiers' Own Dramatic Stories* (JR Books, 2010).

Scannell, Vernon, *Argument of Kings: An Autobiography* (Robson Books, 1987).

Shears, Philip J., *The Story of the Border Regiment 1939–45* (Nisbet & Co. Ltd, 1948).

Shipster, John, *Mist Over the Rice Fields: A Soldier's Story of the Burma Campaign 1943–45 and Korean War 1950–51* (Leo Cooper, 2000).

Stewart, P. F., *The History of the XII Royal Lancers (Prince of Wales's)* (Oxford University Press, 1950).

Summers, Julie, *The Colonel of Tamarakan: Philip Toosey & The Bridge on the River Kwai* (Pocket Books, 2006).

Synge, W. A. T., *The Story of the Green Howards 1939–45* (Privately printed, 1952).

Taylor, Eric, *Women Who Went to War 1938–46* (Robert Hale Ltd, 1988).

Taylor, Keith, and Stewart, Brian, *Call to Arms: Officer Cadet Training at Eaton Hall 1943–1958* (Privately Published, 2006)

Terry, Roy, *Women in Khaki: The Story of the British Woman Soldier* (Columbus Books Ltd, 1988).

Thompson, Julian, *Dunkirk: Retreat to Victory* (Pan Books, 2009).

Torday, Jane, *"Wish Me Luck As You Wave Me Goodbye:" A Selection of Northumbrian Memories of World War II* (The Spredden Press, 1989).

Tout, Ken, *By Tank: D to VE Days* (Robert Hale Ltd, 2010).

Turner, Barry, and Rennell, Tony, *When Daddy Came Home: How Family Life Changed Forever in 1945* (Hutchinson, 1995).

Twigg, Reg, *Survivor on the River Kwai: The Incredible Story of Life on the Burma Railway* (Penguin Books Ltd, 2014).

Tyrer, Nicola, *Sisters in Arms: British Army Nurses Tell Their Story* (Phoenix, 2009).

Urquhart, Alistair, *The Forgotten Highlander* (Abacus, 2011).

Ustinov, Peter, *Dear Me* (Penguin Books, 1978).

Ward, S. G. P., *Faithful: The Story of the Durham Light Infantry* (Thomas Nelson & Sons Ltd, 1962).

Warwick, Ernest, *Tamajao 241: A POW Camp on the River Kwai* (Paul-Leagas Publications, 1987).

Watts, J. C., *Surgeon at War* (Digit Books, 1955).

Whicker, Alan, *Within Whicker's World* (Coronet Books, 1987).

White, Peter, *With the Jocks: A Soldier's Struggle for Europe 1944–45* (Sutton Publishing Ltd, 2002).

Whitehouse Stanley, and Bennett, George B., *Fear is the Foe: A Foot Slogger from Normandy to the Rhine* (Robert Hale Ltd, 1997).

Whitelaw, William, *The Whitelaw Memoirs* (Headline, 1990).

Wingfield, R. M., *The Only Way Out: An Infantryman's Autobiography of the North-West Europe Campaign August 1944–February 1945* (Hutchinson, 1956).

Wilson, Dare, *Tempting the Fates: A Memoir of Service in the Second World War, Palestine, Korea, Kenya, Aden* (Pen & Sword Ltd, 2006).

Wilson, David, *The Sum of Things* (Spellmount Ltd, 2001).

Wilson, James, *Unusual Undertakings: A Military Memoir* (Leo Cooper, 2002).

Woollcombe, Robert, *All the Blue Bonnets: The History of the King's Own Scottish Borderers* (Arms & Armour Press, 1980).

——, *Lion Rampant* (B & W Publishing, 1994).

Chapters and Articles

Corrigan, Imogen, '"Put that Light Out": The 93rd Searchlight Regiment Royal Artillery', in Lee, Celia, and Strong, Paul Edward (eds), *Women in War: From Home Front to Front Line* (Pen & Sword Ltd, 2012), pp. 77–86.

French, David, '"Tommy is no Soldier": The Morale of the Second British Army in Normandy, June–August 1944', *The Journal of Strategic Studies*, Vol. 19, No. 4 (December 1996), pp. 154–78.

Ford, Douglas, '"A Conquerable Yet Resilient Foe": British Perceptions of the Imperial Japanese Army's Tactics on the India-Burma Front, September 1942 to Summer 1944', *Intelligence and National Security*, Vol. 18, No. 1 (Spring 2003), pp. 65–90.

Griffith, P. G., 'British Armoured Warfare in the Western Desert 1940–43', in Harris, J. P., and Toase, F. H. (eds), *Armoured Warfare* (Batsford, 1990).

Jones, Edgar, and Ironside, Stephen, 'Battle Exhaustion: The Dilemma of Psychiatric Casualties in Normandy, June–August 1944', *Historical Journal* 53.1 (2010), pp. 109–28.

Kaushik, Roy, 'Discipline and Morale of the African, British and Indian Army units in Burma and India during World War II: July 1943 to August 1945', *Modern Asian Studies* 44, 6 (2010), pp. 1255–82.

Natzio, Georgina, 'Homeland Defence: British Gunners, Women and Ethics during the Second World War', in Lee, Celia, and Strong, Paul Edward (eds), *Women in War: From Home Front to Front Line* (Pen & Sword Ltd, 2012), pp. 87–100.

Strachan, Hew, 'Training, Morale and Modern War', *Journal of Contemporary History*, Volume 41 Number 2 (April 2006), pp. 211–27.

Wykes, Alan, 'The British Soldier', in *History of the Second World War*, Volume 7 Number 16 (Purnell & Sons Ltd, 1968), pp. 3109–11.

Index